The Encyclopedia of Infant and Toddler Activities

for Children Birth to 3

Revised Edition

Edited by Donna Wittmer, PhD

Gryphon House
www.gryphonhouse.com

Copyright

©2017 Gryphon House, Inc.

Published by Gryphon House, Inc.

P. O. Box 10, Lewisville, NC 27023

800.638.0928; 877.638.7576 (fax)

Visit us on the web at www.gryphonhouse.com.

Library of Congress Cataloging-in-Publication Data

The cataloging-in-publication data is registered with the Library of Congress for ISBN 978-0-87659-733-0.

Bulk Purchase

Gryphon House books are available for special premiums and sales promotions as well as for fund-raising use. Special editions or book excerpts also can be created to specifications. For details, call 800.638.0928.

Disclaimer

Gryphon House, Inc., cannot be held responsible for damage, mishap, or injury incurred during the use of or because of activities in this book. Appropriate and reasonable caution and adult supervision of children involved in activities and corresponding to the age and capability of each child involved are recommended at all times. Do not leave children unattended at any time. Observe safety and caution at all times.

Acknowledgments

• • ● ● ● ● • • •

Thank you to the contributors to the original *Encyclopedia of Infant and Toddler Activities for Children Birth to 3*:

Sandy L. Scott, Holly Dzierzanowski, Phyllis Esch, Mollie Murphy, Edda Sevilla, Megan Friday, Monica Hay Cook, Shelly Larson, Renee Kirchner, Jackie Wright, Susan Grenfell, Sandy Packard, Jean Potter, Margery K. Fermino, Michelle Larson, Kate Ross, Michelle Barnea, Virginia Jean Herrod, Christina Chilcote, Maxine Della Fave, Anna Granger, Jodi Kelley, Carol Crumley, Devon Kramer, Bev Schumacher, Karyn F. Everham, Jennifer Gray, Gail Morris, Peggy Asma, Sarah Hartman, Kimberly Smith, Shyamala Shanmugasundaram, Elizabeth Noble, Patti Moeser, Erin Huffstetler, Glenda Butts, Ann Scalley, Laura Durbrow, Jean Lortz, Mary Jo Shannon, Nedra Weinreich, Audrey Kanoff, Sunny Heimbecker, Jennifer Rydin, Elaine Commins, Kathy Wallace, Mary Brehm, Jill Martin, D'Arcy Simmons, Shelley Hoster, and Diane Shatto.

Contents

Foreword

· · ● ● ● ● ● · ●

Parents often feel a surge of overwhelming awe and love for their newly birthed baby. Less often, however, have they taken lots of child-development courses that explain developmental norms, trajectories, and theories about how babies develop stage by stage and how best to support early development. Even more rarely have new parents taken courses that include practical experiences to encourage participating in, as well as carefully observing, the ways in which seasoned and well-trained caregivers embed learning activities in daily routines as they care in nurturing ways for infants and toddlers. Sometimes, professional care providers who provide emotional nurturing for babies have also not had sufficient opportunities for in-depth learning of ways to promote early learning in very young children.

This encyclopedia can serve as a treasure chest for parents and for infant-toddler caregivers. It provides a treasure trove of activities in a great many domains that are important for adults to consider when planning activities. The book addresses a myriad of developmental areas by providing interesting and stage-appropriate activities.

Among the varied activities provided are those that clearly address fundamental goals that caregivers need to accomplish to ensure an optimal developmental trajectory for each little person. Every baby deserves to have each caregiver foster:

- a loving, secure attachment to each person who is given the precious trust of caring for a baby or toddler;

- the early blossoming of receptive and expressive language abilities;

- pleasure in singing and listening to, as well as moving and dancing to, music;

- curiosity and love of learning—even the youngest baby is entranced by a mobile over the crib that swings in the air when the baby kicks or swipes a hand at it;

- delight in trying and mastering new activities, whether tasting new foods, rolling playdough into long snakes, scribbling a picture with a marker, blowing soap bubbles, trying to dress a doll or teddy bear, or handling and exploring a toy with focused attentiveness and persistence;

- early, passionate interest in age-appropriate books, carefully chosen so that infants and toddlers come to treasure them and love to have a special book read over and over;

- early emotional development of empathy—the ability to understand, accurately interpret, and care about another's feelings—as well as willingness to be helpful and kind when another person has troubles;

- love of the outdoors and nature and gentleness with creatures, such as flowers, plants, and tame animals;

- enjoyment of spatial and perceptual challenges in games that require simple counting abilities and estimations of distances and mass in order to accomplish an activity; and

- enhancement of young children's bodily strength and skills in climbing, swinging, running, skipping, jumping, and other gross motor activities that enhance gracefulness and self-confidence.

Of special importance and adding to the usefulness of the activities in this encyclopedia, the suggestions provided will increase a caregiver's awareness of the many different developmental goals that can be reached by arranging for a given activity. For example, when an adult provides props for dress-up pretend play, then such play can enhance toddlers' physical motor skills, fine motor control, prosocial interaction skills with peers, planning and sequencing skills, and language abilities.

Each of the activities provided in this encyclopedia is designed to enrich children's development in many areas as well as the domain that is the main focus of the activity. For example, learning to cut with a pair of safe scissors, in which eye-hand coordination and dexterity are a special focus, also can enhance a toddler's executive-planning skills, creativity, artistic imagination, and vocabulary enrichment. Remembering how to use this or any other safe tool also enhances a young child's memory skills.

This encyclopedia is so rich in activity suggestions that a caregiver, regardless of a particular child's personal preferences, will be able to choose at each stage of development some activity that really appeals to that special little person and will further that little one's positive growth and development. Adults who are searching among the rich array of activities can find suggestions that will feel comfortable in each domain of learning and will fit the unique skills or preferences of a particular child. Browsing through the many activities may also spur an adult to increase his or her own creativity in creating further experiences and activities with the same generous goals—to promote the optimal flourishing of each precious little child in care!

Alice Sterling Honig, PhD
Professor Emerita of Child Development
Syracuse University

Introduction

If you are looking for hundreds of ideas to help infants and toddlers grow and learn, this book is for you. More intellectual growth occurs in the first three years of life than at any other time. Not only does the brain grow during this period, but the structures that support learning now and in the future also are created.

Infants, toddlers, and two-year-olds process information every waking minute. They do this by observing, tasting, listening, smelling, and touching. These very young children try out different actions and learn from them. They are active learners who energetically shake, bang, drop, push, pull, roll, bounce, and move objects. They are constantly looking for patterns in interactions, in how objects work, and in how language is structured. They have goals, such as learning what a ball does; strategies, such as licking, tasting, bouncing, rolling, shaking, and pushing the ball; and theories about how things work, such as balls roll, but square blocks do not. They will be very surprised if they find a square object that also rolls. As they explore and experiment, they develop expectations for how relationships, objects, and the environment will act. The rapid growth in the first three years of life is nothing short of miraculous.

Whether you are a teacher, caregiver, parent, or family member, you are key to what and how the children learn about themselves, others, and the world. The experiences you provide for the children in your care play a crucial role in the process of hardwiring their brains for learning and loving. You provide the opportunities for young children to develop and learn in the emotional, social, language, cognitive, and motor domains. You also influence how children approach play and learning. Are they motivated, curious, and persistent in their learning? Can they manage their feelings, actions, and behaviors with the support of familiar adults? Do they demonstrate flexibility in their actions and behaviors? These **self-regulation** skills that young children develop with you will provide a foundation for their present and future learning.

We know that infants, toddlers, and two-year-olds thrive within safe, secure, affirming, affectionate, and motivating relationships. These relationships provide many opportunities for loving and learning at home and in care and education programs. Responsive relationship-based care is vital for children's brain development, secure **attachments**, energy and desire to learn, and sense of well-being. Young children need to know that they can trust adults to keep them safe, be encouraging, and make learning enjoyable. They develop confidence in their own abilities within warm, consistent, sensitive, caring relationships.

We also know that culture—what individuals and groups value and believe—influences all aspects of life and learning. These values and beliefs guide the decisions about who families want their children to be and what they want them to learn. We hope that you talk with families concerning their goals, hopes, and dreams for children and then consider which activities best support those goals.

How This Book Is Organized

Teachers, child care directors, and other early childhood professionals who work with infants and toddlers contributed many of the activities. This book provides an array of activities that are responsive to children's goals, interests, needs, and strengths and that support learning through children's exploration and discovery. Many of the activities happen during normal daily routines such as transitions, napping, and snacking. All activities support learning across emotional, social, language, cognitive, and physical and motor domains; however, some have a special focus on particular domains. Other activities are written for the learning areas in a program room—creative, dramatic play, literacy, math, outdoors and nature, and sensory/science. There is a section on fingerplays and rhymes that adults can relish with young children. The last section includes activities for working with families. All the activities are fun and enjoyable and are developmentally appropriate for very young children.

This book is organized within the following categories:

- Domains: emotional development, cognitive development/discovery, fine- and gross-motor development, language development, and social development

- Learning Areas*: construction, creative explorations, dramatic play, literacy, math, outdoor play/nature, and sensory/science

- Routines: arrival; songs, fingerplays, and rhymes; transitions; snack time; nap time; cleanup; and departure

- Working with Families

***Note:** Cognitive development and discovery can happen anywhere for infants, toddlers, and two-year-olds. Specific activities to support cognitive development are listed in that chapter. Similarly, fine- and gross-motor development can happen in a variety of settings. Specific activities to support motor development are listed in that chapter.

Age Ranges

Within each category, the activities include the age range for which the activity is best suited. Think of the activity selections as a continuum. For example, some are appropriate for infants; others can be adapted to work with infants, toddlers, and two-year-olds. Suggestions for adaptations in the activities will help you adjust to fit the interests and abilities of the children in your care.

Infant activities, signified by this symbol , are for babies up to twelve months old. The activities fit easily within an infant's daily routine of feeding, eating, diapering, and playing and will build relationships and support learning at the same time. Most of the activities for infants include language, literacy, and relationship opportunities.

Toddler activities, signified by this symbol , are for children from twelve to twenty-four months of age. Children this age enjoy dumping and filling, opening and closing containers, as well as crawling and walking through obstacle courses. They are developing both their large muscles in their arms and legs and their small muscles in their hands. Activities that engage toddlers' eyes and hands together build **perceptual** and **eye-hand coordination skills**. Activities that support emotional, social, language, and literacy activities are very important during these years. Toddlers' **receptive** (words they understand) and **expressive** (words they can say) vocabularies increase every day when they are given opportunities to engage in interactive, reciprocal sounds, gestures, words, and early sentence conversations. Many of the activities for toddlers recognize that they develop friendships, learn to be **prosocial**, and learn to negotiate conflicts within supportive adult-child relationships.

Some activities are appropriate for both infants and toddlers and are signified with both symbols. These activities include adaptations for children who are in these age groups. Children these ages need opportunities to actively explore their environments without being placed in containers, such as car seats, infant seats, jump seats, and entertainers. The activities emphasize opportunities to play with new materials and to experiment and discover something new every day. Activities that build secure relationships with adults and peers are the key to the success of these children. Infants need nurturing, and toddlers will want to explore but will need to return to their favorite adults for emotional energy.

Activities for two-year-olds are signified by this symbol: 🚶.

Two-year-olds, from twenty-four to thirty-six months of age, love using crayons, paint, and playdough to create. Language and literacy activities are crucial for this age. Almost every activity builds on books that two-year-olds love to look at and listen to. Many songs and fingerplays are appropriate for this age group to learn. Dramatic play opportunities increase as two-year-olds begin to pretend while feeding dolls, stir pretend food in pots and pans, and imagine that they are dogs or cats.

Some activities, such as Discovery Bottles, are appropriate for children of all ages and abilities, with adaptations to make the activity easier and more challenging. Infants will visually enjoy the bottles, and older infants and toddlers will experiment with rolling them. Older toddlers and two-year-olds can help make the discovery bottles, experimenting with what materials make their creations glow, sparkle, light up, and make interesting sounds.

Activities

Each activity includes a list of needed materials. You will probably already have most of them on hand, and families are great resources for materials. You might want to ask local businesses whether they have items they want to donate, such as empty cardboard boxes. Note: Only teachers and caregivers should use certain materials. Give children only the materials that they can use safely.

The "More to Do: Extensions and Adaptations" section provides ideas for adapting the activities for children's interests and abilities. This section also offers ideas for using books and songs that build on the opportunities for learning provided in the activity. There are enrichment ideas to extend the activity into other areas of the curriculum, such as dramatic play, language, literacy, art explorations, and outdoor play/nature. Because of the extensions and adaptations, there are many activities within activities, allowing and supporting the activity to be offered for many days and weeks and revisited when you think children's interest will be sparked again.

It is critical that you know the children in your care and select activities that are interesting, challenging, and allow for success. Psychologist J. McVicker Hunt called this *meeting the match*, and developmental psychologist Lev Vygotsky's work helped us think about the **zone of proximal development**. These terms mean that we find activities that are both challenging enough to spark children's motivation and are easy enough that children can successfully complete them with effort. Use your judgment to decide whether an activity is appropriate for an individual child or a group of children. Adapt activities to take into account children's individual strengths, interests, and needs. Children with special needs may need adaptations in some specific domains but not in others.

Determining the Appropriateness of an Activity
· · ● ● ⬤ ● ● · ·

- Does it meet one or more children's needs and strengths?

- Does it spark the interest of a child or many children?

- Does it provide for developmental levels—infants, toddlers, and/or two-year-olds?

- Does it support learning in a variety of developmental domains—motor, communication, thinking, social, emotional, and cultural?

- Does it support a child doing many different things with the toy or material?

- Does it support gender-neutral, multicultural thinking and nonviolent, prosocial behavior?

- Can the material or the activity be offered as an opportunity for children rather than as a forced activity?

- Can the material or experience be adapted for children with special needs?

- Are vocabulary-rich expansion interactions suggested?

Source: Wittmer, Donna, and Sandra Petersen. 2017. *Infant and Toddler Development and Responsive Program Planning: A Relationship-Based Approach,* 4th ed. New York: Pearson.

Some activities provide a list of related books, songs, and rhymes. These enhance and support concepts that children are learning in the activity. For example, during an activity, children may have opportunities to learn prosocial skills, names of emotions, colors, sorting skills, and concepts such as on/off, up/down, in/out, and the names of animals. The books and songs chosen provide more opportunities to learn those skills and concepts. Look in this section for both original and new versions of familiar songs and rhymes.

The "Opportunities for Learning" section highlights the possibilities that the activity offers for children's learning. They are not learning objectives that you make sure all children learn. Rather, they define the potential that each activity has for children's learning. They are based on North Carolina's *Foundations for Early Learning and Development* (ncchildcare.nc.gov/pdf_forms/NC_foundations.pdf) and on the *Head Start Early Learning Outcomes Framework* (https://eclkc.ohs.acf.hhs.gov/hslc/hs/sr/approach/pdf/ohs-framework.pdf).

Some activities have a section called "What We Know." This section offers developmental information to support your understanding of how and why to use the activity with the children in your care.

Glossary

A glossary of terms appears on pages 269 through 271. The terms that appear in boldface in the text are defined there.

Final Thoughts

Safety

Safety is the first and most important requirement for any activity. Review all activities before presenting them to the children, using your knowledge of the developmental needs of the children in your care. Test all materials with a choke tube to be sure that they do not pose a choking hazard.

Qualities of Successful Activities

Any activity you do with very young children should meet their need for secure relationships with their primary caregivers. Children should receive responsive, positive, warm interactions—not scolding, harsh, authoritarian interactions. Children must be loved, nurtured, cherished, and comforted when they are distressed.

Activities should provide respect for each child's individuality, development, and culture and should offer language and communication models and responsive interactions with children. Activities should be responsive to individual children and group interests, goals, needs, strengths, and culture. Create an individualized program by adapting and extending activities for children's different ages, stages, cultures, and interests.

Activities should provide prosocial models and support children learning prosocial behavior for present and future social and academic success. Caregivers should demonstrate empathy for children's feelings, needs, and distress and should help children understand emotions, feel empathy for others, and express emotions in healthy ways.

Activities should offer levels of symbolization—a real object, animal, or person; photos or pictures of objects, animals, or persons; or dramatic play, letters, and words—in many activities to support cognitive, language, and literacy development. Language and literacy experiences, in particular, are the key to children's ability to communicate, socialize successfully, and learn to read.

Create enriched environments that are not only individually effective by age, stage, and culture but are also enticing, beautiful, calm, and interesting. Encourage problem solving as basic to children's lifelong learning. Create schedules that ensure that children have time to explore in an enriched environment and have opportunities to come back to adults for comfort, energy, and safety. Ensure that teachers understand that all opportunities have possibilities for language, literacy, emotional, social, motor, and cognitive learning. **Scaffold** learning by helping children learn how to learn. For example, rather than finishing a puzzle for a child, help the child learn strategies for doing a puzzle.

Understand the importance of knowing, observing, and documenting children's learning.

And work closely with families, always.

Section 1
DOMAINS

- Emotional Development
- Cognitive Development/Discovery
- Fine- and Gross-Motor Development
- Language Development
- Social Development

Emotional Development

What Are You Feeling?

Materials

None

What to Do

1. Observe and respond to the physical and verbal communication cues of infants. These might be yawns, turning away from you, burbles, wiggling, moving feet, crying, clinging tightly, throwing herself back when she is in your lap, nestling against your shoulder, or other cues.

2. Try your best to figure out what a child is communicating to you. For example:

   - When an infant turns her head away from you, she is signaling that she needs a break from the interaction. Wait until the infant is ready to engage again.

   - Throwing herself backward is a strong disengagement cue. The infant may be feeling very uncomfortable in the situation.

   - Burbles and drooling may mean the infant needs less stimulation.

   - Smiles say, "I like interacting with you."

3. As you become familiar with a child's cues, you will be able to guess what she needs. The infant will let you know if you guessed wrong, but take heart! We caregivers hardly ever get our responses right the first time. Being responsive means being a detective of infants' communication cues. As Magda Gerber, infant-toddler specialist, would say to a baby: "I don't know what you want, but I will try to figure it out."

4. Be responsive and alleviate a child's stress if you can. Stress can have negative consequences for the infants' brain development.

Songs: Lullabies are very soothing to an infant.

What We Know

Infants need responsive interactions with adults from birth to develop secure attachments, learn language, and develop self-confidence. They need opportunities to take a turn in an interaction. When adults are responsive, infants learn that language is a tool for communication (Tamis-LeMonda, Kuchirko, and Song, 2014) and that they can be effective communicators. Infants also develop expectations for positive adult-child interactions and feelings of **self-efficacy**—"I can make something happen"—when adults smile back at an infant (Mcquaid, Bibok, and Carpendale, 2009).

- Emotional development: Help the child develop the expectation of consistent, positive interactions through familiar adults who are responsive to her needs. This leads to secure attachments with her primary caregivers.

- Language development: Use both nonverbal and verbal communication to engage the child in interactions. Children can process the sounds and words in lullabies.

- Cognitive development: When adults respond to a baby's communication cues, they actively influence the child's world. This gives the child the confidence to explore her environment and learn.

Baby Faces Books

Materials

Construction paper

Scissors (adult use only)

Baby or parenting magazines

Glue

Markers

Clear contact paper

Hole punch (adult use only)

Ribbon or yarn

What to Do

Ahead of Time:

1. Cut different colors of construction paper into 6" x 6" squares. Make four to ten squares.

2. Cut out enough pictures of babies from the magazines to put a different face on each paper square. Try to find large close-ups of faces and different expressions and emotions. If you like, you can take photos of the children in your care and use them to create a *Baby Faces* book. Try to capture photos of children with different emotional expressions.

What We Know

- At eight months of age, some babies will reach out to peers in distress (Liddle, Bradley, & Mcgrath, 2015).

- Even at six months of age, infants show a preference for looking at videos of same-age infants. Nine-month-old infants will look longer at pictures of infants their own age than at those of children of different ages (Sanefuji, Ohgami, & Hashiya, 2006).

3. Glue the pictures onto the fronts and backs of the construction paper pages.

4. Place the pages in the desired order. Print the words *Baby Faces* on one square to make the title page.

5. Cover the pages with clear contact paper. For each page, cut a piece of contact paper twice as wide as the page and about a half inch longer on each side. Fold the sticky side of the contact paper over both sides of the construction paper page and overlap the contact paper to seal it around the edges. Cut a ½" rounded border around each page, making each one about the same size.

6. Punch two holes on the left side of each page, and tie the pages together with a ribbon or piece of yarn.

With the Children:

1. As you look through each page with a baby, point to and talk about the parts of the face. The child will use sustained attention as he focuses on the pictures.

2. Watch the infant's eyes. Where is the infant looking? Follow his cues and talk about what he is finding interesting.

3. Talk about the emotions expressed in each picture. Make that expression on your own face. The baby might try to make the expression, too.

More to Do: Extensions and Adaptations

For Toddlers and Two-Year-Olds:

- When using photos of children in your room, write the first name of the child at the bottom of the page.
- Use magazine pictures of toddlers and two-year-olds on the pages.

Suggested Books:

Baby Faces by Margaret Miller

Baby Faces by DK Publishing

Baby Faces by Kate Merritt

Opportunities for Learning

- Emotional development: Infants will learn about the feelings of others. Eventually, they will show empathy toward other babies in distress and reach out to them.

- Language development: The children will respond to and use a growing vocabulary as they learn the names of different feelings, watch their teacher express emotions, and hear the names of different expressions. They can learn *sad, happy, angry, disappointed, surprised,* and so on.

- Literacy development: Two-year-olds will show interest in print if their name is written at the bottom of a photo of themselves. This activity provides a foundation for reading.

Mirror Face

Materials

Unbreakable child-safe mirror

What to Do

1. Sit down with an infant. Look into the mirror and make faces that illustrate different emotions, such as happy, sad, scared, and so on. Use the word for each emotion as you make the face.

2. Tell the child what each facial expression means: "I'm smiling because I'm happy."

More to Do: Extensions and Adaptations

For Toddlers and Two-Year-Olds:

- Encourage the children to make different facial expressions to you and in the mirror.

- Ask them how they feel when they make a face: "Oh, I see you are frowning. How do you feel?"

Song: "If You're Happy and You Know It"

What We Know

Children may begin to recognize themselves in a mirror around eighteen to twenty-four months of age. In studies by Beulah Amsterdam in 1972 and Mark Nielsen and Cheryl Dissanayake in 2004, the researchers secretly made a mark on toddlers' faces. If the toddlers touched the mark when looking in a mirror, they were said to have **self-recognition**. Children younger than eighteen months typically ignored the mark and acted like there was another child in the mirror.

Suggested Books:

If You're Happy and You Know It , Clap Your Hands! by David Carter

If You're Happy and You Know It! by Jane Cabrera

Opportunities for Learning

- Emotional development: By playing this game with you, children will begin to understand and express emotions. They will develop a sense of self and begin to recognize themselves in a mirror. Over time, they will begin to develop impulse control when they learn how to express emotions with words rather than falling apart when they are angry or sad.

- Language development: Children will begin to understand and use feelings words, such as *happy, angry, or sad*. (Two-year-olds might say, "Me so mad," or "Me so sad.") They will also learn words for actions, such as *clap, stomp, boo-hoo*.

- Cognitive development: Children will begin to make the connection between their feelings and their actions (**cause and effect**). They will learn that when they are sad, an adult will comfort them, and when they are angry, an adult will help them manage that feeling in helpful ways.

Describing Emotions

Materials

Magazines

Cardboard

Clear contact paper

Ribbon or yarn

Scissors

Glue

Hole punch (adults use only)

What to Do

Ahead of Time:

1. From the magazines, cut out photos that show children with a variety of emotions.

2. Glue the photos to the cardboard, and cover them with clear contact paper.

3. Punch holes in one side of the cardboard.

4. Repeat until you have several pages.

5. Tie the pages together to make a book about feelings.

With the Children:

1. When the children are looking at the book, be sure to name the feeling depicted in each photo. Use language to say how you know what emotion is being expressed; for example, "The girl is smiling. I think she is happy."

2. You can use these books when conflicts occur to help children begin to realize what the other child is feeling.

3. As the children look at the faces in the book, they will be maintaining focus (with support) on photos of children their own age.

More to Do: Extensions and Adaptations

For Infants:

- Describe the emotion for the infant. Make the faces yourself, and notice how the infant reacts.

- If the child has a home language other than English, use words in a language that the child speaks. For example, say the word for the emotion in English and then in Spanish.

For Toddlers and Two-Year-Olds:

- Describe the emotion for younger toddlers.

- Encourage older toddlers and two-year-olds to describe the emotion. Start with choice questions, such as, "Is the baby feeling sad or happy?" After the child can label some emotions, ask an open-ended question, such as, "How does the baby feel?"

- Relate the emotion expressed in the photo to the child's experience; for example, "Remember when you felt so sad because Tamara took your doll away from you? Your face looked very sad."

- Look at the book with several two-year-olds together. Encourage them to tell each other a time when they felt sad, happy, afraid, and so on.

- Use words in a language that the child speaks. For example, say the word in English and then in Spanish.

For Two-Year-Olds:

- Write the name of the emotion on the bottom of each page. Say excitedly, "This word says *sad*. Look, the word *sad* starts with an *S*." Do not pressure children to know the letter. When you tell the child the name of the letter, you are helping the child begin to learn the name of the letter.

> ## What We Know
>
> When eighteen to thirty-month-olds were encouraged by their parents to label and explain emotions while the parents were reading books to them, the children later helped and shared with others more frequently (Brownell et al., 2013). Learning about emotions may help children realize that others have feelings, too. In contrast, children who have been exposed to aggression between parents have more difficulty regulating their feelings of sadness, withdrawal, and fear (Raver, Blair, and Garrett-Peters, 2014).

Suggested Books:

Baby Faces by Margaret Miller

Baby Faces by DK Publishing

Baby Faces by Kate Merritt

Baby Happy, Baby Sad by Leslie Patricelli

Opportunities for Learning

· · · • • ● • • · ·

- Emotional development: The children will learn to recognize and interpret others' emotions and to begin to manage their own emotions.

- Social development: The children will feel empathy for others' feelings and show care and concern toward others.

- Language development: The children will begin to understand and express the names for feelings.

- Literacy development: The children will develop beginning knowledge of the alphabet when an adult points out letters and words.

How Do You Feel Today?

Materials

Circle pattern

Markers

Old catalogs or magazines

Craft sticks

Paper or tagboard

Glue

Scissors (adult use only)

What We Know

The names of different emotions are important for children to learn. The language experiences that children have in the early years make a difference in their language learning and later reading ability (Duff et al., 2015). Children need to hear many responsive and encouraging words in the first three years.

What to Do

Ahead of Time:

1. Trace around the circle pattern to make circle shapes on paper.

2. Cut out the circles to use for faces.

With the Children:

1. Ask the children to look through old catalogs or magazines and find people who look happy, sad, angry, silly, and scared. Help the children identify the emotions: "Oh, that person is smiling. She must be happy."

2. Cut out the pictures for the children, or let two-year-olds use child-safe scissors to cut out the faces. **Note:** It will be challenging for toddlers and many two-year-olds to look through magazines and stay on task as they find faces that represent different emotions. For some individuals or groups, the teacher may need to have the faces cut out, ready to glue onto the circles and craft sticks.

3. Help them glue the pictures onto the circles. As the children look through magazines and glue faces on the circles, they will maintain attentiveness, effort, and persistence.

4. Help them glue a craft stick to the back of each face to make feeling sticks.

5. Put several faces out at a time. Describe an emotion. Encourage the children to look for and hold up the face that matches the emotion. Do not expect toddlers and two-year-olds to know the names of very many emotions. They are just learning to understand and name them.

More to Do: Extensions and Adaptations

For Older Toddlers and Two-Year-Olds:

- This is a choice-time activity. Make it available at a learning center with a teacher present, so that the teacher can work with small groups of children who choose to do the activity.

- Place the feeling sticks in a flowerpot of Styrofoam close to the door that children enter in the morning. Ask the children to pick up a stick that matches how they feel that morning. Encourage them to show it to a parent and/or teacher.

- Use the labels for emotions often to help children learn the words that match the feeling.

- Ask children how a friend feels. See if they can find the face that matches their friend's face.

Opportunities for Learning

· · • • ● • • · ·

- Emotional development: The children will develop a sense of self as they think about how they feel and how to connect to others. They will begin to understand and express emotions. They will develop empathy as they think about how another person feels.

- Social development: The children will develop a sense of self with others and begin to understand friendship. They will develop social understanding as they learn to "read" the faces of others and think about how others feel.

- Language development: The children will understand and use an increasing number of words, such as *happy, sad, angry, scared, silly, circle, stick, glue, friend,* and the names of friends.

- Cognitive development: The children will problem solve as they try to figure out how to glue the faces and sticks to the circles.

- Physical/Motor development: The children will develop fine-motor skills and eye-hand coordination as they glue and handle the stick. They will use safe behaviors as adults remind them how to hold the stick so that they and others feel safe.

Cognitive Development/ Discovery

Peekaboo

Materials

Handkerchief or soft cloth large enough to cover the infant's face

What to Do

1. Place a handkerchief over the baby's head and pretend you cannot find him.

2. Say, "Where's (baby's name)?"

3. When the baby takes off the handkerchief, get excited and say, "There's (baby's name)!"

4. Encourage the baby to put the handkerchief on his head by himself.

5. Say, "Peekaboo!" after you know the infant or young toddler is comfortable with the game.

More to Do: Extensions and Adaptations

For Infants:

- Do this activity with infants who you know will not be upset when the cloth is placed over their faces. If an infant begins to fuss, then stop the activity and try again at another time.

- Place the handkerchief over your face and say, "Where's (your name)?"

- Most infants older than six months of age will pull the cloth off their own faces. As they play with you, they will develop initiative and curiosity.

- Some infants will wait until the adult removes the cloth. They are demonstrating impulse control and self-regulation. This may become a game for the infant to be quiet and lie still with the cloth on his face.

What We Know

Usually by eight months of age, infants will physically look for objects that are out of sight. However, very young infants visually expect objects to reappear after they watch the objects go behind a screen (Bertenthal, Gredebäck, and Boyer, 2013). They may look for their special caregivers (**person permanence**) before they have object permanence.

For Young Toddlers:

- Young toddlers may start the game themselves and want you to play along.

- Young toddlers still delight in peekaboo games and may begin to say the words themselves.

Suggested Book: *Peek-A Who?* by Nina Laden

Opportunities for Learning
• • • ● • • •

- Emotional development: The children will develop expectations for sensitive, caring interactions with responsive adults. They will build attachment and trust with adults when the adult is predictable and responsive. They will learn to take turns in responsive interactions.

- Language development: The children will learn their names and the meaning of the word *peekaboo*.

- Cognitive development: The children will develop **person** and **object permanence** when the adult hides her face with the cloth.

- Physical/Motor development: The children will use fine-motor skills as they reach toward their own or an adult's face and pull off the cloth.

Did I Do That?

Materials

Toys that make sounds when touched, shaken, pushed, or pulled

Ankle rattles

What to Do

1. Make the toys available to the infants. Younger infants will gradually learn to reach for a toy.

2. For older infants, place the toys on the floor. They may reach or crawl to a toy.

3. As the children interact with the toys, talk about what they are doing: "I heard a rattle. Did you make that sound?" Encourage them to repeat their actions.

4. As the children interact with the toys, they will maintain focus and demonstrate persistence, with support from an adult. This is the beginning of self-regulation and **executive**

functioning. They will show interest in and curiosity about objects, materials, or events.

More to Do: Extensions and Adaptations

For Young Infants:

- Help them make something happen and repeat their actions to make it happen again. Observe the infant with the toy. Does the infant repeat an action to get the same effect?

- Observe the child's thinking: Does the infant poke, push, or hit a toy to make it work? How does this change over time?

- Infants must sleep on their backs, but they need some tummy time during the day. Place a toy in front of an infant who is on his tummy.

- When young infants coo or smile, respond with enthusiasm. The infant will probably smile or coo again.

For Older Infants:

- Safe instruments such as small pianos allow children to make sounds by touching a key.

- Books are wonderful toys to offer older infants. They may lie on their backs while holding a small book in the air, or they may sit on your lap while you hold the book. Many older infants can turn the pages of board books, and with each turn of a page there is a surprise. They enjoy making things happen.

- When older infants babble, say a first word, or make a noise with a toy, respond with excitement. The infant will probably do the action again.

What We Know

When infants actively explore objects, they learn more about the objects than if they just observe actions (Gerson and Woodward, 2014). When three-month-old infants successfully pulled or moved a mobile with reaching movements, those infants reached more frequently at other times than did infants who were just allowed to observe the mobile (Needham et al., 2014). Exploring toys and making something happen increases learning.

- Emotional development: The children will develop a sense of identity and belonging. They will show an awareness of self and confidence in their own abilities in relationships with others.

- Language development: The children will use nonverbal communication (gestures) and language (coos, babbles, first words) to engage others in interaction. They will learn the words *book, toy, lap,* and the phrase "You did it!"

- Cognitive development: The children will develop expectations for how objects, toys, and people work and how the children can make them work. They will develop an understanding of cause and effect as they act on their social and physical environment. They will use a variety of strategies to solve problems, such as figuring out how a toy makes noise.

- Physical development: The children will demonstrate eye-hand coordination and fine-motor skills when they handle different types of toys.

Where Did the Monkey Go?

Materials

Shoe box

Familiar items, such as toys

What to Do

1. Turn the shoe box upside down, and place a familiar item, such as a stuffed monkey, underneath the box as the child watches.

2. Ask, "Where did the monkey go? Can you find it?"

3. If the child needs help, tap on the box, peek underneath, or sing the following song to the tune of "Frère Jacques."

    Where's the monkey? Where's the monkey?
    Can you find it? Can you find it?
    Look under the box. Look under the box.
    There it is. There it is.

4. As the children search for the toy, they will demonstrate initiative and curiosity. Curiosity piques as a favorite toy is hidden.

What We Know

Babies have a basic knowledge of number (Spelke, 2011). Young infants are puzzled if three objects go behind a screen but only two come out from behind it..

More to Do: Extensions and Adaptations

For Older Infants:

- During snack, put cereal under a bowl or cloth for the child to find and eat.

- Hide your face with a cloth, then pull it off and say, "Peekaboo! Here I am."

- Show the infant that you are hiding a toy under a cloth. Wait to see if the infant pulls off the cloth and looks for the toy. If the infant doesn't, then pull off the cloth and say, "There it is. The toy is under the cloth." Try the activity again on another day.

- Hide a crawling infant's foot with a cloth, and see if the infant pulls off the cloth. Say, "Oh, where's your foot? There it is. Your foot is under the cloth."

For Toddlers:

You'll need two shoe boxes. Hide an object under one shoe box (or cloth) first and see if the toddler can find it. If the toddler can find it, then hide it under the first shoe box again. Next, take it out and show the toddler, and then hide it under a second shoe box. The toddler may continue to look under the first shoe box even though you've shown the toddler that you moved the object to the second shoe box. Older toddlers will usually look under the second shoe box because of their previous experience with objects and knowing that they exist, even when out of sight. Be sure to use the words *under* and *over* often when playing this game.

Suggested Books:

Pop-Up Peekaboo! Colors by DK Publishing

Pop-Up Peekaboo! Farm by DK Publishing

Pop-Up Peekaboo! Woof! Woof! by DK Publishing

Pop-Up Peekaboo! Playtime by DK Publishing

Pop-up Peekaboo! Meow! by DK Publishing

Opportunities for Learning
• • • • ● • • • •

- Social development: The children will develop expectations of consistent, positive interactions with familiar adults.

- Language development: The children's vocabulary will increase as they understand and use an increasing number of words, such as *under, over,* and *monkey.*

- Cognitive development: The children will develop object permanence, **spatial relationships**, and problem-solving skills.

- Physical/Motor development: The children will begin to coordinate hand and eye movements to perform actions. This develops as children handle toys and manipulate a cloth or a shoe box.

How Things Work—
An Adventure Walk in the Room

Materials

None

What to Do

1. Hold an infant in your arms or walk with older children. Walk around the room, showing them how things work. For example, flick a light switch on and off, open and close a drawer, or turn a water faucet off and on.

2. Describe what is happening with rich, specific language. With a younger child say, "I'm turning the light on. I'm turning the light off." With older children say, "When I flip this switch up, it turns the light on. When I flip the switch down, the light turns off."

3. If it is safe and healthy, allow the child to touch the objects and try to do the actions, too. This activity will give the children an opportunity to show interest in and about objects, materials, and events. They may want to do the activity again and again as they seek to understand the world around them.

What We Know

Children need many active hands-on experiences with concepts such as on/off and up/down before they begin to understand their meanings and say the words. Infants' language development benefits when adults repeat words (Newman, Rowe, and Ratner, 2015).

More to Do: Extensions and Adaptations

For Infants:

Do the activity with individual infants so that they have a chance to hear the words you use and see the action.

For Toddlers and Two-Year-Olds:

- Take two children at a time on the adventure walk, so that both can hear your words and see what is happening.
- Assure the other children that they will get a turn also. Then, keep your promise and go ask other children if they want a turn.

Suggested Book: *If You Give a Moose a Muffin* by Laura Numeroff

- Emotional development: The children will express a range of emotions. This activity will often make children laugh when they are surprised at the actions. They will take safe risks in learning. You can help them feel safe while exploring by modeling the actions first.

- Social development: The children will form relationships and interact positively with other children as they take turns trying the action.

- Language development: The children will participate in conversations with peers and adults in one-on-one and small-group interactions. They will ask and answer questions to seek help, get information, or clarify something that is not understood. They will increase understanding and use of vocabulary as adults emphasize words, such as *on, off, up, down, light, faucet, water, switch, moose,* and *muffin*.

- Cognitive development: The children will learn about cause and effect when they watch the adult flip a switch and a light comes on. They will use spatial awareness when they open and close a door. They will build scientific knowledge as they explore their environment and experience how things work.

- Physical/Motor development: The children will demonstrate gross-motor skills (arms) and fine-motor skills (hands) and perceptual skills (eyes and hands together) as they interact with items in the room.

Discovery Bottles

Materials

5 clear plastic bottles in a variety of sizes	Water
Vegetable oil	Food coloring
Dish soap	Glitter
Sequins	Small plastic animals
Craft glue	Duct or packing tape

What to Do

Ahead of Time:

1. Fill a bottle with equal amounts of water and oil. Add food coloring.

2. Fill four more bottles almost full with water. Add dish soap and food coloring to one bottle, glitter and food coloring to the second bottle, sequins and food coloring to the third bottle, and food coloring and some small plastic animals that float and sink to the fourth bottle. Be creative! Fill the bottles with different items that might be of interest to the children.

3. Secure the lids with craft glue so that the children are unable to open the bottles. Tape the lids securely. Display these bottles in the discovery center.

With the Children:

1. Encourage the children to investigate the different bottles. They might shake or roll them.

2. Follow the children's cues. Talk with the children about what they see in the bottles, including the differences and similarities in the bottles.

More to Do: Extensions and Adaptations

For Infants and Young Toddlers:

- Fill bottles of different sizes so small hands can hold on to some of the bottles.
- Adults can hold the bottles up to the light and encourage the young child to look through them.
- Infants who are on the floor on their backs can hold up the bottle to look at and through it.
- Infants practicing tummy time can play with the small bottles.
- Encourage walkers to hold a bottle while they walk. This increases balancing skills.
- Read *Ten Little Babies* by Gyo Fujikawa to several infants in your lap or several who are on the floor.

For Older Toddlers and Two-Year-Olds:

You may make the discovery bottles with several children—depending on the abilities of the children.

Count the number of bottles and the number of animals that they see in the bottles.

Talk about the patterns and colors that they see.

Experiment with which bottle rolls the farthest.

Some bottles will roll in funny ways—encourage the children to roll their bodies in the same way. Then sing the song below and read *Roll Over!* by Merle Peek or *Ten in the Bed* by Penny Dale as small groups of no more than five children gather to do the activity.

Song:

Ask the children to lie on the floor side by side. With each verse, one child rolls away. The children who roll away can stay together as a group rather than feel that they must leave the group. The song can be acted out using the bottles instead of children.

Roll Over!
There were five in the bed,
And the little one said:
"Roll over! Roll over!"
So, they all rolled over, and one fell out. (one child rolls away)

There were four in the bed,
And the little one said:
"Roll over! Roll over!"
So, they all rolled over, and one fell out. (one child rolls away)

There were three in the bed,
And the little one said:
"Roll over! Roll over!"
So, they all rolled over, and one fell out. (one child rolls away)

There were two in the bed,
And the little one said:
"Roll over! Roll over!"
So, they all rolled over, and one fell out. (one child rolls away)

There was one in the bed,
And the little one said:
"Good night!"

Suggested Books:

Roll Over! A Counting Song by Merle Peek

Ten in the Bed by Penny Dale

Ten Little Babies by Gyo Fujikawa

Give Me Eggs—It's Eggciting!

Materials

12 colorful plastic eggs

Basket

Empty plastic egg carton

What to Do

1. Put the eggs in the basket. Place the basket and the empty egg carton on the floor in the discovery or fine-motor learning area.

2. Let the children explore the eggs, carton, and basket freely. Observe what their thinking is about moving eggs. Do they move them one or two at a time? Do they explore how to fit the eggs in the carton? What are their goals? What are they trying to do with the eggs and basket?

3. As the children play, if it doesn't interfere with the children's concentration, talk about the color of the eggs or count the eggs as they move them from the carton to the basket and back again. Use words such as *full, empty, in,* and *out.*

4. Sit in the cognitive-discovery learning area and start reading the books listed below.

More to Do: Extensions and Adaptations

- Increase or decrease the number of eggs and containers depending on the capabilities of the group.
- Provide different types of containers. Children will build spatial understanding as they try to fit the eggs into different sizes and shapes of containers.
- Provide a shoe box with holes on top and on the sides just large enough for an egg to fit through.
- If the eggs are large enough, place toy chicks (too large to cause choking) inside the eggs for children to find.

Suggested Books:

Ten Little Eggs by Jean Marzollo

Ten Chirpy Chicks by Debbie Tarbett

Opportunities for Learning

• • • • **●** • • • •

- Emotional development: The children will develop a positive sense of self-identity as they experiment with and move the eggs.
- Language development: The children will learn new vocabulary, such as *full, empty, in, out, basket,* and *container.*
- Cognitive development: The children will develop object permanence as they close the cover of the carton and open it again. They will develop spatial understandings as they experiment with how to fit the eggs into the carton.
- Physical/Motor development: The children will develop fine-motor skills as they use the small muscles in their hands. They will develop perceptual skills as they judge how to fit the eggs into the carton.

Boxes Galore—Where's the Toy?

Materials

5–8 shoe boxes of different sizes

Toys such as blocks, balls, and plastic cars

Basket or large bowl

What to Do

1. Spread five to eight shoe boxes with their lids on the floor in the fine-motor or cognitive-discovery area.

2. Provide a basket or large bowl, and place toys in the area.

3. Observe how the children remove the lids from the shoe boxes, put a toy inside, and replace the top. Observe their goals and strategies for accomplishing those goals.

4. Let the children put toys in the boxes, take them out, and move them from box to box. As the children explore, they will demonstrate emerging initiative and curiosity.

More to Do: Extensions and Adaptations

- Increase or decrease the number of boxes, depending on the capabilities of the children who come to play the game.

- Hide a toy elephant or other stuffed animal in one box, and then mix the boxes. Ask, "Can you find the elephant? Where did he go?" "I wonder where the elephant is hiding." To make this easier for some children, make sure that the elephant box has a different-colored lid. To make it more challenging, have all the boxes look the same. Do this several times so that children begin to watch carefully where you put the elephant and where the box goes.

- Start reading a book as an informal group gathers to play the game and listen to the story. Have each child hold a stuffed animal that goes with the book, such as a bear, lion, hippo, flamingo, or elephant.

- Take photos of the children to create a display that lists what children are learning.

Suggested Book: Polar Bear, Polar Bear, What Do You Hear? by Bill Martin Jr. and Eric Carle

Song: (Sing to the tune of "Where, Oh Where Has My Little Dog Gone?")

> *Where, oh where has my elephant gone?* (hold palms up)
> *Where, oh where can she be?*
> *With her trunk so long* (put hands in front of mouth for a trunk)
> *And her tail so short* (hold hands behind you)
> *Oh where, oh where can she be?* (hold hands palms up)

Opportunities for Learning

- Emotional development: The children will demonstrate positive feelings about themselves.
- Social development: The children will develop relationships and a sense of belonging with other children.
- Language development: The children will learn new vocabulary, such as names of animals, *in, out, box, lid,* and words in the book.
- Cognitive development: The children will recall information as they remember where the elephant went and will learn by imitation.
- Physical/Motor development: The children will develop perceptual skills as they watch to see where the elephant goes. They will develop fine-motor skills as they use the small muscles in their hands to handle toys and open and shut the boxes.

On/Off, In/Out, Up/Down

Materials

Mechanical toys with on/off switches

Flashlights

Baskets or boxes

Small toys without switches

What to Do

Explore the concepts of on and off, in and out, and up and down with the following ideas:

- On/off: Let the children explore the mechanical toys and flashlights. Encourage them to experiment with the on/off switches.
- In/out: Let the children explore the small toys and the baskets and boxes. Show the children how to put the toys into the baskets or boxes and say, "In." Model dumping the toys out and say, "Out."

What We Know

Psychologist Jean Piaget developed the concept of **cognitive disequilibrium**, which occurs when a person is confronted with information that does not fit with what he already knows. When the children realize that some toys have switches and others do not, they are motivated to create a new idea or **schema** of what a toy is and what it can do. They will experiment to see which toys become active when a switch is flipped.

As the children explore, they will seek information and demonstrate persistence in their actions and behaviors. This occurs when children are offered new toys and allowed to explore them.

More to Do: Extensions and Adaptations

For Young Toddlers:

With young toddlers who are saying one-word sentences, when the toys and lights are switched on, say, "On." When they are switched off, say, "Off."

For Older Toddlers and Two-Year-Olds:

- With children using one-, two-, or three-word sentences, you can use **parallel talk**: "You turned the light on." "You turned the light off." "You put the flashlights in the box." "You took the toys out of the box."

- Encourage the children to explore the toys with switches and those without switches. You can ask, "How are these toys different?"

Suggested Book: In & Out, Up & Down by Sesame Street

Opportunities for Learning
· · ● · ● ● · ● · ·

- Emotional development: The children will show confidence in their own ability. This occurs as children cause events to happen.

- Social development: The children will learn social skills, such as how to take turns with the toys. They will learn prosocial skills and attitudes if an adult encourages a child to help another child who is struggling.

- Language development: Children are learning the concepts of on/off, in/out, and up/down as adults use the words often in direct connection with the action.

- Cognitive development: The children will explore the characteristics of the physical world. They will problem solve how to turn objects on and off and flip switches up and down. They will develop spatial awareness as they move objects in space. They will use their memories as a foundation for more complex actions and thoughts. They will recognize the differences between familiar and unfamiliar objects.

- Physical/Motor development: The children will develop fine-motor skills (use of small muscles in fingers), perceptual skills (using eyes and hands together), and gross-motor skills (using large muscles to sit and balance while holding a toy).

Instrument Fun

Materials

Rhythm instruments, such as drums, tambourines, and shakers

What to Do

1. Make instruments available in a learning center. Stay nearby to support the children who choose to experiment with the instruments.

2. When a child does something with an instrument, such as hits a tambourine, imitate the child's action. Wait for the child to respond. If he does, see how many turns a child will take before stopping.

3. Observe what surprises the children about the instruments. Do they have a hypothesis about how to make noise with each type of instrument? How do the children experiment with the instruments?

What We Know

With a family member and an experimenter, nine-month-olds listened to music twelve times for fifteen minutes a time over the course of one month. The experimenter helped parents and babies tap out the beats in time with the music. Other children played with toys but didn't listen to music. The babies who heard the music and tapped out the beats were better able to detect patterns in sounds, an ability that helps babies learn language (Zhao and Kuhl, 2016).

More to Do: Extensions and Adaptations

For Older Infants, Toddlers, and Two-Year-Olds:

Sit with the children and listen to music, tapping out the beats in time to the music.

For Toddlers:

Toddlers will enjoy instruments that they can shake. These include bells, tambourines, or rain sticks.

For Two-Year-Olds:

Two-year-olds might like wind instruments such as recorders or kazoos. Each child will need his own, however, so that germs are not spread from one child to another.

Sorting the Groceries

Materials

Groceries (real or pretend)

Paper shopping bags or boxes

Pretend refrigerator

Pretend pantry or cupboards

What to Do

1. Bring bagged groceries to class. These can be real food items, or you can use empty boxes, cartons, and packages or play food.

2. Play with one child or a small group of children. Ask a child to select one item from the bag.

3. Ask the children to decide whether the item should go in the refrigerator or on the pantry or cupboard shelf.

4. Continue the activity until all the groceries are put away. As the children explore the groceries, they will develop self-regulation by maintaining focus and sustaining attention with support. They will show persistence and the ability to be flexible in actions and behaviors.

What We Know

Younger toddlers may be able to match objects; for example, if they see a box of cereal on a shelf they may put another box just like it there. Older toddlers and two-year-olds may be able to sort objects by one visible characteristic, such as color, shape, or size.

More to Do: Extensions and Adaptations

For Toddlers:

- Place the bags in the dramatic play area, and observe where children put the food. Encourage them to experiment with where the food fits best. Do they put the items away on shelves or in the refrigerator? Sit in the dramatic play area and name items that children don't know.
- Count the objects with children after they put them on shelves.

For Two-Year-Olds:

- If children are interested, look at the pictures on the cans or boxes of food. Point out one word on the container and excitedly say, "Look, this word says *beans*. *Beans* starts with the letter *B*. Do you like to eat beans?"
- Encourage the children to count with you to find out how many cans or boxes are on shelves or in the refrigerator. Write the numeral on a piece of paper and tape it to the shelf or refrigerator.
- Provide crayons, paper, and pieces of tape so that children can write scribbles, letters, or marks.

Suggested Books:

The Carrot Seed by Ruth Krauss

The Very Hungry Caterpillar by Eric Carle

Opportunities for Learning

- Social development: The children will build relationships with other children by imitating and engaging in play with them.
- Language development: The children will use nonverbal communication and language to engage others and to learn and gain information. They will learn the names of foods, number words, and *warm* and *cold*.
- Cognitive development: The children will actively explore objects and learn the names of different foods. They will recognize differences between familiar and unfamiliar objects, which are memory and sorting skills. They will use objects or symbols to represent something else, such as an empty box representing a real box of food or the word *beans* representing real beans. They will use matching and sorting of objects or people to understand similar and different characteristics, which is emergent mathematical thinking.
- Physical/Motor development: Children will use perceptual information to direct their actions, experiences, and interactions.

Clothespin Drop

Materials

Clean, empty 2-liter soda bottle

Wooden clothespins (without snaps) or crayons

What to Do

1. Place the soda bottles and clothespins together in the discovery area. Observe how children combine the two items.

2. If children do not put the clothespins in the bottles, model how to put clothespins through the top of the soda bottle. As the children try to put items in the bottles, they will show persistence at a task for a short period.

3. Encourage the children to shake the bottle to hear the pins rattling in the bottle.

4. Use the concepts of in and out and full and empty.

More to Do: Extensions and Adaptations

- Put a dot of color on each clothespin, or have the children paint the pins different colors. Name the color of the clothespin as it drops into the bottle.

- Count the clothespins as they go into the bottle. Ask, "How many clothespins will fit in a bottle?"

- For children who have small-motor challenges, use bottles with larger openings.

- At times, encourage two children to cooperate to fill one bottle. Observe how the two children develop strategies so that both can participate. If a conflict occurs, ask toddlers how they would solve the problem. If they can't think of a strategy, then suggest taking turns.

- If children enjoy this activity, find other containers and objects that children can use to fill and empty.

- Read *My First Opposites* and develop activities that demonstrate other opposites, such as open and shut.

Suggested Book: *My First Opposites* by Max and Sid

What We Know

Ask open-ended questions that encourage the children to problem solve to discover the answer. For example, questions and comments such as, "How do you feel today?" or "I wonder how we can get the clothespins in the bottle," encourage children to communicate and experiment.

Bubble Fun and Sculptures

Materials

Nontoxic bubble liquid

Large tub or large container

Water

What to Do

1. Place the bubble solution into a tub or large container and fill with water, creating lots of bubbles.

2. Gather the children near the container of bubbles. Let them experiment with the materials.

3. Demonstrate how to create a bubble sculpture. Discuss the need to be gentle when molding the sculpture.

4. Listen to the words children use as they play with the bubbles.

5. If there is more than one tub, keep them close together for your close supervision and so that toddlers and two-year-olds can see each other's bubble play and talk together.

6. As the children investigate the bubbles, they will maintain focus and sustain attention with support. They will show interest in and curiosity about objects, materials, and events as bubbles appear and disappear. They will use a variety of strategies to solve problems as they experiment with different ways to make more bubbles.

More to Do: Extensions and Adaptations

- Use other materials that are safe for very young children, such as wet sand.
- Provide gloves for the children if you put snow into the tubs.
- Provide small containers that children can fill with bubbles.
- Provide spoons and other safe kitchen utensils, such as small handheld strainers. Some children may prefer to touch the bubbles with a utensil rather than with their hands.
- Take photos and record what the children say. Make a poster to display for the children and their families. Capture the children's discoveries, such as the fact that bubbles pop. List a few opportunities for learning (see below).

Songs: "There Are Bubbles in the Air: Storytime Song"

> *There are bubbles in the air, in the air.*
> *There are bubbles in the air, in the air.*
> *There are bubbles in the air,*
> *There are bubbles everywhere.*
> *There are bubbles in the air, in the air.*

See the website for more verses. Adults can learn the song at https://www.youtube.com/watch?v=U6GtceF5hhU&list=RDU6GtceF5hhU#t=6

Suggested Book: Bubbles, Bubbles by Kathi Appelt

Color and "Just Like Me" Search

Materials

Objects in the classroom

What to Do

1. Show the children an item and name its color.

2. Ask a child to find something in the room that is the same color. Offer help as needed. As the children search for an item of the same color, they will focus and sustain attention on the task.

3. When the child brings back an item of the same color, use specific encouragement that helps children learn language, such as, "You did it. You brought me a red block. Look, it is red just like mine."

More to Do: Extensions and Adaptations

- Provide different colors of paint and crayons in the creative area in the room. After a child returns with an item of color, give a child a crayon of the same color as the object and a big piece of drawing paper. Encourage several children to work together drawing on the paper. Talk about the names of the colors.

- Lay the objects on a table in pairs, sorted by color. Hold up an item and say, "Hmm, I wonder where to put this red block."
- Play the game again on another day, but ask children to find an object just like one that the teacher holds, such as a block, a book, or a crayon.

Song: "If You Are Wearing Red" (Sing to the tune of "If You're Happy and You Know It.")

If you are wearing red, shake your head. (shake head)
If you are wearing red, shake your head.
If you are wearing red, then please shake your head.
If you are wearing red, shake your head.

If you are wearing blue, touch your shoe. (touch shoe)
If you are wearing blue, touch your shoe.
If you are wearing blue, then please touch your shoe.
If you are wearing blue, touch your shoe.

If you are wearing black, pat your back. (pat back)
If you are wearing black, pat your back.
If you are wearing black, then please pat your back.
If you are wearing black, pat your back.

If you are wearing pink, give me a wink. (wink)
If you are wearing pink, give me a wink.
If you are wearing pink, then please give me a wink.
If you are wearing pink, give me a wink.

Suggested Books:

The Colors of Us by Karen Katz

Mouse Paint by Ellen Stoll Walsh

A Color of His Own by Leo Lionni

Opportunities for Learning

- Social development: The children will develop friendships as two of them go off together to find an object the same color as the adult's object.
- Language development: The children will attend to the directions from the teacher and learn more vocabulary as the adult talks about the colors and other features of the objects. They will use increasingly complex language.
- Cognitive development: The children will explore the environment, sort objects, and explore objects' differences and similarities.
- Physical/Motor development: The children will use large muscles in their arms and legs as they move around the room.

Who Lives Here?

Materials

3 boxes of different sizes

3 stuffed animals of different sizes

Labels for the boxes

What to Do

Ahead of Time:

1. Label the boxes *small, medium,* and *large.*

2. Line up the boxes on the floor, and scatter the animals around the boxes.

What We Know

Toddlers and two-year-olds *fast map* words to objects and experiences. This means they can learn new words quickly when the same words are used frequently in different situations and environments by different people (Gershkoff-Stowe and Hahn, 2007).

With the Children:

1. Say, "The bear wants to go home. Where should he go?"

2. Encourage the children with comments such as, "I see you are trying to put the large puppy into the large box." Or, "You are trying to put the large puppy in the small box. Is there a large box for the large puppy?"

3. Using the words *large* and *small* help toddlers and two-year-olds learn the words and concepts of size. Also, use the words *in* and *out* often as children put the animals in the boxes and take them out of the boxes.

4. As the children explore the boxes, they will show imagination in their play and in their interactions with others.

More to Do: Extensions and Adaptations

For Toddlers:

Toddlers may experiment to see if the large puppy fits in the small box and the small puppy in the large box. Encourage them to experiment. Encourage problem solving by asking open-ended questions such as, "How does the small bear feel in such a large home?" "How does the large puppy feel in a small home?" Encourage the toddlers to communicate.

For Two-Year-Olds:

- Some two-year-olds will need to be challenged with more boxes and stuffed animals.
- Point to the labels and say the words often. Excitedly say the names of the letters, too, as you point to them.
- Place the boxes in the creative area of the room, and invite children to color or paint them. Then, put the boxes back in the discovery area of the room.
- Two-year-olds can choose books for the stuffed animals after they are in their homes. Ask the children to find a large book for the large animal, a medium book for the medium animal, and a small book for the small animal.
- Use the words *small, medium,* and *large* in many different contexts. For example, say, "Kareem, can you bring me the small ball?"

Suggested Book: My Very First Book of Animal Homes by Eric Carle

Opportunities for Learning

- Emotional development: The children will learn empathy and show care and concern for the stuffed animal when the adult asks how the animal feels.
- Social development: The children will learn how to negotiate and share with peers.
- Language development: The children will learn new words and the meaning of words such as *small, medium, large, in, out, boxes,* and the names of animals.
- Literacy development: The children will learn to appreciate and handle books and recognize pictures on the covers and in the books.
- Cognitive development: The children will use a variety of strategies to solve problems. They will develop spatial awareness as they fit animals into the boxes. They will organize objects by size. This is **seriation**, a mathematical concept.
- Perceptual, Motor, and Physical development: The children will develop both small and large muscles as they move around and handle the boxes and animals.

Who Says *Moo?*

Materials

Plastic, stuffed, or puzzle pieces of farm animals

Box or cloth

What to Do

1. Let the children play with the animals in the discovery area for several days.

2. After the children have explored the animals, ask a small group if they want to play a game.

3. Take one animal away and hide it inside or under the box or cloth.

4. Make the sound of the animal, such as "moo," "baa," or "meow."

5. Ask the children to name what kind of animal makes that sound. Allow time for the children to guess.

What We Know

Children often want a book read many times. This helps them understand the meaning of the words and story and relate it to their own lives.

6. Once the children guess the correct animal, remove the animal from the box. Continue with the other animals. As you play this game with the children, they will show interest in and curiosity about objects.

More to Do: Extensions and Adaptations

For children who have difficulty with this task, give them a choice. Hold out two animals and say, "Who says, 'Moo?'"

Read the different books listed below to small groups of children who come to play the game. Let children hold an animal as they listen. Encourage them to talk about animals that they have seen and the sounds that the animals make.

Suggested Books:

Who Said Moo? by Harriet Ziefert

My Very First Book of Animal Sounds by Eric Carle

Noisy Baby Animals by Patricia Hegarty

Noisy Farm by Tiger Tales

Discovery Kids: Oink on the Farm by Parragon Books

Opportunities for Learning
. · ● ● ● ● ● · .

- Social development: The children will imitate peers and engage in play with them.

- Language development: The children will increase their vocabulary as they learn the names of animals and the sounds that they make.

- Literature: The children will develop interest in books and the motivation to have books read to them.

- Cognitive development: The children will use objects or symbols to represent something else, such as plastic animals representing live animals.

- Physical/Motor development: The children will use the small muscles in their hands for exploration and play when they handle the small toy animals and books.

Function Junction

Materials

Variety of objects, such as a toothbrush, hairbrush, comb, spoon, cup, and so on

What to Do

1. Sit with one toddler or a small group of toddlers.

2. Show them a few of the objects, and let the children explore them.

3. Ask questions about the objects, such as, "What do you use to brush your teeth?" The children may choose to answer verbally or they may retrieve the object.

4. Repeat with the other items. The children will use their imaginations as they play and explore the items.

5. Support the idea that self-care may differ in diverse cultures.

More to Do: Extensions and Adaptations

For Toddlers and Two-Year-Olds:

- Read the children's book listed below about brushing teeth.

- Ask some open-ended questions such as, "What else do you use when you brush your teeth?" "What do you do before you go to bed?" These types of questions encourage children to talk. Many toddlers and two-year-olds can answer choice questions better than open-ended questions. You could ask while showing the items to a child, "Do you use a toothbrush or a hairbrush to brush your hair?"

For Two-Year-Olds:

In the dramatic play area of the room, provide doll combs, hairbrushes, toothbrushes, spoons, cups, and plastic baby food containers to encourage play.

Suggested Book: *Brush, Brush, Brush!* by Alicia Padron

Song: (Sing to the tune of "Here We Go 'Round the Mulberry Bush.")

> *This is the way we comb our hair,*
> *Comb our hair, comb our hair.* (pretend to comb your hair)
> *This is the way we comb our hair,*
> *Before we go to school.*

You can add other verses based on the objects you bring to the group.

> *This is the way we brush our teeth . . .* (pretend to brush your teeth)
> *This is the way eat our food . . .* (pretend to eat food with a spoon)

Opportunities for Learning

- Emotional development: The children will learn about themselves and self-care. They will show confidence in their abilities.

- Social development: The children will imitate other children to learn and build relationships with peers.

- Language development: The children will increase their vocabulary as they see objects and hear the words at the same time—*comb, brush, hair, teeth, eat.* They will attend to, understand, and respond to language.

- Cognitive development: The children will use pretend play to increase their understanding of culture, environment, and experiences.

- Perceptual, Motor, and Physical development: The children will demonstrate healthy behaviors with increasing independence as part of everyday routines and learn self-care.

Something's Different

Materials

Variety of small toys

Self-care objects, such as a comb and a toothbrush

What to Do

1. Place several similar objects on a table, such as a toy train, car, and airplane.

2. Add one object that is very different from the others, such as a toothbrush.

3. Invite a small group of children to look at the items on the table with you.

4. Point to each item and help them name it.

5. Ask the children to tell what each item is used for and how they use the item. Give lots of time for each response and ask additional questions if needed. As the children explore the items, they will show interest in and curiosity about the objects.

6. Ask the children which of the four items is different from the others. Some toddlers might need help with this cognitive skill, so lead them to the answer by asking questions. For example, ask, "Can you ride in a car?" "Can you ride in a train?" "Can you ride in an airplane?" And "Can you ride in a toothbrush?" After they answer the question about the toothbrush, say, "Then this toothbrush must be . . . (pause to give the children a chance to fill in the word) different from the rest!"

7. Emphasize the discovery by grouping the three similar items together on the table and saying, "We can ride in these. They are the same." Point to the different item, in this case the toothbrush, and say "We can't ride in a toothbrush. It is different from the rest."

8. Continue with other sets of other items such as the following:
   ● Pencil, pen, crayon, bell
   ● Shoe, sock, glove, apple
   ● Orange, lemon, kiwi, block

More to Do: Extensions and Adaptations

Let the children freely play and experiment with all the objects. Notice if they start to sort the items naturally. Comment on what they are doing, for example: "Tony, you have the car, the wagon, and the bicycle together here. How are they the same? Which one is different?"

Opportunities for Learning
● ● ● ● ● ● ● ● ●

● Language development: The children will attend to, understand, and respond to communication and language from others. They will understand and use an increasing number of words, such as the names of objects and the words *different* and *same*, when teachers use the words often.

● Cognitive development: The children will use matching and sorting of objects to understand similar and different characteristics. This is emergent mathematical thinking.

● Physical/Motor development: The children will use perceptual (touch, taste, vision, hearing) information to understand objects, experiences, and interactions. They will develop fine-motor skills as they use their hands for exploration, play, and daily routines.

Fine- and Gross-Motor Development

Eyes, Hands, and Feet

Materials

None

What to Do

1. Gently inform the infant what you are going to do. When a baby's fists begin to open more often, at between one and three months, play with her fingers and put her palms on your face.

2. When the infant is lying on her back, place gentle pressure against the soles of her feet. This pushing against the pressure and exercising helps develop the baby's muscle strength.

3. Be responsive with these activities. Watch for cues from the infant that she is enjoying the activity. If she seems distressed, then stop and try another day. This activity can build trust between you and the infant if you are responsive to the infant's facial expressions and gestures.

4. As you do this activity with the infant, she will show curiosity and express interest in the world around her as she watches your hands and mouth.

More to Do: Extensions and Adaptations

- When a young infant is lying on his back, hold a brightly colored ball about 12 inches from the child's face. Slowly move the ball from one side of the child's face to the other. Observe if the infant's eyes follow the ball.

- Do the fingerplay below. Even though infants won't understand the words, they are processing language—how words are pronounced, the patterns of language, and which words are more likely to follow other words. Infants experience remarkable brain development during the first three years of life. Let children see your hand movements as you say the words.

> **What We Know**
>
> Infants can develop secure attachments with more than one caregiver. When infants feel secure, compared to children who do not feel secure, they communicate more, engage in reciprocal interactions more, count on caregivers to comfort them and help them feel safe, and engage in more prosocial peer interactions (for summary of research, see Wittmer and Petersen, 2017).

Fingerplay:

> *Open, shut them,* (open and shut infant's hands)
> *Open, shut them,*
> *Give a little clap, clap, clap.* (gently clap infant's hands)
> *Open, shut them,* (open and shut hands)
> *Open, shut them,*
> *Put them in your lap.* (put infant's hands in lap)
>
> *Creep them, creep them,* (crawl your fingers up infant's tummy)
> *Creep them, creep them,*
> *Right up to your chin.* (creep hands up to chin)
> *Open up your little mouth,* (open your mouth)
> *But do not let them in.* (bring hands quickly down)

Opportunities for Learning

- Emotional development: The infant will show awareness about himself and how to connect with others as you touch her feet and hands.
- Social development: The infant will develop expectations of consistent, positive interactions through secure relationships with adults.
- Language development: The infant will understand and later use new vocabulary such as *open, shut, clap, chin,* and *mouth.*

Prone Play

Materials

Unbreakable mirror

Toys

Blanket or mat

What to Do

1. This activity encourages the infant to tolerate playing on her stomach. Lie on the floor and put the infant on your stomach. Place her so she is on her stomach and looking at your face.

2. Talk to the infant and play with her in this position.

What We Know

According to the American Academy of Pediatrics, infants must sleep on their backs (**supine**) to prevent **sudden infant death syndrome (SIDS)**. During the day, give infants opportunities to be on their stomachs (**prone**) while being carefully observed.

3. Change to a sitting position, laying the infant across your lap on her stomach.

4. Put an item, such as a mirror, in front of her to look at and touch.

More to Do: Extensions and Adaptations

- Lay the infant carefully on her stomach on a blanket or mat on the floor. Encourage the child to explore the environment and crawl, if she is beginning to crawl, by putting some toys within reach and some just out of her reach.

- Place one infant on her stomach facing another infant, so that the two infants can see each other when they lift their heads.

- Many babies protest when placed on their stomachs. With the support of familiar adults, she will learn to manage her feelings and emotions. Lie on your stomach facing the baby. Try to engage the infant. If the infant cries, then stop and try again another day.

Song: (Sing to the tune of "Here We Go 'Round the Mulberry Bush.")

> *This is the way we lie on our tummy,*
> *Lie on our tummy, lie on our tummy.*
> *This is the way we lie on our tummy,*
> *So early in the morning.*

Opportunities for Learning
· · · ● ● ● ● · · ·

- Emotional development: The infant will use expectations learned through repeated experiences in primary relationships to develop relationships with other adults.

- Social development: The infant will show interest in other children. As infants face each other, watch for signs of interest.

- Language development: The infant will learn and later use new vocabulary if an adult uses words—such as *on, off, tummy* or *stomach, crawl*, and the names of toys—often in context.

- Cognitive development: The infant will use spatial awareness to understand objects and their movements in space as she reaches for toys.

- Physical/Motor development: The infant will demonstrate effective and efficient use of large muscles (gross motor). She will explore the different ways she can move to accomplish goals.

The Encyclopedia of Infant and Toddler Activities for Children Birth to 3

Saucer Spin

Materials

Snow saucer

Blanket for saucer

What to Do

1. Young children need motion activities to develop their balancing system. Find a saucer used for snow sledding.

2. Cover the inside of the saucer (the concave side) with a soft blanket.

3. Sit a child in the saucer and gently rotate it. This will challenge the child to balance himself.

4. Place infants on their backs in the saucer. Gently rotate the saucer.

5. Toddlers can either lie down on the blanket or sit up.

6. After rotating the saucer, pause and wait for the child to give you a signal to do it again or get out.

More to Do: Extensions and Adaptations

- Two children can ride on the saucer together, holding onto each other and keeping each other safe.
- Challenge older children to maintain eye contact with you as their positions change.
- Play music or sing "Row, Row, Row Your Boat" when the child is in the saucer.
- Read the book, "Row, Row, Row Your Boat" while one or two children lie or sit in the saucer.

Suggested Book: *Row, Row, Row Your Boat* by Annie Kubler

Song: "Row, Row, Row Your Boat"

> *Row, row, row your boat*
> *Gently down the stream.*
> *Merrily, merrily, merrily, merrily,*
> *Life is but a dream.*

To hear more verses, visit http://www.songsforteaching.com/nurseryrhymes/

Opportunities for Learning

- Emotional development: The children will manage emotions with the help of supportive adults.

- Social development: The children will show interest in other children and interact positively with them.

- Language development: The children will communicate needs and wants nonverbally and/or by using language when the teacher pauses to give the children a chance to communicate their desires.

- Cognitive development: The children will understand causal relationships. When the teacher pauses rotating the saucer, the children learn that they can communicate their needs and cause a responsive interaction.

- Physical/Motor development: The children will develop balance and core strength when they sit in the saucer.

Bumpy Lumpy Locomotion

Materials

Soft items, such as small pillows, rolled towels, or sponges

Flat washable sheet

Toy (optional)

What to Do

1. Put a few soft items on the floor.

2. Cover the items with a flat sheet.

3. Put an infant down on one side of the sheet.

4. Stand or sit at the opposite side of the sheet and call the infant. You can also use a toy to attract the infant's attention. Encourage the infant to move across the bumpy lumpy surface to you.

5. Observe when infants and toddlers seem surprised by a bump or lump. They may try crawling back and forth over the bumps to explore what they are. As the children try new and challenging experiences, they will use a variety of strategies to solve problems.

What We Know

Rolling over occurs around three to six months, and crawling occurs sometime between seven and ten months. Many infants create ways to move before that, such as scooching on their bottoms, using a commando crawl, or using a combination of movements.

6. The infants and toddlers will move across the sheet any way they can, either by rolling, crawling, or walking. Use parallel talk as the infants move across the sheet: "Tione is crawling. Marcus is rolling. Madu is looking at me."

More to Do: Extensions and Adaptations

- Use textured materials, such as rugs, blankets, or towels, on top of the sheet for the infants and crawling toddlers to crawl on and over.
- To encourage curiosity and object permanence, place soft toys under the corners of towels for the children to discover.

Suggested Book: Flip, Flap, Fly! A Book for Babies Everywhere by Phyllis Root

Opportunities for Learning
· ● ● ● ● ● · ·

- Emotional development: The children will develop a positive sense of identity, self-awareness, and confidence in what they do.
- Social development: The children will become familiar with the peers in their room.
- Language development: The children will respond to and use a growing vocabulary as adults frequently read the book and talk about what the infants are doing and using.
- Cognitive development: The children will use their senses to construct knowledge about the world as they crawl over bumpy things, discover toys under towels, and so on. They will explore the concept of how we move.
- Physical/Motor development: The children will develop large- and small-muscle control as they move and pick up toys.

Obstacle Course

Materials

Pillows

Blocks

Other objects a child can climb over or around

What to Do

1. As infants begin to master crawling, create an obstacle course by stacking pillows and blocks on the floor for babies to crawl over. Encourage the children to explore the obstacle course.

2. Set up the course and observe what crawling infants do. Some will go through the trail from start to finish, and others will crawl over the obstacles on the side.

3. Keep the obstacle course available for as long as children seem interested. Each day they may try different strategies to move through and over the obstacles. As they explore, the children will demonstrate emerging initiative.

4. Observe how several children manage to move together or share space.

What We Know

Children's pointing with their index finger occurs at the end of the first year. When children point, they may seem to be asking what an object is and other times they may want to engage you to look in a wonderful moment of **joint attention** (Begus and Southgate, 2012). When children point, they are often ready to learn the name of an object, person, animal, or action.

More to Do: Extensions and Adaptations

- Create a tunnel, and make toys available for the children to hold while crawling through the tunnel. For example, a child might put a block in each hand and try to crawl while pushing the blocks. Place toys along the way for the children to discover.

- Sit by the obstacle course and read the book *The Day the Babies Crawled Away*. Show the children how the babies in the book crawl. Say, "You are crawling like the babies in the book."

Suggested Book: The Day the Babies Crawled Away by Peggy Rathmann

Opportunities for Learning

- Emotional development: The children will manage emotions with the help of supportive adults. If a child is frustrated, help the child figure out how to solve the problem.

- Social development: The children will imitate and engage in play with peers.

- Language development: The children will use nonverbal communication to engage others. Observe whether a child points to engage you to look at an object. If not, you point at an interesting toy and say its name. See if the child imitates you.

- Cognitive development: The children will increase spatial understandings, a mathematical concept.

- Physical/Motor development: The children will develop gross-motor skills as they use the large muscles in their arms and legs.

Stacking Cups

Materials

Plastic cups

What to Do

1. Find plastic cups of different sizes and colors to stack and put inside each other.

2. Place the cups in the fine-motor or cognitive-discovery learning area, and let the children choose the activity. Toddlers are likely to stay with an activity and persevere if given time to explore materials.

3. Encourage the children to play with the cups, stacking and nesting them. Children will develop the ability to show persistence in actions and behaviors as they stack the cups or put them inside each other.

4. Talk about what a child is doing: "You are stacking the little cup on the big cup! You are putting the little cup inside the big cup."

5. When the cups fall over, say, "Let's do it again."

More to Do: Extensions and Adaptations

- Count the cups as the children play with them.
- Sort the cups of different colors. "Let's put all of the red cups together." "Let's put all of the blue cups together."
- Place two mats on the floor to encourage pairs of children to sit and do the activity together.
- Read the books listed below and compare the colors of the cups to the colors in the book. As you hold the cup up to the picture say, "Look, the butterfly is blue and your cup is blue".

Suggested Books:

Butterfly Butterfly: A Book of Colors by Petr Horáček

Little Quack Loves Colors by Lauren Thompson

What We Know

As an infant or toddler stacks or nests cups, educators can observe and make the task harder or easier depending on what a child can do: add more cups, take cups away, provide larger or smaller cups. In a 2014 study by Hiroshi Fukuyama and colleagues, mothers of older infants were sensitive to their children's ability to nest cups and adapted the activity to make it easier or harder for the children.

Opportunities for Learning

- Social development: The children will show interest in and interact with other children. They will imitate and engage in play with other children.

- Language development: The children will increase understanding and use of vocabulary as an adult points out different colors and sizes: *red, blue, cup, little, big, inside, on*, and number words.

- Literacy development: The children will comprehend meaning from pictures and stories.

- Cognitive development: The children will compare, sort, group, and organize objects. This is mathematical thinking.

- Physical/Motor development: The children will develop fine-motor skills as they use their hands for exploration and play.

Magic Surprise

Materials

Empty tissue box or wipes container

Several colorful handkerchiefs, silk scarves, or soft pieces of cloth

Needle and thread (adult use only)

Scissors (adult use only)

What to Do

Ahead of Time:

1. If you are using a wipes container, slightly enlarge the hole in the top with the scissors.

2. Carefully tie the scarves together at one corner with small knots that will go through the hole or slit at the top of the container used, creating a long length of scarves. Make sure the knots are very tight. Alternatively, you can sew the fabric pieces together end to end to create a chain.

3. Make a large knot at the end of the chain to prevent it from coming out of the container.

4. Stuff the scarf chain into the container. Leave a bit of the end piece sticking out of the opening.

5. Put the box on the floor for the children to discover. Be sure to supervise carefully.

With the Children:

1. When a child discovers the box, she will begin to pull the scarf chain out. She may experiment with how hard to pull the scarf chain.

2. Comment on what the child is doing, "Oh, look! You found a surprise. Wow! Here comes another one. Oh, it's purple. I wonder how many there are. Keep pulling!"

3. Talk with the children about the colors of the scarves, the patterns or designs on the scarves, and the number of scarves in the box.

4. Be prepared to stuff the scarves back into the container many times. As the children explore the scarves, they will show interest and curiosity about objects and materials.

More to Do: Extensions and Adaptations

For Older Toddlers:

- Hold the container and encourage older toddlers to walk backward as they pull out the scarves. This is challenging for many young children.
- Read the book *Butterfly Colors and Counting* by Jerry Pallotta to a small group of children who gather to do the activity. Pretend the scarves are butterflies. Give each child a turn to pull out one "butterfly." Count how many butterflies there are in the container.
- Place butterfly puzzles in the fine-motor area of the room.
- Make butterfly catchers (see activity on page 78).
- Go on a nature walk and look for butterflies.

Suggested Book: *Butterfly Colors and Counting* by Jerry Pallotta

Song: "Do You Know a Butterfly?"

Go to https://www.youtube.com/watch?v=aQ_LPlSl9ms to learn the words and actions of the song.

Wall Puzzles

Materials

Cloth items, such as a sock, mitten, small cloth doll, small hat, and washcloth

Needle and thread (adult use only)

14" x 20" piece of heavy cardboard

Duct tape

Velcro

16" x 22" piece of flannel material

What to Do

Ahead of Time:

1. Securely sew a 2" piece of the hook side of the Velcro to each of the cloth items (sock, mitten, cloth doll, and washcloth).

2. Cover the cardboard with the flannel material. Securely tape the flannel in place by lapping it over the edges of the cardboard and taping the fabric to the back.

3. Attach the flannel board to the wall near the floor, and stick the cloth items to the flannel board.

With the Children:

1. Show the children how to pull the items off the flannel board and reattach them.

2. Talk to them as they play. Comment on the type of item they have pulled off. Tell them what it is and how it is used. For example, "Oh, Deirdre, you have a washcloth. You wash your face with a washcloth." "Sam, you have a sock. Where does the sock go? Yes, on your foot!"

3. The children will focus on this interesting activity for a short period. They will enjoy pulling the items and listening to the sound the Velcro makes. Observe the theories they have about how to pull the items off. Do they pull really hard, softly, up, or down?

4. Supervise this activity closely so that the items do not end up in little mouths. Wash the items after use.

More to Do: Extensions and Adaptations

For Two-Year-Olds:

- Draw an outline of the item on the flannel board. Some children will notice and match the item with the outline when they put the items back on the board.

- Attach a laminated photo (symbol) of a cloth item next to the real item. Encourage children to match the photo with the real item and put them back on the board together.

- Extend this activity to other times of the day by commenting on the names and functions of clothing throughout the day.

- Read the book *Toes, Ears, & Nose!* and talk about body parts related to the cloth item. Provide a mirror so children can look in the mirror.

Suggested Book: *Toes, Ears, & Nose!* by Marion Dane Bauer

Opportunities for Learning

• • • • ● • • • •

- Emotional development: Children will develop a sense of identity and belonging by showing awareness of things they can do and some of their body parts.

- Social development: Children will demonstrate social skills needed to successfully participate in groups as they show awareness of each other as they play and possibly exchange items of clothing from the board.

- Language development: Children will begin to understand and use new vocabulary, such as *washcloth, sock,* "wash your face," and "on your foot."

- Literacy development: Children will recognize pictures of toes, ears, and nose in the book.

- Cognitive development: Children will use objects and symbols to represent something else when they match the photo to the real cloth item.

- Physical/Motor development: Children will demonstrate increasing independence as a part of everyday routines.

Sticky Crawl or Walk

Materials

Contact paper

Packing tape

What to Do

1. Tape a long piece of contact paper to the floor with the sticky side up.

2. Encourage children to either crawl or walk (with shoes on) on the contact paper from one end to the other. Children will be surprised as their feet or hands stick to the paper. Children learn to manage feelings and emotions with the support of familiar adults. They may seek **emotional refueling** (Kaplan, 1978) during a risk-taking activity such as this one.

More to Do: Extensions and Adaptations

- Some children will want to watch the other children rather than do the activity themselves.

- Observe how walking children try not to bump into each other. They are usually very aware of each other.

- Encourage two children to hold hands and cross the "river" together.

- On another day, add colorful cardboard cutouts of frogs, turtles, ducks, and geese for children to maneuver around. Children may try to pick up the animals.

- Record the children and watch the video with them. Use the children's names and describe what each child is doing.

For Toddlers and Two-Year-Olds:

Sing the Busy Feet "It's Warm Up Time" song and model the different actions of the animals.

Find it at https://www.youtube.com/watch?v=MugzDjGDYjo.

What We Know

Crawling infants, toddlers, and two-year-olds may separate from their favorite familiar adults; however, they often return to the adult for comfort and energy. When adults are **emotionally available**, children can often go off to play again. But there may be days that the child wants to stay close.

- Emotional development: Children will develop expectations of consistent, positive interactions and may look to familiar adults for encouragement.

- Social development: Children will engage in play with other children.

- Language development: Children will learn new vocabulary, such as *sticky, stick, stuck, stickier, frog, turtle, duck, geese, on (walk on),* "lift your foot," and so on.

- Cognitive development: Children will use a variety of strategies to problem solve how to move on the sticky surface.

- Physical/Motor development: Children will develop gross-motor skills as they use the large muscles in their legs.

Fun with Balls

Materials

Variety of soft balls, such as textured, sock balls, beach balls

What to Do

1. Keep many different types and sizes of balls in a basket in the gross-motor area.

2. Observe while children experiment with the balls—do they experiment to see how the different balls feel, bounce, and roll?

3. Sit on the floor with a child, and show her how to roll a ball to an adult or to another child.

4. Sit across from the child and roll the ball to her. Say, "Ba, ba, ba, *ball*," as the ball rolls to the child and then reaches her. Encourage the child to roll it back to you.

5. Ask three children to sit facing each other and roll the ball to each other.

What We Know

Schemas develop as a child explores the environment and has repeated experiences with people, objects, and animals. One child may have a schema for banging objects on the floor to make them work. With experience, the child could develop a schema that shaking objects or pushing a button makes toys work.

More to Do: Extensions and Adaptations

For Infants:

- Make sock balls by stuffing socks with polyester fiberfill or other nontoxic stuffing material. Tie a string securely around the end of the ball or sew it shut.

- Use a beach ball that is easy for infants to hit to make it move.

For Toddlers and Two-Year-Olds:

Hang a soft ball from the ceiling, high enough so that children can reach it with their reaching hands but no lower. **SAFETY ALERT:** Do not allow the string to be long enough to wrap around children's necks. Encourage the children to bat the ball with their hands or a paper towel roll to make it swing.

Suggested Books:

Ball by John Hutton

Where Is Baby's Beach Ball? by Karen Katz

Opportunities for Learning

- Social development: Children will develop strong, positive relationships with peers when teachers encourage interaction and cooperation that is responsive to children's needs.

- Language development: Children will use increasingly complex language as adults imitate children's sounds and words and add a few more to model slightly higher complexity.

- Cognitive development: Children will use memory as a foundation for learning as they develop a *schema*—a theory for how things work—for what balls do: roll, bounce, and fly in air when someone throws them.

- Physical/Motor development: Children will coordinate hand and eye movements to perform actions such as rolling or hitting balls.

Caterpillar/Butterfly Collection

Materials

Construction paper in a variety of colors

Glue

Velcro

Empty paper towel rolls

Scissors (adult use only)

Laminator (optional)

2 baskets

Contact paper or paint

What to Do

Ahead of Time:

1. Cut the paper towel tubes in half, and paint them or cover them with contact paper.

2. Glue one side of a piece of Velcro to the top side of the tube to make a "wand." Repeat for all tubes.

3. Cut construction paper into the shapes of butterflies and caterpillars. Laminate them if possible.

4. Glue the other side of a piece of Velcro to the centers of the butterflies and caterpillars.

5. Place the butterflies and caterpillars on the floor, along with the baskets and the tube wands.

With the Children:

1. Ask the children to collect a butterfly or caterpillar by touching it with the wand.

2. Ask a child if she wants to remove the butterfly or caterpillar from the wand and put it in a basket, so she can catch more.

3. Have children place the caught butterflies in one basket and the caught caterpillars in another basket. Children will demonstrate creativity, imagination, and inventiveness as they explore the butterflies and caterpillars.

More to Do: Extensions and Adaptations

- Place the tubes in the art area, and allow the children to paint them.
- Count the number of caterpillars and butterflies that the children catch.
- Comment on the colors of the caterpillars and butterflies.
- Ask, "Are there more caterpillars or more butterflies? Let's count them and see."

Suggested Books:

The Very Hungry Caterpillar by Eric Carle

Caterpillar to Butterfly by Melissa Stewart

Song: (1st and 2nd Verse) "Do You Know a Butterfly?"

Go to https://www.youtube.com/watch?v=aQ_LPlSl9ms to learn the words and actions of the song.

Opportunities for Learning

- Social development: Children will develop the ability to share space with other children.

- Language development: Children will describe familiar people, places, things, and events. They will learn the words *butterfly, fly, caterpillar, wand, stick, basket, in,* and *Velcro.*

- Cognitive development: Children will begin to understand number and quantities during play as they count the butterflies and caterpillars and decide which basket has more. They will learn the difference and connection between a caterpillar and a butterfly.

- Physical/Motor development: Children will develop large muscles as they move around and use their arms and will develop small muscles as they use their fingers and hands on the wands.

Pull Me Fast, Pull Me Slowly

Materials

Pull toys with safe handles

What to Do

1. Place the pull toys in the gross-motor area, away from blocks where children might be building.

2. Children will pick up the handles of the toys and begin walking with them. Observe what techniques the children use to pull the toys. As the children explore the toys, they will be actively seeking to understand how wheels go around and around.

3. Encourage them to "pull it fast" and then "pull it slowly." Model for the children if they don't seem to know the meaning of the words. Say, "The dinosaur (dog, cat) is following you."

What We Know

As children experiment with different ways to move their bodies, they become more coordinated.

More to Do: Extensions and Adaptations

Sit in the learning area and start reading the book *Wheels Go Round* by Yvonne Hooker. Show the children how the wheels on the pull toys go around.

For Young Toddlers:

Young toddlers who are just beginning to walk will find this activity challenging. Allow them to play with the toy. Encourage them to play with the wheels to make them go around.

For Two-Year-Olds:

- Two-year-olds may find this too easy. If so, add push toys so the children must decide about whether to pull or push the toy.
- Ask two-year-olds if they can find any other toys in the room with wheels.
- Sing the song "The Wheels on the Bus" and read the book *The Wheels on the Bus.* Model how to do the actions with the children. Leave the book in the gross-motor area for the children to "read."

Suggested Books:

Wheels Go Round by Yvonne Hooker

The Wheels on the Bus: A Sing 'N Move Book by Simon and Schuster

Song: "The Wheels on the Bus"

Opportunities for Learning

- Emotional development: The children will express positive feelings about themselves and confidence in what they do as they have fun with the pull and push toys.
- Social development: The children will demonstrate the social and behavioral skills needed to successfully participate in groups as children share space, take turns with the toys, and listen together to the stories and song.
- Language development: The children will ask and answer questions to seek help and get information. They will learn new vocabulary, such as *push, pull, around, wheels,* and vocabulary in the books and song.
- Literacy development: The children will develop interest in books as they are read to them and as they explore books in the classroom.
- Cognitive development: The children will compare objects and notice differences and similarities.
- Physical/Motor development: The children will develop both large and small muscles as they pull and push toys.

Happy Trails

Materials

Colored masking tape

Toys

Stickers

Tent or large cardboard box

What to Do

1. Use tape to make a straight line on the floor, or create a trail with tape on both sides.

2. Observe what children do. Do they walk on the tape? Do they stay within the lines? You could say, "Let's follow the trail and see where it goes." As they explore the trail, the children will be demonstrating initiative.

3. Place small stickers and toys along the trail. Encourage each child to pick up one or two stickers and one or two toys as they walk along the trail.

4. Make the trail end in a tent or large box for children to crawl through or provide a surprising end.

More to Do: Extensions and Adaptations

- Read the suggested book to those children who want to hear the story at the beginning of their adventure. Talk about what they think they will find on the trail as they go on their trip.
- Encourage the children to walk through the trail while holding a stuffed animal or a toy.
- Offer small baskets with handles for children to fill as they go on the adventure.
- Use different colors of tape that leads in different directions. Observe if children follow one color of tape to the end.

For Two-Year-Olds:

Support older two-year-olds as they use tape to create their own trails, both inside and outside.

Suggested Book: *Bookee and Keeboo Go on a Trip* by Alfons Freire

---

What We Know

According to researchers Karen Adolph and colleagues (2012), when older infants and toddlers begin to walk, they will walk as much as thirty-seven football fields a day. They are motivated to move when we give them opportunities to do so.

Rocks in the River

Materials

Nonslip carpet squares of different sizes, colors, and shapes

Masking tape of different colors

What to Do

1. Use carpet squares or colored tape to create a path on the floor. Place the carpet squares (different shapes if you can find them) or masking-tape shapes far apart but close enough for the children to walk or jump from one "rock" to another.

2. Use parallel talk. Say, "You are stepping on the round blue rock." "You are stepping on the square red rock." "You are stepping on the square rock." "You are stepping on the triangle rock."

3. Responsively expand children's language. If a child says, "Rock," say, "Yes, a blue rock." Or, "There are two blue rocks!" while pointing to them and emphasizing the S at the end of *rocks*.

What We Know

The typical progression of expressive language development:

- child makes sounds, such as coos and babbling

- child uses gestures and points

- child uses first words

- child uses two words together

- child adds *S* to words for plural

- child adds *ing* to action words

- child **overgeneralizes**, such as using the word *cat* for all four-legged animals

- child **undergeneralizes**, such as using the word *cat* for only his pet cat, not other cats

More to Do: Extensions and Adaptations

- Place the rocks close together to begin, and then separate them more as you think children are ready.

- Encourage two children to jump on the rocks together to keep each other safe.

- Place the rocks on a blue blanket to simulate a river. Find photos of rivers with rocks to show the children.

- Play music or sing the song below. When you stop the music, all the children must be on a rock or touching a rock. No one should leave the game. Encourage the children to help each other find a foothold on a rock.

- To adjust for different ability levels, place the rocks closer or farther apart, and make them either bigger or smaller.

- Count the rocks with the children.

- Later, after they have jumped on the rocks, help children notice different shapes in the environment. Go on a shape hunt outside by taking the carpet squares of different shapes outside and asking children to find items the same shape to place on the carpet shape.

- Find foods of different shapes for snack time.

- Place sponges cut into different shapes in the water table. Find cookie cutters of different shapes to place with playdough or in the sand table. Wet the sand outdoors and give children cookie cutters of different shapes to use as molds.

Song: (Sing to the tune of "Row, Row, Row Your Boat.")

> *Jump, jump, jump to the rock.*
> *Do not fall off yet.*
> *Jumping, jumping to the rock,*
> *Please, don't you get wet.*

Opportunities for Learning

- Emotional development: The children will take risks during play.

- Social development: The children will show care and concern for others.

- Language development: The children will use increasingly more complex language, such as adding *S* to the ends of words for plurals and adding *ing* to the ends of action words. They will learn new vocabulary, such as *rock, river,* and color and shape words.

- Cognitive development: The children will use objects to represent something else (carpet squares symbolize rocks). They will use spatial awareness to understand their movements in space, which is mathematical thinking. They will develop a sense of number and quantity.

- Physical/Motor development: The children will develop balance and core strength.

Amaze Me

Materials

Furniture or large boxes securely attached to the floor

What to Do

Ahead of Time:

Move furniture or use boxes securely taped to the floor to create a maze. When you first offer this activity, create several ways to get to the end.

With the Children:

1. This activity can be done with crawling or walking children. Invite the children to explore the maze.

2. Observe how children follow the maze. Do they problem solve if they reach a dead end? As they explore the maze, the children will show persistence in finding the end.

More to Do: Extensions and Adaptations

- When children have more experience with a maze, create only one way to get to the end with other paths leading to dead ends.
- Encourage two children to go through the maze together.
- Go through the maze with children who are hesitant to enter, or ask an experienced child to help her peer.
- Provide crayons and paper at the end of the maze with children's names on it. Encourage older toddlers and two-year-olds to make a mark each time they go through the maze. Count the marks with the child when she is finished with the activity.

Squeeze Me Tight

Materials

Sponges of different sizes, shapes, and colors

Scissors (adult use only)

Tub

Nonstaining food color (optional)

Water

What to Do

Ahead of Time:

1. Cut the sponges into a variety of shapes.

2. Fill the tub halfway with water. Add food coloring if you wish.

With the Children:

1. Show the children the sponges and talk about the shapes.

What We Know

When teachers of young children point to letters and words, children are more likely to learn the names of them over time, just as children do when an adult points to an object and says the name of it. Children do not feel pressure and enjoy looking at the letters.

2. Ask the children to put the sponges into the water. Observe how children experiment with them. The children will maintain focus during this fun, interesting activity.

3. The children will experiment to figure out how to squeeze the water out of the sponges. This is great for developing small muscles in the hands and arm strength.

4. Act surprised when water comes out of the sponges. Use the words *squeeze* and *squeezing* often.

5. Read the book *The Mitten* by Jan Brett. Talk about the animals squeezing together.

More to Do: Extensions and Adaptations

- Provide separate bins of water for each child, and place the bins close to each other. This sometimes makes it easier for toddlers (and some two-year-olds) to enjoy the experience with each other.

- Provide plastic containers for children to squeeze the water into, fill, and empty.

- Create a sign to place by the activity that says, "We squeeze sponges," with a picture of a sponge or a real sponge glued to the sign.

- Ask two-year-olds what they learned about sponges. Document their answers, and display them with photos for children, parents, and the community to see.

- Provide lemons for children to squeeze into a container. Add sweetening and water, and drink lemonade.

- Talk about what else we can squeeze. Squeeze each other gently.

Suggested Book: *The Mitten* by Jan Brett

Opportunities for Learning

- Social development: The children will share space and materials with other children. They will imitate other children and enjoy being with them.

- Language development: The children will understand and use new vocabulary, such as *sponge, water, squeeze, full,* and *empty.*

- Literacy development: The children will recognize some symbols as adults say, for example, "Look, this sign says, 'We squeeze sponges.' I see a *W* and an *E. W-E* spells *we,*" as you point to the letters.

- Cognitive development: The children will learn the properties of water. They will gain spatial awareness as they fill and empty containers, which is mathematical thinking.

- Physical/Motor development: They will use both gross- and fine-motor skills to solve problems.

Scientists at Play

Materials

Slide bolts

Hasps*

Door locks with keys

Hardware of different types and sizes

Paint (optional)

Drill (optional; adult use only)

Barrel bolts

Drawer knobs

String

Wooden board

Screwdrivers (adult use only)

What to Do

Ahead of Time:

1. If you wish, paint the board.

2. Attach the bolts, door locks, and drawer knobs to the board. Depending on the hardware, this may require drilling pilot holes to make securing the screws easier.

With the Children:

1. Place the board at toddler eye level, and encourage the children to experiment with pushing, pulling, turning, touching, opening, and closing. Observe the strategies they use.

2. **SAFETY ALERT:** Be sure that the string with the key is attached firmly to the door lock so that children can't get the key off.

3. Place the board in the fine-motor or cognitive-discovery learning area. Supervise closely.

More to Do: Extensions and Adaptations

- Observe and document the different strategies that children use to manipulate the bolts, knobs, and keys. Notice how their strategies change with experience. Do they try to turn all of them? Do they change strategies when manipulating bolts and knobs?

- Read the book listed below to give children more experience with fine-motor tasks.

Suggested Book: *Open the Barn Door...* by Christopher Santoro

---

*A hasp is a fastener for a door or lid, consisting of a hinged metal strap that fits over a staple and is secured by a pin or padlock.

- Emotional development: Some children may become frustrated with these tasks. They will manage their feelings and emotions as they persist in mastering the locks and bolts.

- Language development: The children will increase vocabulary when adults talk about opening a door and use words such as *knob, bolt, key,* and *lock.*

- Cognitive development: The children will actively explore objects. They will use a variety of strategies in solving problems.

- Physical/Motor development: The children will develop fine-motor and eye-hand coordination skills as they handle the hardware.

Balance Beam

Materials

Colored masking tape

Photos of children on a balance beam (optional)

Rhythm sticks (optional)

What to Do

1. Make a straight line on the floor with the tape.

2. Help the children walk on the tape line if they need it. Encourage the children to ask for help from an adult or peer to stay on the line. If the children become frustrated, they will begin to manage their feelings and emotions with the support of familiar adults.

3. Show photos of boys and girls on a balance beam holding a baton to help balance themselves. (You can find some on the Internet.) Place the photos by the balance beam.

More to Do: Extensions and Adaptations

- Ask children if they want to hold on to a baton as they walk (as in the photos). If so, they can use a rhythm stick as a baton. Supervise closely.

What We Know

Children will have a difficult time walking toe to heel at this age. They may find creative ways to stay on the line, such as walking sideways or hopping with both feet. Let them experiment with different ways to move.

- Encourage children to hold other children's hands as they walk on the beam.

- Make two balance beams within about a foot of each other so that children can do the activity together while holding hands.

- Take photos for a display. Add the words that children use and information on how children cooperate.

- Think about where children can practice balancing and walking on lines outside.

Song: (Sing to the tune of "Frère Jacques.")

> *Walking, walking, walking, walking*
> *Very carefully, very carefully.*
> *Walking, walking, walking,*
> *Walking, walking, walking.*
> *Won't you walk with me?*
> *Won't you walk with me?*

Opportunities for Learning

- Emotional development: The children will express care and concern about others as children help each other.

- Social development: The children will imitate and engage in play with other children.

- Language development: The children will use increasingly complex language. They will learn new vocabulary, such as *straight, balance beam, balance, baton,* and "you are walking" (adding *ing* to the ends of verbs).

- Literacy development: The children will recognize and comprehend meaning from pictures.

- Cognitive development: The children will use objects and symbols to represent something else.

- Physical/Motor development: The children will demonstrate effective use of large muscles.

Cereal Pour

Materials

Large paper cups

Small paper cups

Dry cereal

Trays

What We Know

The wrist strength of toddlers is not well developed until approximately sixteen months, when they can begin to control a spoon or pour well.

What to Do

1. Place some small and large paper cups on clean trays on a child-size table in the fine-motor learning area.

2. Put a little bit of dry cereal in one cup, and demonstrate how to pour the cereal from one cup to another. The children will develop the ability to show persistence as they try to pour without spilling.

3. Each child's tray should catch the spilled cereal. Let them eat the dry cereal as a snack.

4. While they explore, use parallel talk and expand children's language; use the words *pour, full,* and *empty* often.

5. **SAFETY ALERT:** As with all foods, be sure that a child is not allergic to the food and that the food is approved by the parents to serve to the child.

More to Do: Extensions and Adaptations

- When each child chooses to finish the activity, help the child wash the tray with dish soap and wash her hands with hand soap in the child-level sink.

- Add pouring containers, such as small pitchers, open containers, and a container with holes in the bottom, to the sand and water tables to encourage children to continue pouring. This will help them build fine-motor and perceptual skills and will let them explore their understanding of spatial concepts.

- For children who find this activity easy, offer smaller containers. For children who find it too challenging, provide larger containers.

- Read the book listed below, and talk about other foods that the children eat.

Suggested Book: *Llama Llama Yum Yum Yum!* by Anna Dewdney

Song: (Sing to the tune of "Here We Go 'Round the Mulberry Bush.")

1. Sing the first verse as children pour:

This is the way we pour our food,
Pour our food, pour our food.
This is the way we pour our food,
So early in the morning.

2. Sing the next verse as children clean up:

This is the way we pour our food,
Pour our food, pour our food.
This is the way we pour our food,
And then we eat it all.

Opportunities for Learning

- Emotional development: The children will express a range of emotions if they become frustrated or are successful with the task. They will show confidence in their own abilities and a willingness to try an activity.

- Language development: The children will use nonverbal communication and language to engage others. They will learn new vocabulary, such as *pour, cup, cereal, tray, dish soap, hand soap, big cup,* and *little cup.*

- Cognitive development: The children will develop a sense of quantity as they determine when a cup is full and will hold no more cereal.

- Physical/Motor development: The children will demonstrate increasingly independent self-help skills.

Beanbag Fun

Materials

Beanbags of various sizes, colors, and shapes

Large wastebasket or laundry basket

What to Do

1. Show the children how to toss a beanbag into the containers.

2. Allow the children to choose how close or far away they stand from a container when they toss a beanbag.

3. Count the beanbags as they go into the container, or say the colors of the beanbags as they go into the container.

4. Provide smaller or larger containers as needed to help the children be successful. As the children engage in this activity, they will try new and challenging experiences.

More to Do: Extensions and Adaptations

For Toddlers and Two-Year-Olds:

- Make beanbags by stuffing cloth with different materials, dried beans, rice, or cotton. Observe how children compare the similarities and differences in the bags.

- Show children how to toss the beanbag up into the air and catch it again. This improves balance.

- Encourage two children to sit apart facing each other and gently toss a beanbag back and forth.

For Two-Year-Olds:

- Play Hide the Beanbag. Ask the children to close their eyes while you hide the beanbag in a small area. (This is very difficult for young children and some will peek.) Always leave a portion of the beanbag showing. Let children take turns finding it.

- Ask a child to toss you a beanbag of a specific color, so you can observe for recognition of color.

- Ask a child to toss you a specific number of beanbags, so you can observe for recognition of number.

Suggested Books:

TouchThinkLearn: Numbers by Xavier Deneux

TouchThinkLearn: Colors by Xavier Deneux

Bowling Away

Materials

10 empty 2-liter bottles

Sand

Glue

Duct tape

Different sizes of soft balls, including a beach ball

What to Do

1. Add a cup of sand to each bottle to increase stability.

2. Glue the lids back on, and tape them securely.

3. Set up the bottles like bowling pins, and invite the children to take turns using a soft ball to knock them down. As the children use the bottles and balls in this way, they will be combining objects in a new way—creativity.

4. Optional: If two or three children are playing, count the knocked-down bottles in a cooperative way. The score would be the total of the bottles knocked down by all three children. Encourage them to work together and help each other. **Note:** Competition is not necessary (or desired) to make this activity fun and meaningful. Children will love knocking down the bottles and setting them back up. One child can be the bowler and the other child the pinsetter.

5. Support the children as they choose which ball they want to use and experiment to see which one works best.

6. This can be a fun outdoor activity as well if there is a sidewalk or paved area where you can set up the bottles.

More to Do: Extensions and Adaptations

For Young Toddlers:

Set up two to five bottles close to the child, and use a bigger ball. Add bottles as you think a child or children are ready for more.

For Two-Year-Olds:

- Use smaller bottles, such as soda bottles.
- Help each child keep a score of bottles knocked down with each ball. Use the information to create a simple graph. Try to make the game cooperative, not competitive.

Type of Ball	Turn 1: Number of Pins	Turn 2: Number of Pins	Turn 3: Number of Pins
Large ball			
Small ball			

Opportunities for Learning

- - - ● - - -

- Emotional development: The children will show confidence in their own abilities and may contribute their own ideas about how a game should be played.

- Social development: The children will develop the ability to wait for a turn and will help another child by setting up the pins.

- Language development: The children will understand and use new vocabulary, such as *bottle, ball,* "knock it down," *pin,* "help each other," *large, small, bigger,* and *smaller.*

- Literacy development: The children will make marks and use them to represent objects or actions (if children make marks on a graph).

- Cognitive development: The children will develop a sense of number and quantity as they knock down pins and as older children count the number of pins knocked down. They will develop reasoning and problem-solving skills as children choose the ball to use.

- Physical/Motor development: The children will develop gross-motor skills as they throw or roll the ball and fine-motor skills as they pick up pins and try to set them up.

Butterfly Catchers

Materials

Yarn

Large pieces of tissue paper

Scissors (adult use only)

What to Do

1. Wrap yarn around the middle of a double piece of tissue paper and tie a knot. The result should look like a butterfly. Make as many butterflies of different colors as you need.

2. Throw the butterflies into the air either in a large space indoors or outdoors. Encourage the children to try to catch the butterflies before they land on the ground.

3. Say, "Oh, Desiree caught a blue butterfly." "Jamal caught a pink butterfly."

4. Encourage the children to throw the butterflies up in the air for a peer to catch.

5. As the children interact with the butterflies, they will show imagination in their play and their interactions with others.

More to Do: Extensions and Adaptations

- Some young children may have difficulty catching the butterflies. Allow them to carry the butterflies around and pretend to be butterflies.

- Read the book *Butterfly Butterfly: A Book of Colors.* Encourage the children to talk about the butterflies they have seen. Talk about the many different colors of butterflies.

Suggested Book: *Butterfly Butterfly: A Book of Colors* by Petr Horáček

Song: (Sing to the tune of "The Ants Go Marching.")

> *Butterflies go flying one by one, hoorah, hoorah.*
> *Butterflies go flying one by one, hoorah, hoorah.*
> *Butterflies go flying one by one.*
> *The little one stops to have some fun.*
> *And they all go flying up and around, above the ground.*
>
> *Butterflies go flying two by two, hoorah, hoorah.*
> *Butterflies go flying two by two, hoorah, hoorah.*
> *Butterflies go flying two by two.*
> *The little one stops to tie her shoe.*
> *And they all go flying up and around, above the ground.*

Butterflies go flying three by three, hoorah, hoorah.
Butterflies go flying three by three, hoorah, hoorah.
Butterflies go flying three by three.
The little one stops to scratch her knee.
And they all go flying up and around, above the ground.

Opportunities for Learning

- Emotional development: The children will demonstrate a positive sense of identity as they have fun catching butterflies.

- Social development: The children will interact with other children—imitating, taking turns, and expressing glee.

- Language development: The children will participate in conversations with peers and adults in small-group interactions. They will understand and use new vocabulary, such as *butterfly, fly,* color words, *one, two,* and "up in the air."

- Literacy development: The children will comprehend meaning from pictures and stories.

- Cognitive development: The children will use objects or symbols (paper butterflies) to represent something real (real butterflies).

- Physical/Motor development: The children will engage in active physical play.

Baby Doll Bath Time

Materials

Washable baby dolls of different ethnic groups

Washcloths

Blankets

Mild liquid soap

Water

Small towels

2 washtubs

Small sponges

What to Do

1. Fill both basins with warm water. Add a tiny amount of liquid soap to one of the basins. Leave the other one without soap. Put the dolls and other materials next to the tubs.

What We Know

Toddlers and two-year-olds are becoming more skilled at using their hands—they stack, turn knobs, and put things together.

SAFETY ALERT

Children need constant supervision with this activity. Children have drowned in 2 inches of water.

2. Support the children as they use the washcloths to wash their dolls in the soapy water.

3. Talk about the dolls' faces, noses, eyes, ears, fingers, arms, tummy (stomach), legs, knees, feet, and toes as the children wash those parts of a doll's body. Observe to ensure that your parallel talk is not disrupting the child's focus on the task. If it is, then wait until the child finishes and ask, "Did you wash her fingers?"

4. Show the children how to rinse the doll in the clean water.

5. Some children will find "a dirty spot" after rinsing the doll and "need" to wash it again.

6. Support the children as they dry the dolls with small towels and wrap the dolls in blankets to keep the babies warm. The children will develop persistence as they follow through to give the baby a bath and dry the baby.

More to Do: Extensions and Adaptations

- If you have room, provide four tubs of water, so two children can wash their babies at the same time. Position the tubs so that children are facing each other.

- Provide more self-care items such as a small comb and brush for children to use with the dolls.

- Provide an unbreakable stand-up mirror so children can see themselves washing dolls and can show their "babies" what they look like after their bath.

- Read the book *Where Is Baby's Belly Button?* and use the book to ask whether a child washed all of the body parts.

Suggested Book: Where Is Baby's Belly Button? by Karen Katz

Opportunities for Learning
· · ● ● ● · · · ·

- Emotional development: The children will develop and show care and concern for others as they gently take care of their "babies."

- Social development: The children will develop relationships with other children who are washing a baby at the same time.

- Language development: The children will communicate needs during the activity. They will develop increased vocabulary, such as *baby, doll, tub, sponge, towel, rinse, soap,* and names of body parts.

- Physical/Motor development: The children will develop fine-motor skills as they use their hands to wash the babies.

Laundry Time

Materials

Baby doll clothing or actual baby clothes

Child-size table

Towel

Drying rack

2 washtubs

Mild liquid soap

Clothespins

Water

What to Do

1. Fill both basins with warm water. Add a tiny amount of liquid soap to one of the basins. Leave the other one without soap.

2. Encourage the children to wash each article of clothing in the soapy water and rinse in the plain water. Children may want to do this activity repeatedly over many days as they engage in pretend or make-believe play with other children.

3. Provide a towel for children to lay the clothing on before hanging the clothes so that some of the water is removed and not dripped on the floor.

4. Help them hang the wet clothes on a clothesline or drying rack.

Opportunities for Learning

- Emotional development: The children will express a range of different emotions.

- Social development: The children will engage in play with other children, enjoying each other's company.

- Language development: The children will communicate with other children through gestures, sounds, or words.

- Cognitive development: The children will problem solve how to wash different types of clothing and hang them up to dry.

- Physical/Motor development: The children will develop gross-motor skills as they stand to do the activity. They will develop fine-motor skills as they use the small muscles in their hands to wash the clothes and hang them to dry.

Scoop Out the Ice Cubes

Materials

Food coloring

Ice-cube trays

Water

Newspapers

2 large transparent or white plastic bowls

Tongs and spoons

What to Do

Ahead of Time:

1. Fill the ice-cube trays with water. Add a few drops of bright food coloring to the water.

2. Place the trays in a freezer. When the ice is set, remove from the freezer.

3. Spread old newspapers on the floor.

4. Fill a plastic bowl with water, and place it on the newspapers.

5. Drop the colored ice cubes into the water, and place the tongs and spoons nearby.

With the Children:

1. Ask the children, "How can we catch the ice cubes?"

2. Observe the strategies they use to catch the ice cubes. Do they try to catch them with their hands? Do they try to use the tongs or spoons? The children will demonstrate persistence as the slippery ice cubes slip away.

More to Do: Extensions and Adaptations

- Count the ice cubes that go into the water. Write the numeral on a piece of paper. Count the ice cubes that came out of the water. Are the two numbers the same? Did any ice cubes melt and disappear?

- Several children could do this activity at one time if the ice cubes are placed in a water table.

- On another day, add small plastic animals for the children to retrieve. Draw pictures of the animals on a piece of tagboard, and write the name of each animal by its picture. Check off the animal when it comes out of the water. Don't expect the children to read the words. You are just introducing the idea that the squiggly lines say words.

- Challenge children to try to use the tongs. This can be difficult for some children.

- Emotional development: The children will demonstrate different emotions. This activity may cause children to feel excited and happy or frustrated.

- Social development: The children will work beside other children with or without conflict.

- Language development: The children will use words, signs, or simple sentences to initiate, continue, or extend conversations. They will learn, for example, words for emotions, words for animals, *water, ice cube, bowl, water table,* counting words, *more, gone, disappear, melt, big, little, bigger,* and *smaller.*

- Literacy development: The children will recognize pictures and some symbols, signs, or words. They will make scribbles on paper to represent an object or action.

- Cognitive development: The children will begin to understand **one-to-one correspondence** when counting the ice cubes or animals. They will develop a sense of number and quantity. They may use words such as *more, all gone, little,* and *big.*

- Physical/Motor development: The children will develop fine-motor skills as they retrieve the ice cubes or animals with tongs or a spoon.

Lacing Shapes

Materials

Colored card stock

Stencils of animal shapes (optional)

Pieces of colored yarn

Children's large plastic yarn needles

Scissors (adult use only)

Hole punch

Tape

What We Know

Toddlers and two-year-olds are practicing how to use both hands and eye-hand coordination skills to manipulate toys and objects.

What to Do

Ahead of Time:

1. Cut the colored card stock into basic shapes (square, triangle, and so on), or use stencils to create animal shapes.

2. Using a single-hole paper punch, randomly punch holes in the shapes, being careful not to punch the holes too close together or too close to the edge of the shape. Depending on the age of the child, you might want to punch only three or four holes in the shape.

3. Thread a piece of yarn onto a yarn needle. It is best to use a yarn color that contrasts with the color of the shape, so that the child can clearly see the stitches she makes.

4. Tie a loop in the yarn with a small knot so that the needle cannot be pulled off the yarn.

5. Tape the opposite end of the yarn onto the back of the card stock shape.

With the Children:

1. Show the children how to weave the needle and yarn in and out through the holes in the shape. If a child becomes frustrated, she will learn to manage his feelings with the help of familiar, supportive adults.

2. **SAFETY ALERT:** This is a one-on-one activity with one teacher working with one child. Children should never be left alone with a plastic needle.

More to Do: Extensions and Adaptations

- If handling a needle is too difficult, use a shoelace with the hard sheath ends (aglets). Tie one end to the card, and let the child use her fingers to thread the other end of the shoelace through the holes.

- Some children will wrap the lace around the whole card to put the lace through another hole from the top side. Teachers can decide which children would benefit from help turning the card over each time the lace is put through another hole.

- Some children may prefer to thread the yarn through large holes in blocks.

- If children have difficulty with the task, provide rings (too large for choking) with large holes in them for children to manipulate a piece of yarn or string through.

Suggested Book: Baby Touch and Feel: Colors and Shapes by DK Publishing

Opportunities for Learning
· • • ● • • •

- Emotional development: The children will develop expectations of consistent, positive interactions with adults.

- Language development: The children will understand and use new vocabulary, such as *card*, names of animal shapes, *lace, yarn, needle, in,* and *out.*

- Cognitive development: The children will use a variety of strategies to solve problems. They will often find unique ways of lacing the yarn back and forth through the holes.

- Physical/Motor development: The children will develop fine-motor and eye-hand coordination skills.

Language Development

Baby Conversations

Materials

None

What to Do

1. Listen for the very young infant to make sounds when looking at you. Respond by imitating and expanding the sounds the infant makes. For example, if the infant says, "ah," you could say "ah" or "bah." If an infant says, "ba," you could say, "ba, ba" or "ba ba, ma ma."

2. Initiate a "conversation" by gazing into an infant's eyes and making a sound you know the infant knows how to make. Look expectantly at the infant and wait for the infant to take a turn.

3. At other times, talk to the infant using **parentese**, a special language adults all over the world use when talking to infants. Adults use speech that has an elevated pitch, long pauses, and exaggerated stress on sounds and syllables. This allows infants to process the structure of language more easily.

4. At other times, sing and talk in a normal voice, to help infants learn the structure of the language(s) they are hearing. Infants will begin to regulate their emotions as adults empathize, provide **active listening,** and calm them when they are in distress.

More to Do: Extensions and Adaptations

- Even though you may not speak the infant's home language, try to imitate the sounds the infant makes.

- Recognize that it is beneficial, not harmful, for infants to be exposed to several languages.

Songs: Lullabies

> ### What We Know
>
> There is structure to language, and infants are trying to figure out that structure when adults talk directly to them. Infants who hear the most parentese in a responsive way have more advanced language development than those infants who hear the least parentese (Ramirez-Esparza, Garcia-Sierra, and Kuhl, 2014).

- Emotional development: The children will relate to, trust, and become attached to consistent adults in their lives.

- Language development: The children will learn the structure of language as they listen intently to the language(s) spoken with and around them. They will develop expressive language as they take turns making sounds, babbling, using gestures, or using first words.

- Cognitive development: The children will perform simple actions to make things happen, such as gestures, cries, sounds, or first words.

Babbling: Echo Me, Echo You

Materials

None

What to Do

1. Once a child starts making sounds, such as "ba," "ma," or "da," echo back to him sounds, such as "ba, ba, ba." Eventually the infant will begin to make the same sounds again, just to hear your response. The child will maintain attention as he takes turns making sounds.

2. After a few times of going back and forth, try a new sound. For example, if the child says, "ba," you say, "ba ba, ma ma." At other times try other sound variations such as "me, me"; "la, la, la"; or "go, go."

3. Instead of new sounds, imitate the child's sounds but in a different intonation. For example, a nine-month-old may say, "da, da" seemingly as a statement. You reply, "da da?" raising your tone at the end of the question. Try to express different emotions while repeating the sounds of the infant. See how many turns the infant will make. One parent reported taking thirty-two turns with her infant while both were echoing the sounds, "da da," but in different pitches and tones.

More to Do: Extensions and Adaptations

- Read the books listed below with one infant on your lap or two sitting infants side by side nestled into you, so they can easily see the pictures and hear the sounds and words.

What We Know

Adults who **contingently** babble back to infants and add a few more sounds facilitate infants' learning new sounds (Goldstein and Schwade, 2008). It is important to talk with infants, make eye contact while speaking or listening, repeat the sounds that infants make, give infants an opportunity to take a turn in the "conversation," and sing songs. Infants' brains are processing language from before birth. At birth, infants can hear the differences in all of the languages in the world. Their brains are prepared to learn language(s).

- Place two younger infants side by side on their tummies or two older infants or young toddlers sitting side by side. Listen for the sounds they make to each other.

Suggested Books:

Moo Baa La La La! by Sandra Boynton

What Does Baby Say? A Lift-the-Flap Book by Karen Katz

Opportunities for Learning
• • • ● • ● • • •

- Emotional development: The children will learn how to express different emotions.
- Social development: The children will show interest in and interact with other children.
- Language development: The children will attend to, understand, and respond to communication and language from others. They will take conversational turns in language interactions.
- Cognitive development: The children will demonstrate curiosity in cause-and-effect relationships.

Self-Talk, Parallel Talk, and Expansion

Materials

None

What to Do

1. Use **self-talk** in responsive ways. When doing daily routines, use any opportunity to talk with children. Tell them everything that you are doing. This works well when you are changing their diapers, feeding them, or putting food on a table for older toddlers and two-year-olds: "I'm getting a clean diaper. I'm putting on your diaper. Thank you for lifting your legs. Now, I'm pulling up your jeans."

2. Use parallel talk in responsive ways. *Parallel talk* is talk that you use to describe what the child is doing, rather than what you are doing. You can say, for example, "You are crawling. You are climbing up

What We Know

Infants say an average of ten words at fourteen months. Between eighteen and twenty-four months, they may begin to use two words together. Speaking normally sometimes and at other times expanding the child's level of language slightly when you talk with him helps the child learn language (Tamis-LeMonda, Kuchirko, and Song, 2014).

one step. You are touching the truck." You will be able to tell if the talking is interfering with the child's goals or annoying the child. Most children like that you are paying such close attention to what they are doing.

3. Use **expansion talk** in responsive ways. Expansion talk expands what the child has just said to you. The adult expands the child's sounds or talk by adding meaning or sentence length. For example, a child looks out the window and says or signs *bird*. You could say "Yes, a red bird," which adds both meaning and sentence length. You judge whether the expansion is appropriate for an individual child to understand. Most very young children won't attend or learn if an adult says, for example, "Yes, that is a bird, and it flies south in the winter and back north in the spring."

4. Use **semantic responsive talk**. When you use semantic elaboration, you try to stay on the same topic as the child. If the child says, "Airplane," and points to the sky, try to talk about the sounds, color, and shape of the airplane. The toddler is more likely to take another turn if you stay on the same topic.

5. Read books every day to children. The books listed below repeat words and then add new vocabulary, expanding the language with each verse.

Suggested Books:

Brown Bear, Brown Bear, What Do You See? by Bill Martin Jr. and Eric Carle

Polar Bear, Polar Bear, What Do You Hear? by Bill Martin Jr. and Eric Carle

Panda Bear, Panda Bear, What Do You See? by Bill Martin Jr. and Eric Carle

Opportunities for Learning

- Language development: The children will understand and use an increasing number of words in communication with others.

- Literacy development: The children will comprehend meaning from pictures and stories if adults often read to them.

- Cognitive development: The children will use understanding of causal relationships when adults are responsive to children's language and communication attempts.

Two or More Languages

Materials

None

What to Do

1. Many children will enter programs learning a language other than English at home, but the parents may want the child to learn English in child care. Other children will enter learning two languages. Honor the home language. It is very important to many parents that children learn to speak the home language well.

2. If a child is learning two languages, make sure that children hear both languages frequently and in a variety of circumstances.

3. Create opportunities for the children to use the languages that they hear.

4. Read books to and with the children in each of the languages that are important to their lives.

5. Recognize cultural differences in how language is learned and used. For example, some families engage their children in lengthy conversations, while others do not. Some families ask many questions, while others do not.

6. If a child is not learning either language well, talk with the parents about asking a doctor for a hearing test to rule out medical problems.

Suggested Books: Find many children's books in Spanish and other languages at amazon.com and other websites.

What We Know

It is important to support young children's use of their home language by reading books, singing songs, and using important words and phrases in the child's home language. Children learn two or more languages easily in the first three years and can demonstrate competency in both languages. Learning two languages enhances brain development and executive functioning (Conboy and Kuhl, 2011; Crivello et al., 2016; Engel de Abreu et al., 2012; Kluger, 2013).

Opportunities for Learning

· · ● · ● · · ·

- Language development: The children will increase their vocabulary in the languages they are learning and will increase their use of those languages in a variety of settings.

- Cognitive development: The children will develop increased executive functioning.

Picture Wall

Materials

Magazines

Tape

Scissors (adult use only)

Contact paper

What to Do

1. Choose a topic that interests several of the children in your group or an individual child. The topic may also relate to a book that you are reading to the children.

2. Cut out pictures that relate to the topic, and cover them with contact paper to make them more durable. Some examples of topics and related pictures are:

   - Transportation: cars, trains, bikes, motorcycles, boats
   - Animals: cows, dogs, cats, horses, birds
   - Clothing: shirts, pants, coats, shoes, boots
   - Concepts such as up/down, big/little, tall/short

3. Attach the pictures to the wall at the children's eye level.

4. Talk with the children about details of the pictures.

More to Do: Extensions and Adaptations

For Infants:

- Laminate the pictures and punch holes on the left side of each picture. Tie the pictures together with yarn to make a book for infants. Check the edges and corners to make sure they are not sharp.

- Laminate the pictures and place them by the wall, standing up against the wall, so children can see them. Crawling infants may pick them up and carry them around.

For Toddlers and Two-Year-Olds:

- Create photo books related to different topics. Find or cut pictures to fit into different sizes of photo books. Seal the edges with tape for added security.

- Add the name(s) of the topic and the specific item at the bottom of each page, such as *Transportation* and *Car, Animal* and *Cat.*

What We Know

Infants will enjoy looking at the photos and books and listening to the books and names of the photos. Toddlers will name of few of the photos, and two-year-olds will name many of them. Many two-year-olds will begin to understand that there are many types of objects, such as animals or transportation. They will begin to sort objects by one characteristic.

Suggested Books:

Animals

Discover Kids: Oink on the Farm! by Parragon Books

Discover Kids: Moo on the Farm! by Parragon Books

Doggies by Sandra Boynton

If Animals Kissed Good Night by Ann Whitford Paul

Transportation

Little Blue Truck by Alice Schertle

Sophie's Big Beep Beep Book! by DK Publishing

Opportunities for Learning

• • • • ● • • • •

- Language development: The children will understand and use a growing vocabulary, such as words on a wall and in photo books.

- Literacy development: The children will comprehend meaning from pictures and stories.

- Cognitive development: The children will learn to sort objects into categories.

Rhyming Time

Materials

Books with content that rhymes

What to Do

1. Every day read one or two rhyming books to the children. Infants will cuddle on your lap to listen, toddlers will gather in small informal groups, and two-year-olds will sit for longer periods in small informal groups.

2. Sing the same rhyming song often, until older toddlers and two-year-olds begin to learn the words to the song.

What We Know

Infants are processing language and learning the structure of language as they listen to books. Toddlers and two-year-olds are learning new vocabulary and sentence structures as well as rhyming words.

Suggested Books:

Chicka Chicka Boom Boom by Bill Martin Jr. and John Archambault

Duck in the Truck by Jez Alborough

Is Your Mama a Llama? by Deborah Guarino

Moose on the Loose by Kathy-Jo Wargin

Silly Sally by Audrey Wood

Sheep in a Jeep by Nancy E. Shaw

The Itsy Bitsy Bunny by Jeffrey Burton

The Itsy Bitsy Spider Finger Puppet Book by Parragon Books

Songs:

"Itsy Bitsy Spider"

"Twinkle, Twinkle, Little Star"

"I'm a Little Teapot"

Opportunities for Learning

• • • ● ● ● • • •

- Emotional development: The children will recognize and interpret emotions of animals in the books, with the support of favorite adults.

- Social development: The children will enjoy peer interactions in small groups as they listen and react to the storybooks.

- Language development: The children will ask questions as they listen to stories and will begin to understand and enjoy rhyming.

- Literacy development: The children will relate what happens in stories to their own experiences.

Where Is It?

Materials

None

What to Do

Help infants, toddlers, and two-year-olds learn to understand where body parts are and learn to name the body parts.

More to Do: Extensions and Adaptations

For Infants:

- Name body parts on the child and yourself during typical routines. For example, when feeding a child, say, "You are opening your mouth. You must be hungry. I can open my mouth, too. See? Here is my mouth."
- Read the books listed below.

For Toddlers:

- Young toddlers may point at one or more body parts. This can be challenging, though, because toddlers can't see their own noses, eyes, or ears. They can see their belly buttons, hands, fingers, legs, feet, and toes. Show them their body parts in a mirror.
- Older toddlers may name some body parts when asked; for example, if you ask, "What is this?" as you point to your own nose, an older toddler may reply, "Nose."

For Two-Year-Olds:

- Two-year-olds can learn to recognize and point to more parts of the body, such as elbows, knees, heels, eyelids, and eyebrows.
- Many two-year-olds can learn words for what body parts do—*wiggle, tickle, sneeze, hug, kiss,* and *giggle.* To support this learning, read the following books. They will start adding *ing* to words, as in *kissing, blowing,* and *jumping.*

Suggested Books:

Look at You! A Baby Body Book by Kathy Henderson

Lick! by Matthew Van Fleet

Sniff! by Matthew Van Fleet

Munch! by Matthew Van Fleet

Eyes, Nose, Fingers, and Toes: A First Book All About You by Judy Hindley

From Head to Toe by Eric Carle

Toes, Ears, and Nose! A Lift-the-Flap Book by Marion Dane Bauer and Karen Katz

All of Baby, Nose to Toes by Victoria Adler

All About Me! by DK Publishing

Where is Baby's Belly Button? by Karen Katz

What We Know

Older infants and young toddlers understand and may sign or say words such as tummy or nose and will have approximately ten words by fourteen months of age. Toddlers and two-year-olds express themselves with increasingly complex vocabulary and sentence structure. Older toddlers and young two-year-olds may say, "My tummy," "I kissing," "What dat?" "Kai hot here," or "Me tickling." Many two-year-olds will say multiword sentences with a large vocabulary and will ask what and why.

Fingerplay:

> *Here is* (child's name)'s *eye.* (point to eye or gently touch eyelid)
> *Here is* (child's name)'s *nose.* (gently touch nose)
> *Touch the part that sees.* (gently touch eyelid)
> *Touch the part that blows.* (gently touch nose)

Opportunities for Learning

● ● ● **●** ● ● ●

- Emotional development: The children will demonstrate a positive sense of self-identity and self-awareness as they point to body parts, learn the names, and think about their functions.

- Social development: The children will form relationships with other children when books are read in small informal groups and when children choose to hear the story.

- Language development: The children will respond to and use a growing vocabulary, such as *body*, names of body parts, *sees, blows, wiggle, tickle, sneeze, hug, kiss,* and *giggle.*

- Literacy development: The children will develop interest in books as teachers read the many infant and toddler books about body parts.

- Cognitive development: The children will use their senses to construct knowledge of the world around them as they learn the functions of different body parts.

Yo-Ho: A-Spying We Go

Materials

Empty paper towel rolls, 1 for every 2 children

Scissors (adult use only)

Contact paper or nontoxic paint and paintbrushes

What We Know

Singing songs "lights up the brain," increases vocabulary, and promotes future academic success (Cooper, 2010).

What to Do

Ahead of Time:

1. Cut the paper towel rolls in half to make a "spyglass."

2. Invite the children to decorate the paper towel rolls with paint. Or, you may wish to cover the paper towel rolls with contact paper yourself.

With the Children:

1. Give each child a spyglass made from the paper towel roll.

2. Take a small group of children around the room with their spyglasses to look for specific things in the environment, such as a crayon, a block, a paintbrush, a ball, and so on.

3. Give all the children in the room a turn in a small spying group. Encourage the children to help each other as they look.

4. The children will develop persistence as a small group looks for all the items.

More to Do: Extensions and Adaptations

- Place different stuffed animals around the room with all or part of the animal visible to the children. Sing the following song:

    Going on a lion hunt, and I don't care.
    Got my camera by my side and my binoculars, too.
    Going on a bear hunt, and I don't care.
    Got my camera by my side and my binoculars, too.

- Sing a verse for each hidden animal. If a child spots a bear when you are looking for a lion, wait to pick it up until you sing the verse for that animal. Children will often excitedly remember where they saw that bear when they were looking for the lion. This supports memory development.

- On another day, look for photos of children hidden in obvious places in the room and visible to the children.

- Hide animals or pictures of characters related to a book, such as *The Very Hungry Caterpillar* by Eric Carle. Hunt for food items in the order they are presented in the book.

Suggested Books:

We're Going on a Lion Hunt by Margery Cuyler

We're Going on a Bear Hunt by Michael Rosen and Helen Oxenbury

- Emotional development: The children will manage emotions such as excitement with the support of special adults.

- Social development: The children will develop relationships with their peers as they go on an exciting adventure together and the teacher encourages social interaction.

- Language development: The children will understand and use an increasing number of words, such as the names of animals, items in the environment, *spyglasses*, the names of peers, names of food, *hungry*, and *caterpillar*.

- Cognitive development: The children will develop memory as they remember where an animal was hidden or which foods the hungry caterpillar ate first.

- Physical/Motor development: The children will coordinate hand and eye movements as children hold their spyglasses and look for objects.

Pack 'n' Go

Materials

3 small suitcases

6 sets of doll clothing

What to Do

1. Young children love to put things in containers and take things out. Provide three child-size suitcases and six sets of clothing, such as hats, shirts, pants, and socks, to put in the suitcases and take out again.

2. Ask three children if they want to help pack suitcases and go on a trip together to a special place on the other side of the room. Give each child a suitcase and two sets of each type of clothing.

3. Comment on the names of the clothing if the children do not. Observe which names children then say.

4. Pretend you are going on a trip from one end of the room to another. Unpack and then pack again to go "home."

More to Do: Extensions and Adaptations

For Toddlers:

- Toddlers from eighteen to twenty-four months may know the names of some of the clothing or repeat the names after you.

- Observe if children sort items or just put them in the suitcase.

For Two-Year-Olds:

- Many two-year-olds will know the names of the items and use two or more words together. If not, tell them the names of items, using short sentences: "This is a red shirt." "This is a blue shirt."

- Comment on the colors and patterns in the clothing.

- Challenge children to pack the shirts together, the socks together, and so forth.

Song: (Sing to the tune of "The Farmer in the Dell.")

> *A-traveling we will go.*
> *A-traveling we will go.*
> *Hi, ho, don't you know,*
> *A-traveling we will go.*
>
> *Jack chose a shirt.*
> *Jack chose a shirt.*
> *Hi, ho, don't you know,*
> *A-traveling we will go.*
>
> *Madeleine chose some socks.*
> *Madeleine chose some socks.*
> *Hi, ho, don't you know,*
> *A-traveling we will go.*

What We Know

The typical progression of expressive language development:

- Child makes sounds (coos, babbling)

- Child uses gestures and points

- Child uses first words

- Child uses two words together

- Child adds *s* to words for plural

- Child adds *ing* to action words

- Child overgeneralizes, such as using the word *cat* for all four-legged animals

- Child undergeneralizes, such as using the word *cat* for only his pet cat, not other cats

- Emotional development: The children will develop the ability to self-regulate as they participate in enjoyable activities for longer periods and use words to negotiate play rather than hit or bite.

- Social development: The children will play with other children, exchanging toys and clothing. They will enjoy participating in a common plan—going on a trip.

- Language development: The children will use sounds and words in social situations, such as the names of clothing, colors of clothing, *in, out, trip, pack*, the names of peers, the name of the teacher, and may ask, "Where we go?"

- Cognitive development: The children will explore the environment, making new discoveries.

- Physical/Motor development: The children will develop both fine-motor and gross-motor skills.

Photo Finish

Materials

Camera

Printer

Laminator or clear contact paper (optional)

What to Do

Ahead of Time:

1. Take pictures of different objects in the room, and print them out.

2. Laminate them or cover them with clear contact paper, if desired.

With the Children:

1. Give each child a picture and tell him to look very carefully at it.

2. Encourage each child to look around the room and find the object in the picture.

3. Depending on how large the item is, have the child stand by the item or bring it to you.

4. Ask each child to hold up the picture and the item (or point to the item) and tell the other children what he found.

5. As they look for the items in the photos, the children will demonstrate interest in and curiosity about objects.

More to Do: Extensions and Adaptations

For Toddlers and Two-Year-Olds:

Children will enjoy doing the activity for several days. Give each child a different picture each time. Change the pictures every third day or so to keep the interest and curiosity of the children.

For Two-Year-Olds:

Ask the children to describe the object—color, shape, function, texture, or size (big or little).

Suggested Book:

Brown Bear, Brown Bear, What Do You See? by Bill Martin Jr. and Eric Carle

Change the words and ask, "(Child's name, child's name) what do you see?"

Opportunities for Learning

• • • ● • • •

- Emotional development: The children will show confidence in their own abilities. They will manage feelings and emotions with the support of familiar adults.

- Social development: The children will interact with other children as they take turns talking about their objects.

- Language development: The children will increase vocabulary, such as the names of items; color words; shape words; texture words such as *rough, smooth, bumpy, soft, hard*; and function phrases such as "play with it," "build with it," and "eat with it."

- Literature development: The children will recognize pictures and some symbols, signs, or words as they understand that the picture is a representation of the real object.

- Cognitive development: The children will actively explore people and objects to understand themselves, others, and objects. They will use reasoning to solve problems as they try to figure out where an item is located.

- Physical/Motor development: The children will use perceptual information (touch, hearing, and vision) to understand objects.

Surprise Box

Materials

Shoe box

Sock

Variety of items to place in the box

Scissors (adult use only)

Glue

What to Do

Ahead of Time:

1. Cut an opening in the shoe-box lid large enough for a child's hand to fit into.

2. Cut the foot end off the sock. Glue one open end of the sock to the inside of the hole on the bottom of the lid. This will keep the children from peeking inside the hole to look at the items in the box.

3. Place different items in the box that teach new vocabulary and/or accompany a story that is being read. Try to include a variety of textures, such as smooth, rough, soft, hard, fuzzy, and so on.

4. Set the box in the language, cognitive-discovery, or sensory area in the room.

With the Children:

1. Children will probably want to explore the box but may not know how to put their hands into the opening of the sock and reach deep enough into the box to find an item. Show them how. As they explore what is in the box, the children will demonstrate interest in and curiosity about objects and will manage feelings and emotions with the support of familiar adults.

2. Ask the children to guess what the item is before pulling it out and looking at it.

More to Do: Extensions and Adaptations

For Toddlers and Two-Year-Olds:

- Some children may be fearful of putting their hands in the sock and then into the box. Let them observe other children do the activity. Talk about how all the items are safe for children to touch.

- Children will enjoy doing the activity for several days and predicting what is in their hand while it is in the box. Change the items every third day or so to keep the interest and curiosity of the children.

- Take photos of children's faces as they put their hands into the sock and box, or record what children say. Create a documentation panel of children's emotions and/or language. List the opportunities for learning suggested below. Look at the documentation panels with the children to encourage them to talk about what they were feeling and thinking.

For Two-Year-Olds:

- If there is more than one item in a category, such as rocks or crayons, encourage children to sort the items. Observe how children sort the items. If children do not seem to understand, you could say, "What if we put all of the rocks here and all of the crayons here?"
- Ask the children to describe the object before pulling it out and looking at it, to encourage expressive language development.

Suggested Books:

Tails by Matthew Van Fleet

Fuzzy Fuzzy Fuzzy! by Sandra Boynton

Opportunities for Learning

• • • ● • • •

- Emotional development: The children will show confidence in their own abilities.

- Social development: The children will interact with other children as several children sit by each other to play the game.

- Language development: The children will increase vocabulary, such as the names of items in the box, *sock, hole, in, out,* "pull it out," and texture words—*rough, smooth, bumpy, soft,* and *hard.*

- Literature development: The children will recognize pictures and some symbols, signs, or words when teachers place items from a storybook in the box.

- Cognitive development: The children will actively explore objects to understand themselves, others, and objects. They will use matching and sorting of objects to understand similar and different characteristics. This is mathematical thinking. They will use reasoning to solve problems as they describe the objects and guess what they are.

- Physical/Motor development: The children will use perceptual information (touch, hearing, and vision) to understand objects.

Flip the Flap

Materials

Magazines

Laminator or clear contact paper

Scissors (adult use only)

Velcro

Glue

Felt or flannel material

Flannel board

What to Do

Ahead of Time:

1. Choose pictures of objects, animals, and people with different emotional expressions, and cut them out.

2. Laminate the images, or cover them with clear contact paper.

3. Cut the Velcro into 1½" pieces. Attach one side of Velcro to the back of each photo.

4. Cut the felt or flannel material into 6" or smaller squares.

5. Glue one side of each piece of cloth to the top of each photo so that the cloth covers the photo and can be lifted from the bottom to see the photo.

6. Attach the other sides of the pieces of Velcro to the flannel board. Put several of the flap-covered photos on the flannel board.

7. Place the board in the language/literacy area.

With the Children:

1. Encourage the children to peek under the flaps and name the people, animals, or objects they see. If they do not spontaneously use the words, then excitedly provide the words for them as the children lift the flaps: "Dog!" "Happy man!" "Car!"

2. Change the photos from time to time to keep the children's interest. As the children explore the photos, they will show interest in and curiosity about discovering surprise images.

More to Do: Extensions and Adaptations

- Use photos of animals and their homes so that children can find the two photos that match.
- Use two photos each of children in the group so that children find the two photos that match.
- Use photos of farm animals one day and jungle animals another day.
- Change the photos to match books that you are reading to the children.
- Read the books listed below, and encourage children to lift the flaps gently.
- Encourage two children to sit together by the board and play the game together.

Suggested Books:

Sesame Street: Elmo at the Zoo by Lori Froeb

Peek-a-Baby: A Lift-the-Flap Book by Karen Katz

Opportunities for Learning
• • ● • • ● • • ●

- Emotional development: The children will recognize and interpret emotions shown in the photos.
- Social development: The children will initiate and engage in play with other children.
- Language development: The children will increase vocabulary, such as the names of animals, emotions, and peers.
- Literacy development: The children will handle books and relate them to their own experiences.
- Cognitive development: The children will recognize differences between familiar and unfamiliar people, animals, and objects. They will use pictures of objects to represent something real. This is symbolic representation.
- Physical/Motor development: The children will develop fine-motor skills as they use the small muscles in their hands to pick up the flaps.

Social Development

I Want to See You

Materials

Blankets or mats

What to Do

1. Place two young infants on their backs near each other on the blanket, so that they can turn their heads and see each other.

2. Observe how the infants look at each other. Some infants will reach out to the other child to touch him.

3. Older infants will often crawl to be near other children. They may want to touch the other child. Observe carefully to teach the older infant how to make a connection with another child without poking or pulling the child's hair. Say, "Touch gently."

> **What We Know**
>
> Younger infants often show great interest in each other, using sounds to get another child's attention, stretching their feet out to touch each other, and mirroring each other's sounds (Selby and Bradley, 2003). Older infants may crawl to each other, point toward a toy, or hold up a toy to show a peer (Brownell, Ramani, and Zerwas, 2006).

More to Do: Extensions and Adaptations

Sing the following song with two infants together. Sit on the floor with back support so that several crawling infants can come to you for hugs when they need them. Allow the infants to move freely. Do not put them in containers such as entertainers, car seats, or infant seats.

Song: (Sing to the tune of "Twinkle, Twinkle, Little Star.")

> *Twinkle, twinkle, little* (child's name), (open and close hands)
> *What a wonderful friend you are.* (point to the child)
> *From your head to your toes,* (point gently to body parts as you say them)
> *From your knees to your nose*
> *Twinkle, twinkle, little* (child's name),
> *What a wonderful friend you are.*

Friendship Book

Materials

Camera

Photographs of the children

Tagboard or cardboard

Scissors (adult use only)

Glue

Contact paper

Hole punch (adult use only)

Yarn or ribbon

Permanent marker

What We Know

Children can be friends by one year of age (Howes, 1996). They greet each other and choose to be close to a friend. They play more easily with a friend than with a stranger. Toddlers and two-year-olds miss a friend when the friend is absent for a day.

What to Do

Ahead of Time:

1. Take photos of the children when they are together. Try to capture images of them beside each other or doing activities together.

2. Cut the tagboard or cardboard into squares big enough to glue the photos on them.

3. Mount pictures on the cardboard and cover with clear contact paper.

4. Punch holes in one end of the cardboard and tie several together to make a book about friends.

With the Children:

1. When the children are looking at the book, be sure to name the child, the other children in the photo, and what they are doing together.

2. Make the friendship books available in the literacy learning area of the room.

More to Do: Extensions and Adaptations

For Infants:

- Take photos of infants beside each other, looking and smiling at each other, and giving objects to each other.
- Use the names of the children often when looking at the photos.

For Toddlers and Two-Year-Olds:

- Take photos of children greeting and hugging each other, giving an object to a friend, cooperating and sharing with a friend, helping a friend, looking at a book together, and playing together. Notice the many ways that toddlers and two-year-olds are prosocial with each other.
- Write the names of the children in the photo at the bottom of each page.
- Act out the words of the following song with the children while holding up photos of the children with each other.
- With a small group of toddlers and two-year-olds, read the book and talk about what friends do with each other. Write what the children say on a poster and display it for the families and community.

Song: (Sing to the tune of "Twinkle, Twinkle, Little Star.")

> *Twinkle, twinkle, little star,*
> *Oh, what wonderful friends we are.*
> *When we share and when we hug,*
> *When we cuddle all nice and snug,*
> *When we help each other, too,*
> *We are friends, me and you.*

Suggested Book: *Little Blue Truck* by Alice Schertle

- Social development: The children will develop a sense of self with others.

- Language development: The children will increase their vocabulary as they learn the names of the other children and the words *book, picture, friend, head, toes, knees, nose, twinkle, hug, snug,* and *help.*

My Friend, My Friend, Who Do You See?

Materials

Camera

Photo of each child

Cardboard or tagboard

Clear contact paper

Hole punch (adult use only)

Scissors (adult use only)

Yarn

Permanent marker

What to Do

Ahead of Time:

1. Take a photo of each child in your room, and print them out.

2. Cut out cardboard squares large enough for the photos. Make one square per child.

3. Place one photo of a child on each square, and cover the photo with contact paper. Trim the extra contact paper off, and round the edges so that they are not sharp.

4. Punch holes in the left-hand side of each square.

5. Put the pages together, photo-side down, and tie them together with yarn to create a book.

What We Know

Warm, caring, sensitive interactions with adults who read to an individual child or a small informal group build secure attachments with children. Children who experience secure adult-child relationships are more likely to be prosocial with peers (Newton, Thompson, and Goodman, 2016).

A photo is a representation or symbol of the child. It is not the real child. Identifying themselves and other children in photos builds a foundation for reading.

6. Open the book, and write on the first right-hand page: "(Child's name, child's name), who do you see?"

7. Turn the page, and write on the next right-hand page:

8. "I see (next child's name) looking at me. (Child's name, child's name), who do you see?"

9. Continue until each right-hand page has a child's name.

10. For the last photo in the book, simply write, "I see (child's name) looking at me."

11. Cover the writing with clear contact paper.

With the Children:

1. Look at the book and read it to the children. The children will maintain and focus attention with support as they see photos of the children in their room.

2. Point to a photo and ask a child, "Who do you see?" The children will demonstrate curiosity when they are asked this question.

More to Do: Extensions and Adaptations

For Infants:

- Look at the book with an infant on your lap. As you both look at the photo of a child, point to that child in the room and say the child's name.

- Keep the book in a basket on the floor for children who can crawl or for those early walkers in your room.

For Toddlers and Two-Year-Olds:

- Make a book but use photos of the pets of the children.

- Read the book many times with a child. Repetition helps children learn the words and meaning of the book.

- Place the photo book(s) in a comfortable reading area in the room.

Song: "Brown Bear, Brown Bear, What Do You See?"

Hear it on YouTube at https://www.youtube.com/watch?v=ek7j3huAApc

Suggested Books:

Brown Bear, Brown Bear, What Do You See? by Bill Martin Jr. and Eric Carle

Baby Bear, Baby Bear, What Do You See? by Bill Martin Jr. and Eric Carle

Panda Bear, Panda Bear, What Do You See? by Bill Martin Jr. and Eric Carle

Opportunities for Learning

- Emotional development: The children will develop a sense of identity and will understand some characteristics of self as they see photos of themselves and hear their names.

- Social development: The children will show interest in, interact with, and develop relationships with other children.

- Language development: The children will understand and use an increasing number of words, such as *brown, bear, see,* and names of children in the group.

- Literacy development: The children will develop an interest in print as adults point to the photos of the children and the words.

- Physical/Motor development: The children will develop fine-motor skills as they turn the pages of the book.

Handprint Friendship Collage

Materials

Fingerpaint in a variety of colors

Metal pie plates, one per color of fingerpaint

Large piece of paper

Permanent marker

What to Do

Ahead of Time:

1. On the top of the paper, write the words *Handprint Friendship Collage.*

2. Put several colors of paint in the pie tins, and set them out on a table.

3. Lay the piece of paper on the table.

What We Know

Younger children may participate in parallel play—beside each other and usually aware of each other—or in simple social play—taking turns as in run-and-chase games. Older children may participate in complementary and reciprocal social play—a joint activity that has a common plan such as going on a trip—or may engage in cooperative social pretend play in which children have complementary roles—one child is the mom and the other child is the dad (Howes, 1996).

With the Children:

1. Read the book *Hand, Hand, Fingers, Thumb* by Al Perkins to the children. As you sit on the floor and begin to read, those children who want to hear the story will toddle over to sit by you.

2. Bring infants one-by-one and toddlers or two-year-olds in pairs to the table with the paint and paper.

3. Tell the infants what you will do: "I am going to put your little hand in the paint. Then I will put your hand on the paper." Tell toddlers and two-year-olds how to place a hand in the paint and then on the paper.

4. Read the cues of the children as to whether they want to do the activity. Toddlers and two-year-olds may need to watch the activity before they are ready to place their hands in paint. If the children decide to try the paint, they will be trying a new and challenging activity.

5. Wash the children's hands carefully between different colors of paint and when you are finished.

More to Do: Extensions and Adaptations

For Older Infants:

Some infants will resist placing their whole hand in paint. They may be willing to put one finger in the paint and then on the paper. If they aren't willing, try another time.

For Toddlers and Two-Year-Olds:

● Those toddlers who have sensory challenges may resist putting their hands in the paint. Ask them if they would like to put on a plastic glove to do the activity. Toddlers and two-year-olds may also prefer to just use a finger or a thumb.

● You may need to model first, and then ask toddlers or two-year-olds to imitate you.

● Use your thumb to make thumbprints. Add faces by adding eyes, nose, and a mouth to the thumbprints.

Fingerplay:

Clap, clap, clap your hands, (clap hands)
Clap your hands together.
Shake, shake, shake your hands, (shake hands)
Shake your hands together.
Rub, rub, rub your hands, (rub hands)
Rub your hands together.
Wiggle, wiggle, wiggle your hands, (wiggle hands)
Wiggle your hands together.

Ask the children, "What else do we do with our hands?" Then do those actions.

Suggested Book: *Hand, Hand, Fingers, Thumb* by Al Perkins

Opportunities for Learning
• • • • • • • • •

- Emotional development: The children will express positive feelings about themselves and confidence in what they do.

- Social development: The children will form relationships with peers and learn to interact with them.

- Language development: The children will communicate their needs verbally and nonverbally. They will learn new vocabulary, such as *hand, fingers, thumb, handprint, paint, friends, clap, shake, rub, wiggle*, and how we use different parts of our bodies.

- Cognitive development: The children will use objects or symbols to represent something else (a handprint is a symbol for a real hand). They will use spatial awareness as they decide where to place their handprint on the paper.

- Physical/Motor development: The children will use fine-motor skills as they move their hands and make a handprint (or two).

Color Hands—Making Green Together

Materials

Blue fingerpaint

Yellow fingerpaint

2 pie plates

Newspaper or plastic shower curtain or tablecloth

What We Know

Friends may express glee when they are together (Løkken, 2000). Toddlers and two-year-olds laugh, giggle, twirl, and play simple games with each other. They express joy at being together.

What to Do

Ahead of Time:

1. Cover a table with newspaper or a plastic tablecloth.

2. Set out the paint in the pie tins on the table.

3. If you wish, this activity can be a continuation of the Handprint Friendship Collage.

With the Children:

1. Read the books *Mix it Up* by Hervé Tullet and *Maisy's First Colors* by Lucy Cousins to the children. Sit on the floor and begin to read. The toddlers and two-year-olds who want to hear the story will toddle over to sit by you.

2. Do the activity with two toddlers together. Ask them whether they would like to make green together. Other toddlers can be choosing other activities available in the room.

3. Ask one toddler to put his hand in the blue paint and the other toddler to put her hand in the yellow paint.

4. Read the cues of the children to see if they want to do the activity. Toddlers and two-year-olds may need to watch the activity before they are ready to place their hands in paint.

5. Ask the children to put their hands together and see what happens. Spots of green should appear where the colors mix together. Talk with the children about the changes in the colors. Talk about the names of the colors as they appear. As the children explore the colors, they will demonstrate curiosity, attention, and persistence.

6. Wash the children's hands carefully when finished.

More to Do: Extensions and Adaptations

For Older Toddlers and Two-Year-Olds:

● Use different colors, such as yellow and red to make orange, or red and blue to make purple.

● Have a large piece of paper available so that the children can make a handprint on it.

● Read the books many times. Children enjoy hearing special books repeatedly.

Suggested Books:

Mix It Up by Hervé Tullet

Maisy's First Colors by Lucy Cousins

Song:

The More We Get Together
The more we get together, together, together
The more we get together, the happier we'll be.
'Cause your friends are my friends,
And my friends are your friends.
The more we get together, the happier we'll be.

Change this to say *play together, dance together,* or *paint together*.

Row, Row, Row Your Boat Together

Materials

Row, Row, Row Your Boat by Jane Cabrera (optional)

Large piece of cardboard

What to Do

1. Read the book *Row, Row, Row Your Boat* by Jane Cabrera to a small group of children, or sing the song "Row, Row, Row Your Boat." As you begin to read, the children who are interested will toddle over to listen. Let them come and go as they please. Be sure to hold the book so the children can see the pictures.

2. Place the cardboard on the floor; if you can, bend the sides up to look more like a boat.

3. Invite the children to sit on the "boat" and pretend that they are rowing. Show them how to do this motion.

4. Read the book or sing the song again as they row.

5. Provide small rugs for children who need to define their space on the cardboard boat.

What We Know

Observe times when toddlers and two-year-olds help or comfort a peer. Toddlers and two-year-olds are capable of caring and exhibiting helpful behaviors with peers. Many young children try to comfort a peer in distress and may even go get an adult to help (Dunfield and Kuhlmeier, 2013; Kawakami and Takai-Kawakami, 2015).

More to Do: Extensions and Adaptations

For Toddlers:

Young toddlers will have a difficult time pretending; however, they may be able to imitate the adult and older children.

For Toddlers and Two-Year-Olds:

Other children in the room will hear and see the small group acting out the story. They may toddle or run over to be a part of the action. Ask the children in the boat to help the new children find a place to sit.

Suggested Book: Row, Row, Row Your Boat by Jane Cabrera

Song: "Row, Row, Row Your Boat"

Opportunities for Learning

• • • ● • • •

- Emotional development: The children will develop self-regulation and impulse control (executive functioning) as they sit in a small space.

- Social development: The children will develop relationships with peers. They will develop prosocial skills as they are encouraged to work together to "row" the boat and to help find room for children who may join the group.

- Language development: The children will understand and use increasingly complex language as they listen to and act out the story: *row, boat*, the names of animals in the book, and spatial relationships.

- Cognitive development: The children will use pretend play to increase understanding of culture, environment, and experiences.

- Physical/Motor development: The children will develop body control and balance as they experience sitting in the boat. They will use safe behaviors as adults comment on keeping each other safe in the boat.

Look What I Can Do

Materials

None

What to Do

1. Gather the children in a circle. Be sure to create small groups of children so that each can have a turn.

2. Have them take turns going into the middle of the circle and doing an action. For example, the child might clap, jump, hug another child, or shout, "Hooray!"

3. After demonstrating something she can do, encourage the other children to imitate the action.

4. Add a chant:

   Everybody do it, do it, do it.
   Everybody do it, do it.
   Jump like me.

5. Let the children take turns until everyone has had a chance to demonstrate an action.

6. This activity helps children to feel comfortable with being the center of attention.

What We Know

Imitation is one of the primary ways that children learn. They begin to imitate actions when they are older infants and continue to imitate more complex actions during their toddler and two-year-old years (Meltzoff, 2011).

More to Do: Extensions and Adaptations

For Toddlers:

- If there are toddlers in the group who have difficulty thinking of an action, give the child a choice. For example, ask the child if he wants to jump or wave (actions that you know the child can do).

- Allow children who do not want a turn to watch the others.

For Toddlers and Two-Year-Olds:

- Some children may feel shy and not want to perform. Respect them and allow them to watch the other children. Give them suggestions for actions that you know they can do.

- Children on the autism spectrum may have difficulty imitating other children. Choose one movement that you know a child can do and model just that movement.

- Read the book *From Head to Toe* by Eric Carle, and model for the children how to imitate the actions of the animals.

Suggested Book: *From Head to Toe* by Eric Carle

Silly Shoe Mix-Up

Materials

Children's shoes

Large canvas bag

What to Do

1. Ask each child to remove one shoe.

2. One at a time, ask the children to come forward and put their shoe in the bag. Not all children will want to give up a shoe. Some children may have become emotionally attached to their shoes. Allow them to participate by observing.

3. After all the children's shoes are in the bag, dramatically shake the bag to mix them all up.

4. Have the children take turns removing a shoe from the bag.

5. When a child is holding a shoe from the bag, tell her to find the owner of the shoe right away. Ask the child to look carefully at the shoe that remains on each child's foot to find the owner.

6. The children will have fun as they try to find the owners of the shoes.

What We Know

There may be conflict among the children; however, this provides an opportunity for teachers to support children's perspective-taking and cooperation skills.

More to Do: Extensions and Adaptations

- Some children may need help putting a shoe back on.
- Encourage all children (especially observers) to work together to help match the shoes.
- Sing the song below when a child pulls a shoe out of the bag.
- Take photos of the children's shoes, and create a poster. In big letters, write *Shoes*.
- Count the shoes as they go into the bag.
- Describe the color and pattern of the shoe that a child pulls out of the bag.

Song: (Sing to the tune of "Old MacDonald Had a Farm.")

> (Name of child) *has a shoe.*
> *E-I-E-I-O*
> *Who owns the shoe, me or you?* (point to everyone)
> *E-I-E-I-O*

Suggested Book: Ask children to take off their socks and then read *Ten Tiny Toes* by Caroline Jayne Church.

Opportunities for Learning

· · ● · ● ● ● · ● · ·

- Emotional development: The children will build self-regulation skills and impulse control as they wait for their shoes to be found.

- Social development: The children will develop social understanding and enjoy their peers as they participate in a small-group activity.

- Language development: The children will learn and use new vocabulary, such as *in* and *out* and the names of colors and patterns as adults use the words often during the activity. They will develop foundations for early reading skills as the adult points to the word *Shoes* on the poster and says, "This word is *shoes*." They will begin to recognize letters as the adult points to the letters and says, "S-H-O-E-S spells *shoes*."

- Physical/Motor development: The children will use and improve small-motor and self-care skills as they take off and put on their shoes.

Section 2
Learning Areas

- Construction
- Creative Explorations
- Dramatic Play
- Literacy
- Math
- Outdoor/Nature Play
- Sensory/Science

Note: Cognitive development and discovery can happen anywhere for infants, toddlers, and two-year-olds. Specific activities to support cognitive development are listed in that chapter in the previous section. Similarly, fine- and gross-motor development can happen in a variety of settings. Specific activities to support motor development are listed in that chapter in the previous section.

Infant Classroom Diagram

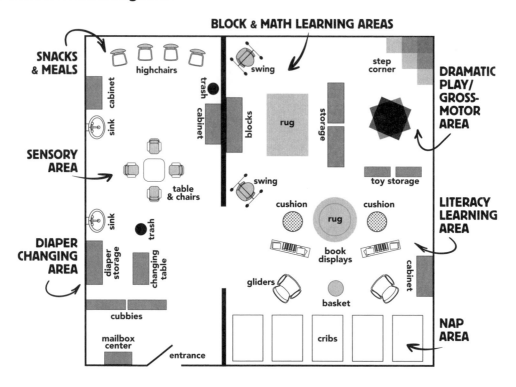

Toddler and Two-Year-Old Classroom Diagram

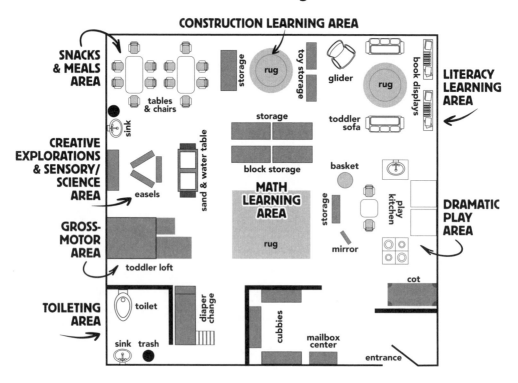

The Encyclopedia of Infant and Toddler Activities for Children Birth to 3

Construction

Purpose of a Construction Learning Area

A construction learning area provides toys and materials that encourage children's building, stacking, combining, and creating with blocks of different sizes and materials; transportation toys; toy animals and people; traffic signs; and building bricks such as Duplos, Mega Bloks, and Legos.

Infant Block Area

For infants, the block and math learning areas are often combined. This area includes low, stable shelves; labeled, dishwasher-safe plastic baskets for materials; soft and washable blocks of various sizes; sensory blocks; and safe-sized toy people and animals.

Please refer to the classroom diagram on page 120.

Toddler and Two-Year-Old Construction Learning Area

This area includes low, stable shelves; labeled, washable, see-through baskets; unbreakable mirrors; blocks of all shapes, colors, and textures; Velcro cloth blocks; Duplos; all types of vehicles; wooden animals and persons; stuffed animals; toddler-safe toy tools and a tool bench; natural materials; and board books.

Please refer to the classroom diagram on page 120.

Dump It Out and Fill It Up

Materials

Containers with large openings, such as baskets, plastic containers, or colored tinplate pails of various sizes

Assorted materials, such as spools, clothespins, large pegs, small blocks, and small cars (**SAFETY NOTE:** Use materials that do not pose a choking hazard.)

> ### What We Know
>
> The element of surprise helps babies learn and motivates them to explore the environment (Stahl and Feigenson, 2015).

What to Do

1. Older infants, toddlers, and two-year-olds love to dump and fill. They are so excited that something can be full one minute and empty the next—and it is even better when they get to do it themselves.

2. Fill the containers with different objects. If possible, have some objects that make a noise and some that have different colors. Use some containers that will make a noise when a toy is dropped into it.

3. Set the activity up in an activity center, and allow the children to choose the activity. Stay nearby to support the children and observe their interests.

4. If the children hesitate to empty the containers, encourage them by turning the containers upside down. Encourage them to refill the containers. Let them do this again and again.

5. Use the words *in, out, full,* and *empty* and color and counting words often as the children dump and fill. However, note if your language seems to distract the children from the task at hand. If so, then wait until the children engage you again.

6. As the children explore the items and containers, they will maintain focus and sustain attention with support. They will show interest in and curiosity about objects, materials, or events.

More to Do: Extensions and Adaptations

For Toddlers and Two-Year-Olds:

- Add materials such as large wrapping paper tubes so that children can send small cars down the chute into a container. Children are often so surprised when the car zooms out of the chute.

- Count the objects as they go into a container.

- Comment on the color of objects.

- If using clothespins, allow older toddlers and two-year-olds to paint them.

- Encourage older children to sort (classify) the objects, such as cars in one container and clothespins in another, or blue clothespins in one container and red clothespins in another.
  - Add dump trucks to the activity center on another day. Continue filling and emptying the dump truck outside in a sandbox.
  - Add boxes and a few larger items on another day. Make small holes in the sides of the boxes for children to try to put toys through.

Opportunities for Learning

- Emotional development: The children will develop a sense of identity and belonging. They will show confidence in their own abilities through relationships with others.

- Social development: The children will develop relationships with peers by showing interest in other children and engaging in play with them.

- Language development: The children will use increasingly complex language in conversation with others. They will understand and use an increasing number of words in communication with others, such as *in, out, full, empty,* color and counting words, *clothespins,* and *dump truck.*

- Cognitive development: The children will use a variety of strategies in solving problems to fill and empty the containers. They will use spatial awareness to understand objects.

- Physical/Motor development: The children will coordinate hand and eye movements to perform actions.

Baby Stacking Blocks

Materials

Blocks, large enough to be safe but small enough for children to hold

What to Do

1. Place blocks in front of sitting infants. Observe as the children play with the blocks. What are their schemas? Do they mouth, bang, shake, or throw them?

2. Model placing one block on top of another. Use self-talk as you move the blocks by saying, "Look, this block is on this block."

What We Know

When educators use eye contact and positive, warm expressions, infants and toddlers are more likely to listen and take a turn in the interaction. Imitation is one of the primary ways that older infants and toddlers learn (Meltzoff, 2011).

3. Take the block off and hand it to the infant. Observe what the infant does with the block. If he is interested and ready developmentally, the child will try to place the block on the other. If the infant does place the block on the first block, hand the infant a second block. Continue until the infant stops trying to stack the blocks.

4. As the children explore the blocks, they will pay attention and try to reproduce interesting and pleasurable effects.

More to Do: Extensions and Adaptations

- Use other toys, and demonstrate how to place one item on another item. For example, place a toy figure on a toy truck.
- Place the child on a mat and say, "You are sitting on the mat" as you pat the mat.
- Place an item under another item and say, "The truck is under the blanket."

Opportunities for Learning

- Social development: The children will trust adults who are sensitive, kind, and present with them.
- Language development: The children will process language spoken to them in a responsive way while actively involved in an activity.
- Cognitive development: The children will explore the environment and gather information through the senses. They will imitate hand motions of the adult.
- Physical/Motor development: The children will demonstrate strength and coordination of the small muscles in their hands by grasping blocks.

Hammering

Materials

Large blocks of Styrofoam

Plastic toy hammers

Crayons or dried-out markers (without lids)

Safety goggles or swim goggles

What to Do

1. Put out Styrofoam on a child-sized table. You can use one large piece for the group or smaller pieces for individuals.

2. Demonstrate how to hammer the crayons or markers into the Styrofoam. Start by holding a crayon or marker in one hand and tapping it with the hammer until it can stand on its own. Take your supporting hand away, and hammer the crayon or marker the rest of the way in.

3. Let children experiment to solve the problem of engaging the crayon or marker. They may use the head, the side, or the end of the hammer. Or, they may decide to push the crayon or marker in with their hands. Let them explore a variety of strategies as they figure out how to use the hammer with the crayon or marker and Styrofoam.

4. The children should wear safety or swim goggles. You may want to limit the number of children at the table at one time for safety reasons.

More to Do: Extensions and Adaptations

- Cover the surfaces of different Styrofoam pieces with tempera paint mixed with glue (to help the paint adhere). Allow the older children to help do this. Encourage the children to sort the colors of the crayons or markers to the color of the Styrofoam piece.

- Children may want to glue the pieces of Styrofoam together for a creation. If the Styrofoam is one large piece, comment on how the children are cooperating to make one sculpture that you will hang on the wall.

- Sing the song while children hammer. Encourage them to hammer with two hammers (one in each hand) during the second verse. Write the words to the song on a large poster board. Point to the words as you sing them. Add the names of the children in the group on the poster. Point to it when you sing that child's name, and say, "Look, this word says, *Megan. M-E-G-A-N.*" If you do this, make it fun for children.

Song:

> (Child's name) *hammers with one hammer,* (pretend to hammer with one hammer)
> *One hammer, one hammer.*
> (Child's name) *hammers with one hammer,*
> *All day long.*
>
> (Child's name) *hammers with two hammers,* (pretend to hammer with two hammers).
> *Two hammers, two hammers.*
> (Child's name) *hammers with two hammers,*
> *All day long.*

Weighty Block Building

Materials

Empty milk and juice cartons

Small boxes

Spoons or small child-size plastic shovels

Colored contact paper

Scissors (adult use only)

Sand

Packing tape

What to Do

Ahead of Time:

1. Rinse and dry several milk or juice cartons.

2. Cut off the tops of the cartons.

3. Place the cartons in the block area inside or the sandbox outside.

With the Children:

1. Encourage the children to scoop sand into the openings of the cartons. Let them add different amounts of sand so the cartons have different weights. (Make sure that they are not too heavy. You can always add new ones with different weights.)

2. Flatten any protrusions, and securely seal the openings with tape. You may need to tape on a piece of cardboard.

3. Wrap colored contact paper around the cartons, including the ends.

4. Encourage the children to build! They will experience various weights as they build with the blocks. They will show interest and curiosity about objects (the cartons) as they lift them and use them.

More to Do: Extensions and Adaptations

- Emphasize the words *light, heavy, easy*, and *hard* with the children. Ask, "Is this block light or heavy?" "Is it easy or hard to lift?"
- Read the books listed below and act out the opposites, such as *look up* and *look down*.
- On another day, add Velcro pieces to all sides of the cartons, so that children can make trains, stack the blocks more easily, and practice fine-motor skills.
- Include one carton that is heavy enough that two children must cooperate to move it, but not so heavy that it would hurt a child's foot if it fell on it.
- Extend the activity to outdoors by going on a hunt for heavy and light items. Observe children's thinking as they discover that what is heavy to one child may be light to another.

Suggested Books:

Opposites by Sandra Boynton

What's Up, Duck: A Book of Opposites by Tad Hills

Quiet LOUD by Leslie Patricelli

Yummy YUCKY Leslie Patricelli

Animal Houses

Materials

Blocks

Stuffed animals in a variety of sizes

What to Do

1. Read a book about animal homes. Let the children who are interested gather to listen.

2. Place stuffed animals of different sizes in the construction area.

3. Tell the children that the animals need a home. Ask the children if they will help build a home for a stuffed animal. There is no right or wrong for this activity. The idea is to encourage the children to build in whatever way they think is appropriate.

4. As the children build, they will problem solve to make the home the right size for the animal or to use the blocks in a way that they wish. Listen to the words the children use, and comment on the choices they make: "I see that you are building a top on the house. You are building a roof."

What We Know

The responsiveness of adults to young children's interests and actions supports children's cognitive development. When adults are intrusive and didactic when playing with children, the children's cognitive scores are lower. (McFadden and Tamis-Lemonda, 2013). Observe how children use materials. Encourage children to experiment with how to build houses. Support their learning by providing interesting materials, wondering how to solve problems with them, following children's leads during play, and scaffolding learning when children become frustrated.

More to Do: Extensions and Adaptations

- Provide masking tape for children to make roads from one house to another.
- Add cardboard boxes to the construction area, and encourage the children to use them to make animal homes.

Suggested Books:

Animal Homes by Jennifer Bové

Welcome Home, Bear by Il Sung Na

My Very First Book of Animal Homes by Eric Carle

Opportunities for Learning
· • • ● • • ·

- Emotional development: The children will learn to recognize and interpret others' emotions and to begin to manage their own emotions.

- Social development: The children will show interest in and interact with other children as they play together. The children will learn how to negotiate and share with peers.

- Language development: The children will use gestures or language to communicate needs to adults and peers. They will learn new vocabulary, such as *block*, animal names, *home, wall, roof,* and *door.*

- Cognitive development: The children will problem solve as they try to figure out how to use the blocks to build the animal homes.

- Physical/Motor development: The children will develop large- and small-muscle control as they move and place the blocks.

Creative Explorations

Purpose of a Creative Explorations Area

A creative explorations learning area encourages children to make discoveries with color and texture and to create, imagine, invent, and express feelings with art materials. For infants, the sensory area and creative area are often combined. Infants create by combining materials in new ways; for example, placing toys on sticky contact paper. Older infants may use large crayons and fingerpaint with close supervision.

Toddler and Two-Year-Old Creative Explorations Area

For toddlers and two-year-olds, furniture and equipment include easily cleaned, child-size tables and chairs; easels for one, two, and four children; shelves to store materials safely and shelves to display materials that are always available to the children, such as paper and crayons. The learning area often includes many types of paper, paints, crayons, chalk, tape, paste or glue, paintbrushes and sponges, and collage and recycled materials. Most toddlers and two-year-olds will need close supervision as they use these materials.

Please refer to the classroom diagram on page 120.

My Baby Footprints

Materials

Nontoxic paint

Large piece of paper or 1 small piece per child

2 small tubs

Warm water

Washcloth and towel

Newspaper or plastic tablecloth

What to Do

1. Ask family members for permission to make paint footprints. Tell them that you will respect children's cues concerning whether they want to do this activity. Tell them that you will help the child wash her feet after the activity.

2. Spread newspaper or a plastic tablecloth on the floor.

3. Place a tub of paint on the newspaper or tablecloth, and place the paper near the paint.

4. Place a tub of warm water and a washcloth and towel nearby.

5. Bring one infant at a time to the area to make footprints.

6. While holding the child, place one of the child's feet into the paint. Immediately help the child place her foot on the paper, making a footprint.

7. Have fun with the infant while washing her foot—count her toes in English, Spanish, and the child's home language, or play "This Little Piggy."

Suggested Books:

Mouse Paint by Ellen Stoll Walsh

Bright Baby Colors by Roger Priddy

This Little Piggy by Child's Play

Fingerplay:

This Little Piggy
This little piggy went to market. (wiggle the big toe)
This little piggy stayed home. (wiggle the long toe)
This little piggy had roast beef. (wiggle the middle toe)
This little piggy had none. (wiggle the ring toe)
And this little piggy cried, "Wee wee wee!" all the way home. (wiggle the pinky toe)

- Emotional development: The children will express a range of emotions—fearful, happy, upset, sad. The hope is that they will mostly be happy during this activity.

- Social development: The children will develop expectations of consistent, positive interactions through secure relationships with adults who are kind, patient, and caring.

- Language development: The children will respond to sounds and words in several languages. They will understand new vocabulary, such as food, *toes, wiggle, piggy, paint*, colors of paint, and *footprint*.

- Cognitive development: The children will develop a sense of number as the teacher counts toes.

My Toddler Footprints

Materials

Nontoxic paint

1 small piece of paper per child

2 small tubs

Washcloth and towel

Butcher paper

2 child-size chairs

Warm water

Newspaper or plastic tablecloth

What to Do

1. Ask family members for permission for the child to make paint footprints. Tell them that you will respect children's cues concerning whether they want to do this activity. Tell them that you will help each child wash her feet after the activity.

2. Spread newspaper or a plastic tablecloth on the floor. Place the tub of paint and the small pieces of paper on the newspaper or tablecloth.

3. Place a tub of warm water and a washcloth and towel nearby.

4. Lay a long piece of butcher paper on the floor. Place a chair at each end of the paper.

5. Invite a child to sit in a chair and remove his shoes and socks. Inform the toddler of everything you and she are going to do.

6. Ask the child if she wants to put her foot in the paint.

7. Ask the child if she wants to put her foot on a small piece of paper to send home. Help her make a footprint on the small paper, if she wishes.

8. After placing her foot on the small piece of paper, the child may need to dip her foot in the paint again. Then help the child walk for ten paces down the butcher paper.

9. Help the child sit in the other chair without getting paint on anything. Excitedly count the number of footprints.

10. Help her wash her feet in the tub of warm water, dry her feet, and put her shoes on. Have fun counting toes in English, Spanish, and the child's home language.

11. Let all the children who want to do the activity have a turn.

More to Do: Extensions and Adaptations

For Toddlers and Two-Year-Olds:

- Some children may prefer to watch. Provide chairs along the side of the butcher paper for those children to sit on. Offer the activity again to give the child who is hesitant another chance to do the activity.

- Before the child walks on the butcher paper, encourage the child to make one print on a small piece of paper that can be displayed or sent home. The child may have to put her feet back into the paint before walking on the butcher paper.

- Write down what the children say while doing the activity, and then display the children's words with the large butcher paper for children and families to see.

Song:

> I see a blue foot (point to toddler's foot)
> Yes, I do.
> I see a blue foot (point to toddler's foot)
> You can see it, too! (hold up foot for toddler to see)

Suggested Books:

Mouse Paint by Ellen Stoll Walsh

Bright Baby Colors by Roger Priddy

Bear Sees Colors by Karma Wilson

Painting Like a Painter

Materials

Sponge roller painters, different sizes

Small unbreakable containers

Nontoxic tempera paint

1 large piece of paper or small pieces, 1 per child

What We Know

Creativity for toddlers and two-year-olds is experimentation, problem solving, and having fun with different materials. Children explore the materials' possibilities.

What to Do

1. Read one or more of the books listed below. Talk about colors.

2. Put a small amount of paint into several containers.

3. Invite the children to dip the sponge rollers in the containers and roll them on paper.

4. Observe the children as they make patterns on the paper. Observe the strategies children use to paint with the rollers. The children will use creativity to increase their understanding and learning as they create with what are possibly new tools for them.

5. When dry, hang the paintings on the wall with the title, "We Rock and Roll."

More to Do: Extensions and Adaptations

For Toddlers:

Find small sponge rollers that painters use to paint trims or windowsills. Small hands can hold this type.

For Two-Year-Olds:

- Add other materials, such as small adult-size paintbrushes and rocks, to dip into the paint and then on the paper. Only use rocks if you feel that your group will use them safely.
- On another day, encourage children to paint the rocks different colors.
- Encourage children to mix red and blue to make purple, yellow and red to make orange, yellow and blue to make green, red and green to make brown, and white and red to make pink.
- Two-year-olds could possibly paint to correspond to a feeling. Sing the song below as they create, and observe if they change their style based on the feeling.

Song:

If You're Happy and You Know It
If you're happy and you know it, paint away.
If you're happy and you know it, shout hooray!
If you're happy and you know it,
Then your face will surely show it.
If you're happy and you know it, paint away.

Consider singing it with the words *sad, excited,* or *angry.*

Suggested Books:

The Mixed-Up Chameleon by Eric Carle

Mouse Paint by Ellen Stoll Walsh

Bright Baby Colors by Roger Priddy

Mix It Up by Hervé Tullet

Opportunities for Learning
· · • · • · • · • · ·

- Emotional development: The children will learn to express a variety of emotions.
- Social development: The children will observe other children and imitate them.
- Language development: The children will use language when communicating with a peer with the support of an adult.
- Cognitive development: The children will demonstrate an awareness of the effects of certain actions with the different painting tools. They will develop early scientific skills through exploring how different painting tools work and what happens when colors mix.
- Physical/Motor development: The children will coordinate eye and hand movements.

Making and Playing with Playdough

Materials

1 cup salt

1 cup warm water

Measuring cup

Airtight containers

Small rolling pins, small blocks, crayons for poking, and so on

4 cups flour

Mixing bowl and spoon

Food coloring (optional)

Plastic placemat

What We Know

Using materials in different ways sparks brain development.

What to Do

1. Make the homemade playdough with the children's help. Mix together the salt and flour.

2. Add the water and food coloring, and mix the ingredients together.

3. Turn out the dough onto a placemat, and knead until smooth. Encourage the children to knead the dough and make shapes.

4. Store the playdough in airtight containers.

More to Do: Extensions and Adaptations

For Toddlers:

- Give each child a small tray and some playdough to use on the tray. This defines the space for the toddler and prevents conflicts.

- Comment on what children do: "Desiree is pounding the playdough with her fist." "Esphyr is poking the playdough with his finger." "Menena made a little ball." Children may imitate each other or continue their own experimentations with the playdough.

- Add new utensils on different days to encourage children's experimentation.

For Two-Year-Olds:

- Read the book listed below. Ask the children what color they would like to make their playdough. Experiment with adding a different color to each batch of playdough.

- Store each color in a separate airtight container, although you can expect that children will share playdough with each other and the colors will soon be mixed.

Suggested Book: *Spot Looks at Colors* by Eric Hill

- Social development: The children will develop expectations of consistent, positive interactions through secure relationships with respectful, sensitive, and consistently warm adults.

- Language development: The children will respond to sounds and words in several languages. They will use new vocabulary, such as *playdough, pounding, roll, ball,* and the names of utensils.

- Cognitive development: The children will use understanding of causal relationships to act on the physical environment.

Super-Soft Playdough to Cut

Materials

Several pairs of child-safe scissors

6 tablespoons vegetable oil

2 cups salt

Food coloring (optional)

2 bowls

Measuring spoon

Saucepan

4 cups water

4 cups flour

8 tablespoons cream of tartar

Small rolling pins

Measuring cup

Mixing spoon

Stove

What to Do

Ahead of Time:

1. Combine the water and oil in one bowl.

2. Combine the flour, salt, and cream of tartar in another bowl.

3. Combine the two mixtures in a saucepan, and add food coloring (if desired).

4. Cook over medium heat, stirring constantly.

5. When the playdough starts to dry out on the bottom, remove it from the heat. It will be lumpy and will look less solid than you think it should be—this is very important! It will look like pudding.

6. Knead it as best you can on a flat surface until it cools and comes together and is no longer sticky.

7. Store the playdough in an airtight container.

With the Children:

1. Allow the children to experiment with the playdough, poking, pushing, pounding, and rolling it.

2. Model how to pull and roll the playdough to make snakes. As the children explore what the playdough can do, they will develop the ability to show persistence in their actions and behaviors.

3. Help the children to roll out several playdough snakes about ½" in diameter.

4. Invite the children to explore how to cut the playdough with the child-safe scissors. Encourage the children to keep their thumbs up when they use scissors. This is an excellent activity for children who are beginning to learn how to cut using scissors. The playdough doesn't flip up like paper does, and this is surprisingly easy for little fingers to do. They can learn the proper way to hold scissors and begin to strengthen the muscles needed to cut paper successfully.

More to Do: Extensions and Adaptations

For Toddlers and Two-Year-Olds:

- Some children, especially toddlers, will have difficulty using scissors. Allow them to pull the playdough apart to make snakes.
- Model asking questions, such as, "Where do you think snakes live?"
- Count the number of snakes each child makes.
- Ask the children if they want to put their snakes on a piece of green paper for snakes in the grass. Children may need to glue the snakes to the paper.
- Allow them to decorate their snakes with glitter glue.
- Ask the children if they would like to take their snakes for a stroll while they sing the following song.

Song: (Sing to the tune of "The Ants Go Marching.")

> The snakes go slithering one by one, hoorah, hoorah!
> The snakes go slithering one by one, hoorah, hoorah!
> The snakes go slithering one by one,
> The little one stops to have some fun.
> And they all go slithering,
> Down and around, all over the ground.

The snakes go slithering two by two, hoorah, hoorah!
The snakes go slithering two by two, hoorah, hoorah!
The snakes go slithering two by two.
The little one stops to tie her shoe.
And they all go slithering,
Down and around, all over the ground.

The snakes go slithering three by three, hoorah, hoorah!
The snakes go slithering three by three, hoorah, hoorah!
The snakes go slithering three by three.
The little one stops to scratch her knee.
And they all go slithering,
Down and around, all over the ground.

Suggested Books:

The Snake Who Said Shhh by Jodie Parachini and Gill McLean

Don't Take Your Snake for a Stroll by Karin Ireland

Opportunities for Learning

• • • • ● • • • •

- Social development: The children will show interest in and interact with other children.

- Language development: The children will increase their understanding and use of language to communicate. They will learn vocabulary such as *slithering*, number words, color words, *grass*, *snake*, and *stroll*.

- Cognitive development: The children will learn early mathematical concepts, such as counting their snakes. They will learn where animals live.

- Physical/Motor development: The children will coordinate hand and eye movements to perform actions. They will adjust their reach and grasp to use scissors.

All about the Process

Materials

Paper   Crayons

Child-size table and chairs

What to Do

1. Place the paper and crayons where children can reach them every day, with a table and chairs nearby.

2. Encourage the children to make marks, circles, and so forth on their papers. As the children explore the materials, they will use creativity to increase understanding and learning as they create with what are possibly new tools for them.

3. Some older two-year-olds may want to say what the picture is or tell you something about it. Listen to what they have to say.

4. Children are likely enjoying the process of creating rather than making a product. Comment on the child's effort, specific colors she uses, any shapes you see, and so on, rather than saying, "That's good," or "Good job."

Suggested Books:

A Color of His Own by Leo Lionni

The Mixed-Up Chameleon by Eric Carle

Mouse Paint by Ellen Stoll Walsh

Spot Looks at Colors by Eric Hill

Bright Baby Colors by Roger Priddy

The Colors of Us by Karen Katz

Mix It Up! by Hervé Tullet

Opportunities for Learning

• • ● ● ● ● • •

- Emotional development: The children will learn to express a variety of emotions.

- Social development: The children will observe other children and imitate them.

- Language development: The children will use language when communicating with a peer, with support of the teacher.

- Cognitive development: The children will demonstrate an awareness of the effects of certain actions with the different painting tools. They will develop early scientific skills through exploring how different painting tools work and what happens when colors mix.

- Physical/Motor development: The children will coordinate eye and hand movements.

Tear It Up

Materials

Old catalogs and magazines

Waxed paper

Paper towels

Cardboard

Tissue paper

Sandpaper

Glue

What to Do

1. Toddlers love to tear things. Let them tear pages from old magazines and catalogs.

2. For an additional sensory experience, add textured papers such as tissue paper, waxed paper, sandpaper, and paper towels.

3. As the children tear the paper, talk about the sensations they are experiencing. "Doesn't this tissue paper feel soft?" "This waxed paper feels slippery." "This paper towel is so hard to tear." "This sandpaper feels so rough."

4. Talk about the colors of the papers as the children are tearing. "I see you are tearing red paper, Lewis." As the children explore the paper textures, they will develop the ability to show persistence in their actions and behaviors.

5. Listen to the children and encourage their language. Observe their fine-motor skills.

6. Provide glue and sturdy pieces of cardboard. Encourage each child to use her torn pieces of paper to create a unique, colorful, and creative collage in whatever way she chooses.

More to Do: Extensions and Adaptations

For Toddlers:

Rather than offering glue bottles, which can be difficult for toddlers to squeeze, consider providing nontoxic paste and a paste stick. **SAFETY ALERT:** Young toddlers often put paper and paste into their mouths. Observe carefully to prevent this from happening.

For Two-Year-Olds:

Many two-year-olds will be able to squeeze a glue bottle. However, they will need close supervision to not completely cover the back of the paper, the table, and themselves with glue.

Contact Paper Art

Materials

Contact paper

Scissors (adult use only)

Tissue paper pieces

Feathers, leaves, bows, ribbon, twigs, and other collage materials

Magazines

Tape

Wrapping paper scraps

Basket or bin

What to Do

Ahead of Time:

1. Cut small pieces of contact paper, and tape them sticky-side out to a table.

2. Tape a large piece of contact paper to the wall with the sticky side out.

3. Cut out photos of animals, people, and objects from old magazines.

4. Set out a basket or bin filled with the photos, tissue and wrapping-paper scraps, and different collage materials to stick on the contact paper.

With the Children:

1. Let the children explore the materials. Watch as they discover that items will stick to the contact paper. How do they react? Encourage them to place the items where they would like on the contact paper.

2. As the children explore the materials, they will show eagerness and curiosity with each new possibility for creating.

3. Provide this as a choice activity so that children can stay with the activity if they like, developing their attention and persistence skills. This also provides time for one teacher to be with a small group of children who choose to do the activity in the creative area.

More to Do: Extensions and Adaptations

For Toddlers and Some Two-Year-Olds:

Toddlers may hesitate to place items on the sticky surface, and they will certainly try to pull them back off. If a child hesitates, then model for the child how to decide where to put an object by placing it over, then on, the sticky surface. Say, "Hmm, let me see. I wonder if I should put the feather here (holding the feather above the surface). No, I think I'll put it on the top part. There, I like that. Now, you try it. Where do you want to put the feather?"

For Two-Year-Olds:

Let two-year-olds experiment with light and heavy objects, such as a feather and a toy car. Wonder with the child by saying, "I wonder if this car is too heavy to stick. What do you think? Should we try it?" Or, "Which is heavier, the feather or the toy car?" "Which is lighter?"

Suggested Book: *What's Up, Duck? A Book of Opposites* by Tad Hills

---

Opportunities for Learning

- Emotional development: The children will express a variety of emotions when creating.
- Social development: The children will enjoy the company of others, share materials, and communicate with each other.
- Language development: The children will understand and use an increasing vocabulary as adults and peers communicate. They will learn words such as *sticky, stuck, stick,* the names of objects, *heavier,* and *lighter.*
- Cognitive development: The children will actively explore people and objects.
- Physical/Motor development: The children will develop an ability to control and refine small muscles.

Yarn Painting

Materials

Nontoxic tempera paint in a variety of colors

Construction paper of different colors

Scissors (adult use only)

Spill-proof containers

Yarn

Plastic tablecloth or newspaper

What to Do

Ahead of Time:

1. Cover a child-size table with a plastic tablecloth or newspaper. Move the chairs away from the table.

2. Fill the spill-proof containers with paint, and place them in the middle of the table.

3. Cut the yarn into pieces that the children can easily handle, and set those on the table.

4. Put out some construction paper for the children to use.

With the Children:

1. Give each child a piece of paper, a piece of yarn, and one container of paint.

2. Help the child dip the yarn into the container of paint and drip the paint onto her paper as many times as she would like.

3. When she is finished with one color, give her another piece of yarn and a different container of paint.

4. Repeat the process as long as the child would like to continue creating. The children will use creativity to increase understanding and learning as they create with what are possibly new tools for them.

5. As the children explore, talk about the colors of paint and yarn, what happens if colors mix, the lines created, sharing the paint, and using their words to ask another child for paint.

6. Over several days, make sure each child has a chance to paint if she would like.

7. Over the next few days, notice colors everywhere—in clothing, in the sky, and in the room. Read the following storybooks.

The Mixed-Up Chameleon by Eric Carle

Mouse Paint by Ellen Stoll Walsh

Bright Baby Colors by Roger Priddy

Mix It Up! by Hervé Tullet

Opportunities for Learning

• • • ● ● ● • • •

- Emotional development: The children will show confidence in their own abilities within secure relationships with special adults.

- Social development: The children will observe other children and imitate them.

- Language development: The children will use language when communicating with a peer, with support of the teacher.

- Cognitive development: The children will demonstrate an awareness of the effects of certain actions with different painting tools. They will develop early scientific skills through exploring how different painting tools work and what happens when colors mix.

- Physical/Motor development: The children will coordinate eye and hand movements.

It Looked Like Spilt Milk

Materials

It Looked Like Spilt Milk by Charles G. Shaw

Nontoxic white paint

Cotton balls

Dark-blue paper

Spoon

What to Do

1. Read *It Looked like Spilt Milk* by Charles G. Shaw to a small group who gather around you when you start reading the book.

2. After finishing the story, give each child a piece of dark-blue paper folded in half.

3. Help each child spoon a small amount of white paint on one half of the paper.

4. Help the children fold the paper over to cover the paint with the other side of the paper. Have them rub their hands over the paper to create a unique design.

5. Ask them to open the paper carefully to discover their creations. As the children explore the paint and paper, they will demonstrate initiative and show curiosity about objects and experiences.

6. If desired, the children can refold the paper to change their design. Provide cotton balls for children who want to stick them onto their paintings. The idea here is not to create a specific scene, such as a sky or clouds, but to let the children explore what happens when paint is pressed between two halves of paper.

7. When finished, open the paper and allow it to dry.

More to Do: Extensions and Adaptations

For Two-Year-Olds:

- Two-year-olds may want to make more than one picture. If they do, put the pictures together and make a book like the *It Looked Like Spilt Milk* book. Put the pages together with the child, and have the child help punch two holes on the left side. Tie yarn through the holes to keep the pages together.

- Encourage older two-year-olds to guess what each picture looks like—a bunny? a cat?

Suggested Book: *It Looked Like Spilt Milk* by Charles G. Shaw

Opportunities for Learning

- Emotional development: The children will develop a sense of identity with others as they play together.

- Social development: The children will enjoy the company of others, share materials, and communicate with each other.

- Language development: The children will understand and use an increasing vocabulary as adults and peers communicate. They will learn words such as *spilt, milk, clouds, cotton balls, on, off, fold, unfold, half, blue,* and *white.*

- Cognitive development: The children will actively explore objects.

- Physical/Motor development: The children will develop an ability to control and refine small muscles.

Creative Creating

Materials

Variety of surfaces, such as bubble wrap, corrugated paper, waxed paper, sandpaper, cardboard, tagboard, the inside of shoe boxes, large and small boxes, construction paper, fingerpaint paper, and contact paper

Painting/coloring tools: pastry brushes, paintbrushes, golf balls, leaves, sponges, toy cars, feathers, crayons, squeeze bottles

Variety of textures such as sand, coffee grounds, and glitter

Nontoxic tempera paint or fingerpaint

Glue

What to Do

Ahead of Time:

1. Decide which materials you wish to offer. For example, add sand to paint or glitter to glue, and provide some interesting surfaces and tools to use with these materials.

2. Spark the creative process by changing the surfaces, the textures of glue and paint, and the tools that young children use each week. Keep the crayons, paper, and paint available each week. When children trust that these will always be available, their interest and skills will advance with use.

With the Children:

1. Encourage the children to explore the materials you have offered this week.

2. Let them try, for example, to make prints by placing a piece of paper over a bubble-wrap painting or fingerpaint paintings. Rub softly and another creative piece appears.

3. As the children discover new materials each week, they will show eagerness and curiosity with each new possibility for creating.

Snow in the Night

Materials

Black construction paper

White chalk

Camera

What to Do

1. Read a book about snow and winter.

2. Give each child a half sheet of black construction paper and a piece of white chalk. Encourage the children to explore the chalk on the paper. This is a great visual for young children. Instead of the usual dark color on light paper, they see a light color on dark paper.

3. Listen to the words the children use as they explore the chalk and paper. As the children explore the materials, they will show eagerness and curiosity with each new possibility for creating.

4. Take photos of children as they do the activity. Display the children's drawings, and add the photos, a list of vocabulary used by the children, and a list of the learning opportunities that took place.

More to Do: Extensions and Adaptations

- Expand learning about winter, snow, dark, and light into other learning areas in the room and outdoors. If your weather allows, bring snow into the water table in the sensory area. Have children wear gloves to play in the snow so their hands won't freeze.

- Place a blanket over a table to create a "dark" area. Add flashlights so that children can play with light.

Suggested Books:

Lisa and the Snowman by Coby Hol

Snowballs by Lois Ehlert

The Snowy Day by Ezra Jack Keats

Opportunities for Learning

- Emotional development: The children will express a variety of emotions when creating.

- Social development: The children will enjoy the company of others, share materials, and communicate with each other as they create.

- Language development: The children will understand and use an increasing vocabulary as adults and peers communicate. They will learn words such as *half, snow, day, night, cold, winter, dark, light, on, off,* names of colors and shapes, and spatial words such as *above, over, high,* and *low.*

- Cognitive development: The children will actively explore objects.

- Physical/Motor development: The children will develop an ability to control and refine small muscles.

Easels for Two

Materials

Easel

String

Paper

Paintbrushes

Nontoxic paint

What to Do

1. Make easels and paint available every day if you can, so that children can trust that these materials will be available. Skills and experimentation increase if easels and paint are available every day.

2. On most days, provide nontoxic paint and several paintbrushes for each child to use alone. On some days, however, tie two paintbrushes from the top of the easel with strings that are long enough so that a child can hold onto a paintbrush and dip it into the paint. Ask if two children want to paint together. The children will need to problem solve to figure out the best way to cooperate while painting.

3. As they figure out how to use the easel together, the children will develop the ability to show persistence in actions and behaviors.

Song: (Sing to the tune of "Row, Row, Row Your Boat.")

Share, share, share your easel
Share it every day.
Happily, happily, happily, happily,
This is how we play.

More to Do: Extensions and Adaptations

- Think about how children can cooperate in other learning areas and times of the day. Children can cooperate rolling a pumpkin indoors or outdoors, carrying a bucket of blocks outside, or wiping off a table. Watch for opportunities for children to cooperate, and use the word *cooperate* often.

- For children who are learning to cooperate, pair an older child with a younger child to share the easel. Ask the older child to help the younger child.

What We Know

Two-year-olds probably won't work together on a joint goal while painting. Rather, many children will enjoy painting beside a friend, each experimenting with his own creation.

Opportunities for Learning

- Social development: The children will show interest in and interact with other children in cooperative ways.

- Language development: The children will increase their understanding and use of language to communicate. They will learn words such as *easel, paint, paintbrush, share, cooperate,* and the colors of paint.

- Physical/Motor development: The children will coordinate hand and eye movements to perform actions. They will adjust their reach and grasp to use tools.

The Encyclopedia of Infant and Toddler Activities for Children Birth to 3

Dramatic Play

· · ● ● ● ● ● · ●

Purpose of a Dramatic Play Learning Area

The dramatic play learning area provides opportunities for children to try out different identities and roles with others; to pretend, imagine, and engage in symbolic play; to act out different experiences they have had; and to express feelings, such as how they feel in a doctor's office or at the kitchen table.

Infant Dramatic Play Area

A dramatic play area for older infants includes dolls and small doll beds; props for dolls; puppets; hats, mittens, and shoes; boxes of various sizes; and a playhouse to crawl through.

Please refer to the classroom diagram on page 120.

Toddler and Two-Year-Old Dramatic Play Area

A dramatic play area for toddlers and two-year-olds often includes a child-size kitchen with furniture and props, including a stove, table, chairs, cooking and eating utensils, placemats, and shelves for "food." Other materials include clothing from different cultures and professions; costumes; dolls representing different ethnic groups; doll furniture and supplies; puppets; a full-length mirror; and home items, such as toy telephones, a lawnmower, and a cash register. A variety of boxes encourages pretend play, as they can be homes for animals and dolls or cozy places to sit. Other settings, such as a doctor's office, a zoo, a library, a post office, a veterinarian's office, or beauty shop may be set up near the kitchen/home area. A home area is comforting for children who want to be able to go back "home."

Please refer to the classroom diagram on page 120.

Dress Me Up

Materials

Culturally relevant clothing

Full-length unbreakable mirror

What to Do

1. Provide clothing that older toddlers and two-year-olds can put on easily—socks, large shoes, hats, loose jackets.

2. Observe what the children do and what they talk about as they put on clothing. What are their strategies for putting on clothing? As they explore the clothes, the children will show imagination in play and interactions with others.

3. Stay with the children who choose to go to the dramatic play area to help them put on and take off the clothing.

4. After children put on clothing, encourage them to look in the mirror. Talk with them about what they have on, what they are doing, and the colors of their clothes. Have them look in the mirror with a friend. Ask, "What do you see?"

5. Change out the clothing often to represent different cultures, professions, and families.

More to Do: Extensions and Adaptations

- To extend the activity to other learning areas and days, check your reading corner. Does it include many books that represent different genders and cultures?

- Add posters to the room with pictures of people from different cultures. Talk to the children about what people in the pictures are wearing and why. For example, those who live in Alaska may need warmer clothing. Those people who live in a warmer climate may need cooler clothing. Talk with the children about what they wear when it is cold or warm outside.

- Some children will need extra help with putting clothes on. Ask other children to help that child; however, be aware that the child may want a favorite teacher to help.

Suggested Books:

Clothes by Sterling Publishing

My Clothes/Mi Ropa by Rebecca Emberley

What We Know

Older toddlers and many two-year-olds will probably not be role playing, as in one child playing a firefighter and another child pretending to be a dog. They will, however, engage in using pretend objects to cook, eat, drink and will pretend to feed dolls and put them to bed.

Pet Week

Materials

Stuffed animals, such as dogs, cats, gerbils, fish, mice, hamsters, horses, donkeys

Plastic or wooden animals

Gauze

Scissors (adult use only)

Props such as boxes, pet carriers, leashes, and plastic bowls

Photos of pets

Magazines

Laminator

What We Know

Younger toddlers will love to play with the animals and the props. Older toddlers and two-year-olds may pretend to feed the animals, give them water, and take them for walks.

What to Do

Ahead of Time:

1. Ask parents to send in photos of the children's pets or to allow children to bring in their favorite stuffed animal. Make copies of the photos and laminate them for durability.

2. Cut out pictures of pets from magazines, and laminate them.

3. Place the photos in the dramatic play area.

4. Place stuffed, plastic, and wooden animals in the dramatic play area.

5. Make a special place in the dramatic play area for pet homes, places to feed pets, and places to take them on walks.

6. Choose one stuffed animal, and wrap gauze around one of its legs to pretend that it has an injury.

With the Children:

1. Ask children to find the photos of their pets and show them to other children. If a child does not have a pet, he can choose a photo of a pet that he would like to have.

2. Ask each child to describe his pet—big or little, small or tall, color, length of ears and tail, and so on—and to talk about what the pet does each day. If a child does not have a pet, he can describe a pet that she would like to have.

3. Ask the children to show you how they take care of their pets, using the stuffed animals and props. As the children explore the materials and props, they will show imagination in play and interactions with others.

4. To help young children show care and concern for others, including animals, hold up the stuffed animal with a bandage on its leg and say, "Oh, no, this pet has a hurt leg. It has a boo-boo. What should we do?"

5. Read the book *All Better!* by Henning Lohein.

More to Do: Extensions and Adaptations

For Toddlers:

SAFETY ALERT: Check the size of the plastic animals to prevent choking.

For Toddlers and Two-Year-Olds:

- Extend learning about animals and caring for pets into the snack area with healthy animal crackers and into the construction area with stuffed animals that need block houses.

- Invite a few children to sit in a circle with their pets on their laps. Say the following rhyme for each child as you go around the circle:

    (Child's name) *has a* (type of pet). (point to a child to hold up her pet)
    What do you think of that?
    She takes care of it every day
    In the most wonderful, loving way.

Suggested Books:

My Pet Animal Book by David Eastman

Explore My World Baby Animals by Marfe Ferguson Delano

All Better! by Henning Lohein

- Emotional development: The children will develop a sense of identity by learning about their own and others' pets. They will express care and concern for others.
- Social development: The children will imitate and engage in play with other children.
- Language development: The children will communicate needs and wants nonverbally and with language as they ask for help with their pets. They will learn new words, such as *dog, cat, gerbil, pet, fish, hamster, horse,* and *leash.*
- Cognitive development: The children will use pretend play to increase understanding of culture, environment, and experiences.
- Physical/Motor development: The children will increase fine-motor skills as they use the small muscles in their hands to feed and take care of their pets.

Oh, My Baby

Materials

Culturally diverse dolls

Small bottles, cups, bowls, and spoons

Doll bed

Comb

Kitchen set with pots and pans

Child-size rocking chair

Baby blankets

Doll clothing

Toothbrushes

Doll stroller

What to Do

Ahead of Time:

Create a doll nursery in the dramatic play area. Add dolls, doll clothing, and doll equipment.

With the Children:

1. Observe how the children take care of the dolls. What do they know how to do?

2. Ask the children what they think babies need. Is there a baby in their house? Do they know any babies?

3. Using a doll, model taking care of it in gentle ways. Say things such as, "Oh, baby's hungry. Let's feed him." Use a dish and spoon to pretend to feed the doll. Encourage the children to help you feed the dolls.

4. Describe all your actions as you do them. For example, "I think baby's sleepy. Let's put him to bed."

5. Model and talk about other ways to take care of the doll, such as burping, changing her clothes or diaper, combing his hair, brushing his teeth, singing to him, reading to him, and walking him in a stroller.

6. Invite the children to help you with the doll or get their own doll to play with. The children will show imagination in their play and interactions with others.

More to Do: Extensions and Adaptations

- Give each child a doll to prepare for nap time. Have them lie down next to their dolls for a nap. Encourage the children to take turns calling out, "Sleep tight," to their dolls or another friend.

- Place the books listed below in the dramatic play area, along with some pillows. Pick up a book and start reading it. Encourage the children to look at the photos in the books.

Suggested Books:

Buenas Noches, Luna by Margaret Wise Brown

Everywhere Babies by Susan Meyers

Goodnight Moon by Margaret Wise Brown

How Do Dinosaurs Say Goodnight? By Jane Yolen

Kiss Good Night by Amy Hest

What We Know

Toddlers and two-year-olds may pretend to feed a baby doll with a toy bottle or a toy spoon and bowl, try to wrap a doll in a blanket, and put the doll in a doll bed.

Stages of symbolic play:

- Older infants will explore how objects move and make noise. They may make the noise of a truck as they play with a toy truck.

- Toddlers may pretend to do actions that are very familiar to them, such as drink from a cup or use a banana as a telephone. Toddlers may also imitate adults' actions, such as feeding a doll with a toy spoon and bowl.

- Two-year-olds may play make-believe and pretend that they are someone or something else, such as a dog or a mother.

Opportunities for Learning

- Emotional development: The children will express care and concern toward others.

- Social development: The children will imitate and engage in play with other children.

- Language development: The children will learn from communication and language experiences with adults and peers. They will learn words such as *doll, blanket, burping, comb, hair, sleepy, hungry, rocking, feeding, holding,* and *baby.*

- Cognitive development: The children will use pretend play to increase understanding of culture, environment, and experiences.

- Physical/Motor development: The children will increase fine-motor skills as they use the small muscles in their hands to hold, rock, and dress dolls.

Going to the Farm

Materials

Stuffed animals: cow, pig, goat, sheep, duck, chicken, horse, and so on

Photos of farm animals

Plastic farm animals, several of each kind

Toy barn

Boxes

What to Do

1. If possible, make a trip to see farm animals so that children have the real-life experience to draw on.

2. Add toy farm animals, photos, and a barn to the dramatic play area, leaving the kitchen, table, and chairs in the area so children can go back "home."

3. Pretend with the children that you are taking a trip to the farm. When appropriate, you can say, "I want to see what farm animals are here today. Let's see, here is a cow and here is a goat." "Where should they go to sleep tonight?" "What should we feed them?" "I think the cows want to sleep together. Where are all of the cows?"

4. Observe as the children play with the animals. What do they seem to know about farms and animals?

5. As the children explore and play with the farm animals, they will develop self-regulation and maintain focus and sustain attention with support. They will show persistence and the ability to be flexible in their actions and behaviors.

More to Do: Extensions and Adaptations

For Toddlers:

SAFETY ALERT: Check the size of the plastic animals to prevent choking.

For Toddlers and Two-Year-Olds:

- Extend the activity by hiding plastic farm animals in the sandbox inside or outside. Give the children shovels and buckets. Let them discover the animals and name them.
- Place books about farms and farm animals in the dramatic play area. Seat yourself comfortably on pillows and begin looking at the books. With the children, match the pictures in the book to the stuffed and plastic animals.
- Provide posters of farm animals eating, sleeping, and playing on the farm.
- Encourage them to use the boxes to create homes for the animals.

Suggested Books:

Are You a Cow? by Sandra Boynton

Counting Cows by Woody Jackson

Cow Says Moo! by Parragon Books

Fun on the Farm: A Pop-Up Book by Helen Rowe

Little Cow by L. Rigo

Moo Moo Brown Cow by Jakki Wood

Oink on the Farm! by Parragon Books

Who Is Hiding on the Farm? by Cindy Bracken

Song: "Old MacDonald Had a Farm"

Ask each child to hold an animal (or two) and show it to everyone when you sing about it.

Opportunities for Learning

• • • • • • • • •

- Social development: The children will build relationships with other children by imitating and engaging in play with them.

- Language development: The children will use nonverbal communication and language to engage others to learn and gain information. They learn words such as the names of animals, *barn, fence, in,* and *out.*

- Cognitive development: The children will actively explore objects and learn the names of different animals. They will recognize differences between familiar and unfamiliar objects, which are memory and sorting skills. They will use objects or symbols to represent something else (a plastic animal or picture in a book represents the real animal). They will use matching and sorting of animals to understand similar and different characteristics, which is emergent mathematical thinking.

- Physical/Motor development: The children will use perceptual information to direct their own actions, experiences, and interactions.

On the Go

Materials

Chairs   Cardboard

Nontoxic paint

What to Do

Ahead of Time:

1. Create Stop and Go signs out of cardboard and paint.

2. Set up chairs to look like seats in a car.

With the Children:

1. Children love to pretend they are going places. Invite them to pretend they are going for a ride in a car. Tell them that the chairs are the car.

2. Invite them to pretend to open the car door and close it again. If more children join the activity, encourage other children to make room for them and find chairs for them.

3. Count the number of children before you take off on a pretend adventure.

4. Encourage them to pretend to buckle themselves in and then act like they are driving.

5. Demonstrate how to turn an imaginary steering wheel. Move your body from side to side when turning corners. Ask, "Where should we go?" to encourage problem solving and language development.

6. Talk about all the things you see along the side of the road.

7. Hold up the Stop and Go signs, and encourage the children to stop, then go. As the children play, they will maintain focus during this fun, interesting activity.

8. Ask everyone, "How are you feeling today?" If they don't answer, offer a choice question, "Are you feeling excited or scared?" "Are you feeling happy or sad?" "Why?"

9. Sing the songs listed below as you travel along.

10. When you get back "home," remind the children to unfasten their seat belts and open and close their doors to get out.

11. If children are interested, pretend to go on a boat, bus, airplane, or different types of trucks. Talk about where each type of vehicle may be going. For example, if children pretend they are driving a truck you could ask, "Are you taking cookies or milk to the grocery store?"

More to Do: Extensions and Adaptations

For Toddlers:

Toddlers may not be pretending to go on a trip; however, they will enjoy the activity with other children and the teacher.

For Toddlers and Two-Year-Olds:

- Adapt the activity for children who have difficulty sitting in a chair. Provide a large box for those children to sit in to go on a trip. Draw a steering wheel on the inside of the box. Extend the activity into other learning areas and days by providing posters, singing songs, and reading books about other forms of transportation.
- Add transportation vehicles to the water and sand tables in the sensory learning area and in the sandbox outdoors.
- Leave the chairs in the dramatic play area. Children may start their own traveling game.

Songs:

"The Wheels on the Bus"

"A-traveling We Will Go" (Sing to the tune of "The Farmer in the Dell.")

> *A-traveling we will go.*
> *A-traveling we will go.*
> *Oh, what fun it is.*
> *A-traveling we will go.*

Suggested Books:

Little Blue Truck by Alice Schertle

El Camioncito Azul by Alice Schertle

Little Blue Truck Leads the Way by Alice Schertle

My Car by Byron Barton

Toot Toot Beep Beep by Emma Garcia

My Bus by Byron Barton

Wheels on the Bus by Jerry Smath

Planes by Byron Barton

Opportunities for Learning

- Emotional development: The children will show care and concern toward others as they include other children in the activity. They will understand and use words for feelings as they answer the teacher's questions about how they are feeling.

- Social development: The children will share space and materials with other children.

- They will imitate other children and enjoy being with them.

- Language development: The children will understand and use new vocabulary, such as the names of vehicles, *transportation, seat belt, safe, stop, go, toot-toot, beep-beep*, and the functions of different types of vehicles.

- Literacy development: The children will recognize that the words on the Stop and Go signs are symbols that have meaning.

- Cognitive development: The children will learn one-to-one correspondence as the group counts the children who go on a trip. They will gain spatial awareness as they make room for more children. They will use pretend play to increase understanding of culture, environment, and experiences.

- Physical/Motor development: The children will use fine-motor and gross-motor skills as they move chairs and pretend to handle the steering wheel.

My Special House

Materials

Large boxes	Box cutter or X-ACTO knife (adult use only)
Nontoxic tempera paint	Paintbrush
Glue	Child-safe scissors
Fabric scraps	Pillows and rugs
Stickers	Stuffed animals

What We Know

Some children will choose to go to a quiet alone space to regulate their feelings and behavior. These types of spaces help children relax and become calm.

What to Do

Ahead of Time:

Use a sharp knife to cut an opening in each box large enough for a toddler to go through. Cut several windows in the sides of the boxes.

With the Children:

1. Explain to the children that they are going to help make a special place.

2. In the creative area of the room, help them paint the boxes with tempera paint.

3. When the paint has dried, let the children put stickers on the boxes or glue scraps of fabric on the walls.

4. Place the boxes in the dramatic play area. Now they are ready for the children to move into! Invite them to bring in rugs, pillows, books, and stuffed animals. The children will develop self-regulation, as each child has a place to go to control his own behavior and emotions.

More to Do: Extensions and Adaptations

1. The special place can be used in many ways: a quiet corner, a playhouse, a post office, or a bear cave—just change the props inside!

2. Some children may feel uncomfortable being too close to other children. Provide a few boxes for individuals who may have sensory challenges.

3. Use a box as a cozy corner where children can go if they need quiet time and a space of their own. Children should not be sent to the box as punishment. Rather, explain to children that they can go to the cozy corner if they need to be alone or with one friend. Add soft materials and many books.

Suggested Books:

Bear Snores On by Karma Wilson

The Very Quiet Cricket by Eric Carle

The Story of Ferdinand by Munro Leaf

Opportunities for Learning
· · ● · ● ● ● · ● · ·

- Social development: The children will build relationships with other children by imitating and engaging in play with them when they use the box together.

- Language development: The children will use nonverbal communication and language to engage others to learn and gain information. They will learn words such as *home, house, pillows,* the names of stuffed animals, words in the books, and *cozy house.*

- Literacy development: The children will comprehend meaning from pictures and stories. They will handle books and relate them to stories or information.

- Cognitive development: The children will use objects or symbols to represent something else (a picture in a book represents the real object).

- Physical/Motor development: The children will use perceptual information to direct their own actions, experiences, and interactions.

Camping

Materials

Large blue paper

Construction paper

Scissors (adult use only)

Pop-up tent

Flashlights

Binoculars

Backpacks

Marker

Toy fishing pole

Vest

Empty boxes of food

Pictures of people camping

What We Know

Toddlers and two-year-olds benefit from knowing the home/kitchen area is always there for them. They then have a safe place to go when they are back from pretend camping or going to the doctor.

What to Do

Ahead of Time:

1. Cut some fish shapes out of paper. Write the word *fish* on each one. Make the fish different colors and sizes.

2. Make a river by laying a long piece of blue paper on the floor. Place a few fish on top of the paper.

3. Set up the tent, and set out the supplies

With the Children:

1. Talk with them about what camping is, and talk about the supplies needed for camping.

2. Allow small groups of two to four children to explore the tent and supplies.

3. You may want to play with the children to model what people do on camping trips. Pretend to fix food over a fire and sleep in the tent. The children will show imagination in play and interactions with others.

4. Add more materials if the children seem interested.

More to Do: Extensions and Adaptations

For Toddlers:

- Let younger children fish with their hands. Encourage them to sit or kneel by the paper river and reach for the fish.
- Talk about the colors of the fish and count the fish.

For Toddlers and Two-Year-Olds:

- Take camping equipment and materials outside, if weather permits.
- Eat camping food for snack.
- Hide plastic fish of many different colors in the water and sand tables.

For Two-Year-Olds:

- Glue a large magnet securely on the paper fish. Make fishing poles by attaching string with a magnet on the end of a short pole. Encourage the children to go fishing and then throw the fish back in the water.
- Talk about the concepts of large and small, long and short, bigger, smaller, shorter, longer, and larger fish. Put the fish in order by size—this is seriation.

Suggested Books:

BIG Little by Leslie Patricelli

Curious George Goes Camping by Margret Rey and H.A. Rey

Opportunities for Learning

- Social development: The children will imitate and engage in play with other children.
- Language development: The children will learn from communication and language experiences with adults and peers. They will learn new words, such as *camping, tent, fish, river, water, fishing pole,* color words, counting words, *longer, shorter, bigger, smaller, largest,* and *smallest.*
- Cognitive development: The children will use pretend play to increase understanding of culture, environment, and experiences.
- Physical/Motor development: The children will increase fine-motor skills as they use the small muscles in their hands to fish, hold fish, hold dishes, and stir food with spoons.

Literacy

Purpose of a Literacy Learning Area

While literacy experiences occur at many times of the day and in many different areas of the room, the purpose of a literacy learning area is to provide opportunities for children to explore and appreciate books and other reading materials. For toddlers and two-year-olds the literacy area includes a writing area for children to enjoy beginning writing experiences.

Infant Literacy Area

This area often includes a no-climb book stand, so that crawling infants can reach attractively displayed books; comfortable flooring for infants to sit or lie on to explore books; comfortable furniture for adults to sit on to read to infants; a low, stable shelf for puppets and other props; and books that are exchanged often (except for favorite books).

Please refer to the classroom diagram on page 120.

Toddler and Two-Year-Old Literacy Area

This area usually includes no-climb book stands to attractively display books; comfortable flooring and furniture where children can curl up with a book; and comfortable furniture for adults to sit on to read to children. This area also includes pillows and blankets; purchased and handmade photo books displayed so children can see the front covers; interesting, culturally diverse posters; props such as puppets and stuffed animals to accompany storybooks; and many types of books. Exchange the books often (except for favorite books).

Please refer to the classroom diagram on page 120.

Toddler and Two-Year-Old Writing Area

A writing area for toddlers and two-year-olds often includes a child-size table, chairs, writing utensils, a variety of paper, large cloth or wooden letters, large magnetic letters and a magnetic board, and tracing materials.

Read Books to Me—The Important First Year

Materials

Books

What to Do

1. Start when children are approximately three months of age. Sit an infant on your lap, cuddling her in your arms. Show the infant the book and talk about the pictures. Continue reading different books with infants throughout their first year of life.

2. When an infant is lying on her back, lie down on your back by the baby. Hold the book up so that both you and the infant can see it. Look at the pictures, name them, and talk about them.

3. At approximately six months of age, lay the baby on her back on the floor on a comfortable, safe surface. Place infant board books around her. The infant may reach to her side to pick up a book, hold it up, look at it, and probably chew on it. Sit by the infant and read the book to the baby. When you read to an infant, notice what the infant is looking at and talk about that picture. At times, read the book so that the infant can hear the rhythm of language.

4. When an infant is beginning to turn from her back to her tummy, place her on a comfortable surface and put books on one side of her. The infant will likely reach out for and roll over to grasp a book. Sit by the infant and read the story to her, pointing to the pictures as you name them.

5. At approximately eight months of age, infants will crawl to books that are placed in the environment. Infants may even indicate to you with a sound or by holding out a book that they want you to read the book to them. As you read with them, the children will show interest and curiosity in interactions with familiar adults.

6. Adult responsiveness to infants' language—their grunts, coos, babbles, and words—is the key to building secure relationships, language development, and the love of books.

What We Know

Babies are learning which sounds are language sounds and which are other sounds. In the first three months, babies prefer listening to speech compared to many nonspeech sounds, suggesting that humans are born with a bias for speech (Vouloumanos et al., 2010). They benefit from hearing you read books and talk about the pictures.

Seven-month-olds can remember Mozart music passages and can still recall these passages after two weeks of not hearing them (Saffran, Loman, and Robertson, 2000). Remarkably, they prefer to listen to passages that they've heard before and that are played in the same sequence. Similarly, we know that infants love hearing the same books over and over, as they become familiar with the sounds and meaning of language.

Opportunities for Learning

- Emotional development: The children will begin to share emotions with a familiar adult and learn to read facial expressions.
- Social development: The children will develop interest in looking at books with other infants.
- Language development: The children will listen and process language—what sounds and words are more likely to go together and follow each other. They will communicate with adults and peers through gestures, sounds, and words.

The Love of Books

Materials

Books

What to Do

1. Place books in all learning centers in the room, not just in the literacy learning area.

2. In the literacy area, place books in a stand so that young children can see the covers of the books.

3. Anytime is a good time to read a book to a toddler or two-year-old. Read a book when a child brings one to you to read. Start reading a book in a learning area in the room and notice as children come over to listen for awhile. Sit on a bench outside or on a blanket in the shade and start reading a book. Read a book when lunch is late.

4. It is best to read to one or two children who can sit on your lap or close by your side so they can see the book and hear the words. When you start reading a book, children may come and go as you read. Use your voice to express emotions, use props that children can hold, and demonstrate your love of books. These techniques keep children listening and loving books.

What We Know

Toddler responsiveness to a book increases across repeated readings of the same book. Toddlers whose caregivers asked more questions during reading had children with higher expressive language six months later (Fletcher and Finch, 2015). Use **dialogic reading** strategies that include engaging children in a conversation as you read the book and encouraging them to relate their experiences as they are (or not) connected to the content of the book (Whitehurst, Zevenbergen, Crone, 1999).

All about Me Book

Materials

Three-ring binder

Heavy paper or tagboard

Glue

Protective sleeves or photo sleeves

Photos of the children

Marker or pen

What to Do

Ahead of Time:

1. Ask families to bring in photos of the child at home with toys, siblings, family members, and pets. Make copies of these photos, and send the originals back home.

2. Take photos of each child at play and interacting with other children in the room.

3. Glue each photo on a piece of heavy paper or tagboard.

4. Label the bottom of the paper with the child's name and, if appropriate, the names of family members, pets, and so on.

5. Place the paper in a protective sleeve and add the page to the notebook.

6. Continue until you have each child represented in the photo book.

What We Know

Very young children do not learn language from watching DVDs or TV (Roseberry et al., 2009). They need interactive turn-taking where they can see the speaker's face, hear the adult respond, and hear their own voice. "All about Me" books motivate children to engage in interactive turn-taking with peers and adults.

With the Children:

Place the binder where adults and children can look at it and share it with other children. As the children explore the photos of themselves and others and talk about them with a trusted adult or another child, they will sustain attention.

More to Do: Extensions and Adaptations

Use a few photos from this binder to create a portfolio binder for each child. Add artwork; any assessment summaries; photos of the child playing and with friends; samples of language, interests, learning goals; photos of developmental and learning accomplishments, and prosocial behavior. Share the portfolio with family members often, and give the portfolio to the family at the end of the year.

Opportunities for Learning

- Emotional development: The children will demonstrate a positive sense of self-identity and self-awareness.

- Language development: The children will respond to and use a growing vocabulary as adults talk with children about what they are doing, wearing, and feeling.

- Literacy development: The children will show interest in print if their names and a few words are written at the bottom of the photos. This activity provides a foundation for reading.

Color Shopping

Materials

Books about colors

Paint

Small baskets with handles

Card stock

Paintbrush

Marker

What to Do

Ahead of Time:

1. Paint each piece of card stock using a different color. Choose colors that are present in items in your classroom. Let dry.

2. Write the name of the color on each card.

With the Children:

1. Read one or two books about colors.

2. Give each child a card and a basket, and suggest that each child or pairs of children look for an item of that color to put into the basket.

3. When each child has found one or two items, help them talk about what they collected. Hold up the card matching the items and read the name of the color. Say, for example, "Red. This word is *red. R-E-D,*" as you point to the letters.

4. Ask the children to return the items to the areas where they belong.

More to Do: Extensions and Adaptations

For Older Toddlers:

An adult will need to go with the toddler to find objects of different colors. Talk about the color of items as you shop for, say, something blue.

For Toddlers and Two-Year-Olds:

- Extend the activity into other learning areas by commenting on colors in each area and outdoors.
- Place books about colors in many areas of the room.

For Two-Year-Olds:

Encourage pairs of children to work together. They will enjoy being together to find the objects.

Suggested Books:

The Colors of Us by Karen Katz

Mouse Paint by Ellen Stoll Walsh

A Color of His Own by Leo Lionni

My Many Colored Days by Dr. Seuss

Colors by Roger Priddy

- Language development: The children will use nonverbal communication and language to engage others and to learn and gain information. They will learn the names of some colors.

- Literacy development: The children will recognize that squiggly lines say something when the teacher reads, "Red."

- Cognitive development: The children will actively explore objects and learn the names of different colors. They will recognize differences between familiar and unfamiliar objects, which are memory and sorting skills. They will use matching and sorting of objects to understand similar and different characteristics, which is emergent mathematical thinking.

- Physical/Motor development: The children will use perceptual information to direct their own actions, experiences, and interactions.

Squeeze Us In

Materials

The Mitten by Jan Brett

Large adult mitten or pot-holder mitten

Small stuffed animals, such as a bear, mouse, bunny, owl, fox, and hedgehog

What to Do

1. Sit in the literacy area and begin to read the book *The Mitten*. Show the children the large adult mitten.

2. Let each child hold a stuffed animal and put it in the mitten when that animal crawls in the mitten in the book. Ask, "How is the (name of animal) feeling?"

3. Have fun trying to squeeze all the animals in the mitten. The children will maintain focus during this fun, interesting activity.

What We Know

When teachers of young children point to letters and words, children are more likely to learn the words and names of the letters, just as children do when adults point to a refrigerator and say the name of it. Children do not feel pressure and enjoy looking at the letters.

Toddlers will hold books, turn pages, and point to pictures in books.

Older toddlers and two-year-olds will "read" books by holding them, looking at the pictures, naming pictures, and making sounds as if they were reading.

More to Do: Extensions and Adaptations

- Act out the story with each child pretending to be an animal. Encourage the "animals" to squeeze together (as if they were in a mitten). Be aware that some children may experience **sensory overload** and not want to squeeze in a space with other children. Allow them to sit back and not squeeze in. When you get to the part with the sneezing, choose a child to sneeze safely into the crook of his arm.

- Encourage the children to keep each other safe and ask each other, "Are you okay?" as they squeeze together.

- Count the animals as they go into the mitten.

- Provide large old mittens and plastic animals in the sand area inside and out. Emphasize the words *in, out, full,* and *empty.*

- Place several copies of the book in the literacy learning area to encourage several children to "read" together.

Suggested Book: *The Mitten* by Jan Brett

Opportunities for Learning
· · ● ● ● ● ● ● · ·

- Emotional development: The children will show care and concern toward others. They will begin to understand and use words for feelings.

- Social development: The children will share space and materials with other children. They will imitate other children and enjoy being with them.

- Language development: The children will understand and use new vocabulary, such as the names of the animals, *mitten, in,* and *out.*

- Literacy development: The children will recognize symbols (that the images in the book match the stuffed animals).

- Cognitive development: The children will learn one-to-one correspondence as the group counts the animals as they go into the mitten. They will gain spatial awareness, which is mathematical thinking, as they fill the mitten with animals.

- Physical/Motor development: They will use fine-motor skills to stuff the animals in.

ABC Ticket

Materials

Packing tape

Card stock

Pairs of matching pictures

Glue

What to Do

Ahead of Time:

1. Find pictures of or draw identical objects, such as two cats, two balls, and two apples. Glue the images onto card stock, and write the word for the object under each picture.

2. Tape one of each set of pictures to the floor in a large area.

With the Children:

1. Give each child or pair of children a picture card. Tell them their cards are their "tickets." Point out the words underneath the pictures, but do not expect the children to learn the letters or spelling of the words. The idea is to expose them to the written words.

2. Invite them to find the card that matches the ticket. When you say, "Go," the children look for the picture on the floor that matches the one in their hand.

3. When they make a match, ask them to stand on their matching picture.

4. When they are finished, encourage the children to show and tell others about their pictures. Read the word under the picture.

5. Use the words *same* and *different* often. For example, "Mei, you found a ball. That ball is the same as the ball on your ticket." "Jermaine found a cat. The cat is different from the apple on his ticket."

6. Give each child or pair of children a different picture and play again.

More to Do: Extensions and Adaptations

- If you know that a child may have difficulty finding the matching picture, then pair the child with you or with a knowledgeable peer.
- Play Concentration with the cards in the motor or cognitive-discovery area of the room.
- Extend the activity at other times by finding things in the room or outside that are the same or different.
- Encourage children to help each other. This helps develop cooperation and prosocial skills.

> ### What We Know
>
> Some two-year-olds may know the names of some letters, especially ones in their names, if adults have talked with the children frequently about letters.

Opportunities for Learning

- Social development: The children will build relationships with others as they interact with peers.

- Language development: The children will develop receptive language skills as they listen to language and participate in conversations. They will increase vocabulary as they learn the names of items on the cards and the concepts of *same* and *different*. They will use language skills as they participate in conversations.

- Literacy development: The children will begin to develop knowledge of the alphabet and the **alphabetic principle**.

- Cognitive development: The children will begin to learn about symbols—that words and pictures represent real items. They will begin to learn that letters have names and that together the letters have meaning.

Math

Purpose of a Math Learning Area

While math opportunities occur in all the routines and learning areas, a math learning area provides books, toys, materials, and interactions that support children's explorations of numbers, shapes, spatial relationships, measurement, patterns, and organizing information such as classification and seriation.

Infant Math Learning Area

The block and math learning areas are often combined for infants. In addition to items listed for the construction learning area, this area includes soft, wooden, or plastic blocks; geometric shapes; and stacking and nesting toys. Wooden or plastic animals (too large for choking) are wonderful for infant hands. Older infants will enjoy handling Duplos, very easy shape-sorting boards and cubes, and large pegboards. Always include board books in each area.

Please refer to the classroom diagram on page 120.

Toddler and Two-Year-Old Math Learning Area

The toddler and two-year-old math area includes puzzles of different levels of difficulty for sorting, patterning, and counting; assorted wooden or plastic animals, shapes, and containers of different colors and sizes; natural materials and manipulatives; large foam dice; multishape sorters; ring counters and stacking toys; a child-size tape measure; and board books.

Please refer to the classroom diagram on page 120.

> **HINT**
>
> For each puzzle, number the puzzle on the back and then number each piece of that puzzle to match. You'll save yourself lots of time trying to figure out which pieces go with which puzzle.

Let's Count Your Fingers and Toes

Materials

None

What to Do

1. When playing with a baby on your lap, playfully count the infant's fingers and toes. Touch each finger or toe as you count, if the baby likes your touch. Infants learn to manage feelings and emotions with the support of familiar adults.

2. Say, "One finger, two fingers, three fingers, four. Five fingers, six fingers, seven fingers, more. Eight fingers, nine fingers, and here's number ten!"

3. Do the same with the baby's toes.

More to Do: Extensions and Adaptations

- Watch for cues that baby is enjoying the game. If the infant looks away, arches his back, yawns, or fusses, then the infant is telling you that he needs a break from the action.
- Read the book *Ten Little Fingers and Ten Little Toes* by Mem Fox and Helen Oxenbury.
- Focus on math during everyday routines. Diapering is a perfect time to count fingers and talk about numbers.

Suggested Books:

My Very First Book of Numbers by Eric Carle

Counting Kisses: A Kiss and Read Book by Karen Katz

Ten Little Fingers and Ten Little Toes by Mem Fox and Helen Oxenbury

> ## What We Know
>
> Math concepts include **cardinal numbers**, counting, **ordinal numbers**, weight, size, quantity, shapes, spatial relationships, measurement, sorting, and patterns.

Opportunities for Learning

• • ● • ● ● ● • • •

- Emotional development: The children will develop expectations of consistent, positive interactions with adults to develop secure attachments.
- Language development: The children will learn the sounds and rhythm of language when the teacher talks directly to them in a responsive way.
- Cognitive development: The children will develop a sense of number and quantity.

Matching in Many Ways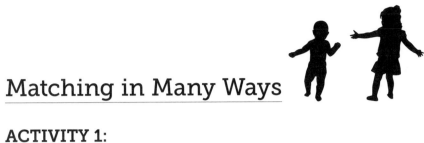

ACTIVITY 1:

Materials

Several pairs of matching socks in distinct patterns and colors

What to Do

1. Separate the socks.

2. Encourage the child to find the matching sock.

ACTIVITY 2:

Materials

Fabric in a variety of textures, such as velvet, satin, cotton, wool, flannel, and fake fur

Fabric in a variety of patterns, such as polka dots, stripes, prints, plaids, and solids

Cardboard

Large shoe box

Glue

Scissors (adult use only)

What to Do

Ahead of Time:

1. Cut the fabric into 4" x 4" squares. Make a few squares of each type of fabric.

2. Cut the cardboard into 4" x 4" squares, one per piece of fabric.

3. Glue a piece of fabric to each piece of cardboard.

4. Cut a 5" slit in the lid of the shoe box. It should be wide enough for the fabric squares to go through.

With the Children:

1. Place the fabric squares and the box in the math learning area.

2. Encourage the children to sort through them and find the squares that match.

3. Encourage children to put the fabric squares back into the box through the slit on top of the box.

More to Do: Extensions and Adaptations

For Toddlers:

- Toddlers will like feeling the textures and looking at the patterns, although most will not be ready to match the squares.
- Toddlers will enjoy the game of putting the fabric squares through the hole on the top of the box and then opening the box to see the squares.
- When playing with a toddler, use the words *same* and *different* as the child plays with the pairs of squares.

For Toddlers and Two-Year-Olds:

- Extend the activity to other learning areas and snack time. Talk about food that is the same and different. Play a hunting game outside by finding objects and things in nature that are the same and different.
- Read books, such as those listed below on opposites, such as up and down, in and out.
- Ask family members to help children notice what is the same and different at home. Send a short list of opposites—in and out, up and down, big and small, loud and quiet—home to families.

For Two-Year-Olds:

Choose four pairs of matching fabric squares. Place the fabric squares in two lines of four fabric squares each. Show the fabric squares to the child. Ask the child to help you turn them over so that the cardboard side is facing up and then mix them up. The child and you can play a traditional matching memory game, turning over two squares at a time until all the matching pairs are found. Use the words *same* and *different* often.

Suggested Books:

What's Up Duck? A Book of Opposites by Tad Hills

Little Quack's Opposites by Lauren Thompson

Opposites by Sandra Boynton

Opportunities for Learning

- Social development: The children will build relationships with others as they interact with peers.

- Language development: The children will develop receptive language skills as they listen to language and participate in conversations. They will increase vocabulary as they learn the concepts same and different, up and down, and in and out.

- Cognitive development: The children will use their senses to construct knowledge about the world.

- Physical/Motor development: The children will develop small muscles, eye-hand coordination, and perceptual skills.

Sort Us Out and Classify Us, Too

Materials

Baskets, boxes, or sorting containers

Pairs of socks in different colors

Day pictures

Card stock

Cat pictures

Bows in a variety of colors

Blocks in different colors

Night pictures

Glue

Dog pictures

What We Know

Toddlers may be able to match items. Encourage them by saying, "Find one just like this." Older toddlers and two-year-olds may be able to sort objects into two groups based on a characteristic, such as color or size. Sorting is a way of organizing information.

What to Do

Ahead of Time:

1. Find photos of cats and of dogs, cut them out, and glue each photo onto card stock.

2. Find photos of daytime scenes and nighttime scenes. Cut them out and glue each photo onto card stock.

With the Children:

1. Choose items for children to sort. For example, begin with letting them sort items by color. Provide blocks in different colors, along with as many baskets or bins as there are colors.

2. Start with the items mixed together. Tell the children that the items need to be put in different baskets.

3. Observe as children play and put the items in baskets. Do they sort them in any way?

4. If they don't sort them, hold up two blue blocks and one red block. Ask, "Which of these are the same?" "Which of these are different?" Or, hold up a red block and a blue block and ask, "Are these the same or different?" Or, "Let's put the blue blocks in one basket and the red blocks in another basket." Model sorting a few blocks and then wait to see what children do.

5. On another day, provide different materials to sort, such as cat photos and dog photos or different colors of socks. Change the materials from time to time to keep the children interested.

More to Do: Extensions and Adaptations

For Toddlers:

Encourage them to find matches for items. For example, show them a photo of a cat, and ask them to find another photo of a cat.

For Toddlers and Two-Year-Olds:

Extend the activity to other learning areas and snack time. Talk about food that is the same and different. Play a hunting game outside by finding objects and things in nature that are the same and different. Read books, such as those listed below on opposites.

Suggested Books:

BIG Little by Leslie Patricelli

Yummy YUCKY by Leslie Patricelli

Opportunities for Learning

· • ● ● ● ● • •

- Language development: The children will use nonverbal communication and language to engage others to learn and gain information. They will learn the names of colors, *same*, and *different*.

- Cognitive development: The children will actively explore objects and learn the names of different colors. They will recognize differences between familiar and unfamiliar objects. They will use matching and sorting of objects to understand similar and different characteristics.

- Physical/Motor development: The children will use perceptual information to direct their own actions, experiences, and interactions.

Shape Me Up

Materials

Shapes, Shapes, Shapes by Tana Hoban

Construction paper in a variety of colors

Scissors (adult use only)

Paper

Markers

What to Do

Ahead of Time:

Cut out different shapes from the construction paper: circle, rectangle, triangle, and square.

With the Children:

1. Read Tana Hoban's *Shapes, Shapes, Shapes* to a small group of children.

2. Give each child a construction paper shape.

3. Tell the group that you are going on a shape hunt with them. Ask the child with a circle to hold it up. Say, "We are going to hunt for a circle shape in our room." Ask the child with the circle, "Where should we go first?" Go with the group to find circles. Hold up the circle shape to see if it matches.

4. Continue until you have found all the shapes in the room. Do this with additional small groups if there are more children in the room. As the children search, they will maintain focus and sustain attention with support.

5. On another day, take a small group outside to look for shapes.

More to Do: Extensions and Adaptations

- Take a camera with you on your shape hunt. Take photos of the children holding up their shape to the matching object.

- Print out the photos and make your own shape book. Below each photo, write the descriptions as told to you by the children.

- Comment positively about how children are helping each other.

Suggested Books:

Shapes, Shapes, Shapes by Tana Hoban

Brainy Baby Shapes and Colors: Rainbows, Circles, and Squares by Brainy Baby

Song: (Sing to the tune of "Where Is Thumbkin?")

> *Where is circle? Where is circle?* (child with the circle holds it up for all to see)
> *There you are, there you are.* (everyone points to the circle)
> *How are you today, circle?*
> *Very well, I thank you.* (child with the circle wiggles the circle)
> *Run and hide, run and hide.* (child hides circle behind his back)

Sing about the rectangle, triangle, and square.

Opportunities for Learning

- Emotional development: The children will manage emotions with the support of familiar adults.

- Social development: The children will interact with other children in a prosocial, helping way.

- Language development: The children will understand and use an increasing number of words to communicate, such as *shape, circle, rectangle, triangle,* and *square.*

- Cognitive development: The children will use matching and sorting of objects to understand similar and different characteristics.

- Physical/Motor development: The children will use perceptual information to understand objects.

Outdoor Play/Nature

Purpose of an Outdoor Play/Nature Learning Area

Outdoor play and a nature learning area give young children opportunities to experience large-motor activities; social experiences with others; creating and building with loose materials; and natural materials such as trees, bushes, leaves, sand, and water.

Infant Outdoor Play/Nature Learning Area

An infant nature learning area includes easy access to a diapering area; shady places for rocking and playing babies; firm mats where babies can lie on their backs, turn over, and crawl; mats of varying levels for climbing; surfaces of different types; and bucket swings.

Toddler and Two-Year-Old Outdoor Play/Nature Learning Area

A toddler and two-year-old outdoor play and nature learning area includes easy access to a diapering and hand-washing area, as well as child-size playground equipment. This area also includes shady places for rocking and reading to children and for quiet play and/or eating; firm mats where children can crawl and sit; surfaces of different types; a shady, quiet area with books and quiet toys; pushing and riding toys; traffic signs; safe water and sand containers; swings of various types, including bucket swings; a short climber and slide on a safe surface; a playhouse; space to run; and short tunnels to crawl through. Include materials, such as boards of various sizes, which the children can safely move from place to place for building. Most important, there should be natural materials that children can explore with all their senses.

Explore a Tree

Materials

Tree

What to Do

1. Bring infants or a small group of toddlers and two-year-olds together to a tree.

2. Explore the colors, textures, and smells of a tree. Place the infant's hand on the bark, encourage toddlers and two-year-olds to touch the tree, and talk about what it feels like (rough, smooth, and so on).

3. Look for any bugs on the tree and point them out.

4. If there are leaves on the tree, help the children feel them. Trace the shape of a leaf with a child's finger. Talk about the color and texture of the leaves.

5. Return to the same tree throughout the seasons to follow the changes that occur in the leaves, flowers, fruit, and so on. As the children explore the tree, they will develop a positive sense of self with nature.

More to Do: Extensions and Adaptations

For Infants:

You will want to hold an infant in your arms. An infant three months and older will probably reach out to touch the tree. Talk about the colors and texture of the bark, leaves, and bugs. Say, "You are touching a tree." "You are touching a leaf." An infant will enjoy listening to the sounds and rhythm of language.

For Toddlers and Two-Year-Olds:

- Take photos of the tree in different seasons, and make a book. It could be titled *Our Tree*.

- Take two or three children together to touch and talk about the tree, leaves, and bugs. This will encourage children to talk to each other. See if they can hold hands and circle the tree. Dance around the tree and celebrate its beauty.

- Ask two-year-olds what questions they have about trees. If they hesitate, model how to ask a question and find the answer.

Rhyme:

> *Bend your branches down* (bend over at the waist)
> *To touch the ground.* (touch your toes)
> *Wiggle your long limbs* (wave your arms side to side)
> *And wave to the sky.* (look up at the ceiling)
> *A gust of strong wind* (blow air through your lips)
> *Blows leaves around.* (fall to the ground)

Suggested Books:

Welcome Spring by Jill Ackerman

Welcome Summer by Jill Ackerman

Welcome Fall by Jill Ackerman

Welcome Winter by Jill Ackerman

Opportunities for Learning

- Emotional development: The children will experience and express a range of emotions.
- Social development: The children will enjoy being with other infants and toddlers.
- Language development: The children will understand many more words than they can speak.

No-Mess Painting

Materials

Buckets

Paved area or a cement wall

Paintbrushes

Water

What to Do

1. On a warm day, fill a few buckets with a small amount of water, and then bring the buckets outside. **SAFETY ALERT:** Watch children carefully. Children have drowned in 2 inches of water.

2. Invite the children to dip their paintbrushes in the water and "paint" the sidewalk, the building, the tables, and so on. As they explore what happens with the water, the children will develop the ability to show persistence in their actions and behaviors. They will use creativity to increase their understanding and learning.

3. The best part of this activity is that when the water dries, there is no mess. But, more important, children love it and learn from it. Children will want to do this repeatedly on warm days. They love to make different marks with their brushes, watch them disappear, and do it again.

More to Do: Extensions and Adaptations

- Toddlers may need smaller brushes, but let them choose the size of brush they can handle easily. This encourages experimentation and problem solving. Some two-year-olds may choose smaller brushes as well.
- After children enjoy painting, read one or more of the following stories to them.

Suggested Books:

Mr. Wishy-Washy by Joy Cowley

Mrs. Wishy-Washy by Joy Cowley

Mrs. Wishy-Washy Makes a Splash by Joy Cowley

Mrs. Wishy-Washy's Splishy Sploshy Day by Joy Cowley

Opportunities for Learning

- Emotional development: The children will manage emotions with the support of familiar adults.
- Social development: The children will trust adults and use them as resources; for example, asking for more water when they need it. They will imitate and engage in play with other children.
- Language development: The children will understand and use new vocabulary and **syntax** when teachers say, for example, "You are painting." When a child is finished, say, "You painted," emphasizing the ends of the words.
- Cognitive development: The children will learn to use a variety of strategies in solving problems. They will use understanding of causal relationships to act on social and physical environments.
- Physical/Motor development: The children will develop both gross-motor and fine-motor skills.

Nature Hide and Seek

Materials

Poster board   Paper

Glue   Markers

Items from nature, such as pinecones, leaves, sticks, rocks, and so on

Small buckets with handles, one per child

What We Know

When young children play outdoors in a free, unstructured way, their emotional, social, cognitive, and motor development grow. Language, too, develops as children engage with educators and peers.

What to Do

Ahead of Time:

1. Gather a variety of natural items found in your outdoor area.

2. Glue examples of each material to the poster board and label them.

With the Children:

1. Give each child a bucket in which to gather nature finds.

2. Show the children the poster board and describe the different objects they are looking for.

3. Take the children outdoors. Display the poster board in a prominent place.

4. Encourage the children to look for the items on the poster board and anything else they find interesting.

5. As the children search for and notice items in nature, they will develop a positive sense of self with nature and will use creativity to increase understanding and learning.

More to Do: Extensions and Adaptations

- Back in the room, let the children glue their items to paper to make a nature collage. Talk with the children about what they found. Describe the colors, size, and textures.

- Encourage two children to go together on the hunt for nature items. Comment on how well the children cooperate with each other.

- Label and empathize with the emotions that children express during this activity.

- If you observe interest in this activity, encourage children to find new items to paste on the poster. Write the name of the object on the poster.

- Do this during every season of the year, and compare items on the posters from different seasons.

- Bring natural items into many of the learning areas in the room—pinecones in the construction area, leaves in the water table, a tree stump for children to examine and sit on, and so on.

Suggested Books:

Welcome Spring by Jill Ackerman

Welcome Summer by Jill Ackerman

Welcome Fall by Jill Ackerman

Welcome Winter by Jill Ackerman

Opportunities for Learning

- Emotional development: The children will experience and express a range of emotions. As they are hunting for items they may express frustration, joy, concern, or disappointment.
- Social development: The children will enjoy being with and cooperating with peers.
- Cognitive development: The children will use memory as a foundation for more complex actions and thoughts as they look at the poster and then go off to find objects.
- Language development: The children will understand and use new vocabulary, such as *leaf, rock, stick, pinecone, acorn, flower, cooperate, cooperated,* and *collage.*
- Literacy development: The children will recognize pictures and some symbols, signs, or words and know that they represent real objects.
- Physical/Motor: The children will develop gross-motor skills as they look for objects and will develop fine-motor skills as they handle the objects and glue them on paper.

Transition with a Red Caboose

Materials

None

What to Do

1. Say this traditional rhyme while transitioning from indoors to outdoors or from outdoors to indoors.

2. Encourage the children to pretend to be a train. The children will use their imaginations as they pretend to be part of a train.

> *Little red caboose, chug, chug, chug,* (make chugging motions with arms)
> *Little red caboose, chug, chug, chug.*
> *Little red caboose behind the train, train, train.* (point behind with thumb in air)
> *Smokestack on its back, back, back,* (pat back)
> *Hurrying down the track, track, track,*
> *Little red caboose behind the train.*
> *Toot! Toot!* (pretend to tug on horn pull)

More to Do: Extensions and Adaptations

As children gather to go outside or inside, give each child a laminated photo of cars on the train. Provide several pictures of a red caboose so that several children can have a turn each time you use this activity. Then say the rhyme.

Suggested Books:

Trains by Byron Barton

The Little Train by Lois Lenski

That's Not My Train by Usborne

What We Know

Reading books, providing a photo of a train, or using the word *train* helps children learn that there are **levels of representation** from the real to the abstract. Levels of representation include, for example, a real train, a photo of a train, a drawing of a train, the sound of a train, a puzzle of a train, and the word *train*. Experiences with materials at different levels of representation provide a foundation for children learning to read the word.

Opportunities for Learning

· · · • · · ·

- Emotional development: The children will practice impulse control as they control their bodies to be a part of a group.

- Social development: The children will enjoy how they feel when interacting with peers and will develop a sense of self with others.

- Language development: The children will learn new words and sing them as they hear a song or rhyme repeated many times. When the books are read, they will learn more vocabulary and complex sentence structure.

- Literacy development: The children will develop emergent literacy skills.

- Physical/Motor development: The children will develop the large muscles in their bodies as they participate in a physical activity. They will learn to control their movements to be safe in a group and to keep their friends safe.

Stop and Go Signs

Materials

2 paint stirrers

Marker

Scissors (adult use only)

Red and green poster board

Heavy-duty stapler (adult use only)

Glue

What to Do

Ahead of Time:

Cut out two large circles, one from the green poster board and one from the red poster board.

With the Children:

1. Read the book, *Red, Stop! Green, Go! An Interactive Book of Colors* by P. D. Eastman to small groups of children.

2. Ask the children who would like to help you create large Stop and Go signs. Tell them that they will be using the signs outdoors at play time.

3. Using large letters, write *stop* on both sides of the red circle and *go* on both sides of the green circle. Let the children help by making marks. The children will maintain focus during this fun, interesting activity.

4. Staple each sign to a paint-stirring stick.

5. During play time, provide riding vehicles and wagons for the children to use. Stand with the Stop and Go signs in the location where "accidents" are most likely to occur.

6. Regulate the children's movement using the Stop and Go signs.

More to Do: Extensions and Adaptations

- Observe the children's interest. If they are interested in signs, take a group for a walk and look for signs. There will be signs for speed limits and the names of streets, yield signs, and danger signs. Ask children what additional signs they would like to make for the playground.

- Ask family members to help their children notice signs and talk about what they say and what they mean.

Suggested Book: *Red, Stop! Green, Go! An Interactive Book of Colors* by P. D. Eastman

Opportunities for Learning

- Social development: The children will share space and materials with other children. They will imitate other children and enjoy being with them.

- Language development: The children will understand and use new vocabulary, such as the names of vehicles, *seat belt, safe, stop, go, sign, green*, and *red*.

- Literacy development: The children will recognize symbols (the words on the Stop and Go signs are symbols).

- Cognitive development: The children will use pretend play to increase understanding of culture, environment, and experiences.

- Physical/Motor development: The children will use fine-motor and gross-motor skills as they ride their vehicles and pull their wagons.

Sensory/Science

Purpose of a Sensory/Science Learning Area

Most of the activities in this book are basically sensory and science activities. Young children use all their senses in activities that promote the following:

- Curiosity: Bring in materials that are new and different to children, such as sandpaper, contact paper, and glue with glitter in it.

- Sense of wonder: Wonder aloud with the children: "I wonder what will happen if I squeeze (drop, bang, throw) this object." "I wonder what the little bear will do next." "I see you are wondering what will happen if you put this block on top of the others."

- Exploring the unexpected: Children wonder about and explore materials, objects, and people more when the unexpected happens. For example, they may place an object with no hole in the middle with the rings that go on a stacking toy. They may place an item that sinks with items that float. Watch a child's eyes when he believes that when you drop an item it drops, but then he sees a toy airplane take off into the sky.

- Experimenting: Observe as children experiment. They may be thinking, "What if I push this button? What if I push the button softly? What if I hammer the button? What if I dump out these blocks? What noises can I make with my lips? How can I get a reaction out of a peer?"

- Testing hypotheses: Observe as they test a hypothesis, such as that balls bounce. Give them several balls and watch as they seem to be asking with their actions, "Do all balls bounce? How high do they bounce? Do some balls bounce higher than others? Are there balls that do not bounce? What else bounces? What else do balls do?"

- Sensory development: The development of sight, smell, hearing, tasting, and touching.

If you'd like to create a sensory/science area for infants, toddlers, and two-year-olds, here are just a few materials, toys, and activities that support exploration.

Infant Sensory Area

The infant sensory learning area is often combined with the creative explorations learning area. In addition to items listed in the creative area for infants, the following materials and toys are added: sensory tubes and balls, fabric pieces of different textures, discovery bottles, clutching toys, and feely boxes with infant-safe materials and toys.

Please refer to the classroom diagram on page 120.

Toddler and Two-Year-Old Science/Sensory Learning Area

The furniture in this area includes water bins and/or tables; light tables; and sand tables and/or bins and shallow pans. Include utensils and equipment for the water and sand tables—cups, funnels, waterwheels, strainers, containers, shovels, and small buckets. Always include natural materials such as leaves, small tree rounds, and bark when you can. Add a feely box or two. Include board books on the five senses and on different materials such as water, sand, textures, and so on.

Please refer to the classroom diagram on page 120.

Feeling Feet, Feeling Good, and Gentle Touches

Materials

Sandpaper

Felt

Stuffed animal

Sponges

Hairbrush

Feather

What to Do

1. Gently stroke the infant's hands and feet while saying his name. Gentle touches help the infant feel safe and loved and help him learn his name.

2. Rub a feather across the infant's feet. Name the object and describe the feeling. For example, "The feather tickles your feet." Gently pass a piece of sandpaper across the soles of his feet. Say, "The sandpaper feels rough."

3. Let the baby touch other items that have interesting textures. Talk about how the items feel. Infants will try new and challenging experiences with the support of a familiar adult.

4. Hold a willing baby and touch a cool window with his hands and feet. Rub the foot gently across the window. Sometimes it makes a squeaking noise.

> ### What We Know
>
> Stress can be a brain changer. The structure of a baby's brain can change in a negative way if the baby experiences **toxic stress** (National Scientific Council on the Developing Child, 2005/2014). Watch for cues from the baby that he likes or dislikes an activity. Always help babies feel safe.

More to Do: Extensions and Adaptations

- Throughout the activity, look carefully for cues from the infant that he is enjoying the activity or is becoming distressed. Some babies are very sensitive to touch and may like the hairbrush but not the feather.

- Try this on several days. Infants benefit when activities are repeated. They learn something new each time.

Suggested Books:

Baby Touch and Feel: Animals by DK Publishing

Touch and Feel Baby Animals by Scholastic

Amazing Baby Feel and Learn! by Kids Preferred

Opportunities for Learning

- Emotional development: The children will show an awareness about self.

- Language development: The children will respond to and use a growing vocabulary as adults frequently read the books and talk about what the infants are seeing and feeling: *rough, smooth, shiny, scratchy, bumpy, furry, tickly.*

- Cognitive development: The children will use their senses to construct knowledge about the world as they touch and see different items in the room.

- Physical/Motor development: The children will develop fine-motor control as they use the small muscles in their hands to hold the safe items and touch the animals in the books.

I Can Make It Move

Materials

Long piece of elastic

Beach ball or inflatable toy

> **What We Know**
>
> A sense of self-worth develops when children successfully influence their environment.

What to Do

Ahead of Time:

1. Blow up a beach ball or another large inflatable toy.

2. Hang it from the ceiling using elastic.

3. Position the object just a few inches off the floor.

With the Children:

1. Position the infants within kicking or touching distance of the object.

2. Be sure to comment whenever the infants move the ball. "Look what you did! You moved the ball." **SAFETY ALERT:** Supervise closely so that the children do not pull the ball down or get tangled in the elastic.

3. As the children explore the ball, they will maintain focus and demonstrate persistence with support from an adult. This is the beginning of self-regulation and executive functioning. They will also show interest in and curiosity about objects, materials, or events.

More to Do: Extensions and Adaptations

For Young Infants:

- Observe the infant with the ball. The first time the infant makes the ball move it may be an accident. However, does the infant repeat an action to get the same effect?
- Observe the child's thinking: Does the infant poke, push, or hit the ball to make it work? How does this change over time?

For Older Infants:

Position the ball so that a sitting infant can touch the ball. Again, supervise closely so that the children do not pull the ball down or get tangled in the elastic.

Opportunities for Learning

· • • ● • • ·

- Emotional development: The children will develop a sense of identity and belonging. They will show an awareness of self and confidence in their own abilities in relationships with others.
- Language development: The children will use nonverbal communication and language (coos, babbles, first words) to engage others in interaction. They will learn new words such as *ball, hands, feet*, and the phrase "you did it!"
- Cognitive development: The children will develop expectations for how objects, toys, and people work and how they can make them work. They will use understanding of cause and effect to act on the social and physical environment. They will use a variety of strategies to solve problems, such as figuring out how to make the beach ball move.
- Physical/Motor development: The children will demonstrate eye-hand coordination and fine-motor skills when they move the ball with their hands or feet. They will develop gross-motor skills when they use the large muscles in their legs to kick.

Senses on the Move:
See, Feel, Listen, Smell, and Maybe Even Taste

Materials

None

What to Do

1. Slowly walk around the room with a baby. A young baby will have his head on your shoulder or chest. An older baby will hold up his head to see while feeling safe in your arms.

2. Stand near something interesting such as a hanging mobile, so the baby can see it and touch it, if it is safe to touch. Encourage the infant to listen to the sounds of the mobile.

3. Talk about what the baby is seeing or hearing. Say, "Look at the shiny mobile. See the colors. Here is red and here is blue," as you point to the colors.

4. Find items in the room that the infant can touch, smell, and for older infants, maybe even taste. Infants will try new and challenging experiences with the support of a familiar adult.

5. Continue until the baby has had a chance to see four or five interesting things or until he grows tired of the activity.

Suggested Books:

What I Hear by Alex Appleby

What I See by Alex Appleby

What I Touch by Alex Appleby

What I Taste by Alex Appleby

What I Smell by Alex Appleby

Song: (Sing to the tune of "Way Down Yonder in the Pawpaw Patch.")

> *Where, oh where is the window?* (pretend to be looking for the window)
> *Where, oh where is the window?*
> *Where, oh where is the window?*
> *Boo! I see the window!* (go to the window and touch it)

Sing about any item, such as a mobile, a rattle, or applesauce.

- Emotional development: The children will manage emotions with the support of a familiar adult.

- Language development: The children will respond to and use a growing vocabulary as adults frequently read books and talk about what the infants are seeing, feeling, smelling, hearing, and tasting: *rough, smooth, shiny, scratchy, bumpy, furry, tickly, loud, soft, yummy, not yummy,* color words, and shape words.

- Cognitive development: The children will use their senses to construct knowledge about the world as they interact with different items in the room.

- Physical/Motor development: The children will develop fine-motor control as they use the small muscles in their hands to touch items that are safe.

Baby Mirrors

Materials

Small handheld unbreakable mirror

What to Do

1. While holding an infant or while the infant is lying on his back, hold the mirror to one side of the infant's face.

2. Ask, "Where's the baby?" to draw the baby's attention to the mirror.

3. When the baby focuses on the mirror, slowly move the mirror over the baby's face from one side to the other. Keep the mirror in his line of vision.

4. Ask, "Where's the baby? See the baby?" This will encourage the baby to follow the mirror as it moves.

5. Continue until the mirror is on the opposite side of the baby's face.

More to Do: Extensions and Adaptations

- Place unbreakable child-safe mirrors around the room. Encourage the babies to look at their own images.

What We Know

While infants won't recognize themselves in the mirror, they will enjoy the sensory experience of seeing, hearing, and touching the infants in the mirror.

- When you read the book *Where's the Baby?* by Pat Hutchins, the phrase, "Where's the baby?" is repeated often. When you say the phrase, hold the small mirror up to the baby and show him his own image.

- If the baby smiles in the mirror, say, "You seem happy. You are smiling. I love your smile," and then smile back at the baby.

- Try to have both the baby's and your face show in the mirror. Point to your nose. Watch to see if some older infants look from your face to your face in the mirror. Point to the baby's nose while looking in the mirror.

Suggested Books:

Where's the Baby? by Pat Hutchins

Baby Loves by Michael Lawrence

Hello Baby! by Lizzy Rockwell

Opportunities for Learning

- Emotional development: The children will begin to understand and express emotions. They will develop a sense of self when they look in a mirror.

- Language development: The children will understand feeling words, such as *happy*, their names, *mirror, look*, "it's you," and "where is baby?"

- Cognitive development: The children will learn the connection between their feelings and their actions (cause and effect). They will learn that when they are sad, an adult will comfort them, and when they are angry, an adult will help them manage that anger in helpful ways.

Texture Blanket

Materials

Baby blanket

5" x 5" (or larger) fabric squares: wool, velvet, corduroy, burlap, satin, terrycloth, fake fur

Sewing machine (adult use only)

What We Know

Sensory explorations, enjoyed with peers and adults or by themselves, build cognitive, emotional, and physical skills in young children. They also support curiosity and a love of learning.

The Encyclopedia of Infant and Toddler Activities for Children Birth to 3

Fabric scissors (adult use only)

What to Do

Ahead of Time:

1. Cut out 5" x 5" or larger squares from a variety of fabrics.

2. Use a sewing machine to attach the fabric squares to the baby blanket. Make sure to stitch everything well, as this blanket will be handled by infants and washed often.

With the Children:

1. Place the blanket on the floor where infants can feel it or crawl across it.

2. Let the babies explore the blanket independently. They will be intrigued by the varying textures. They will try new and challenging experiences and use a variety of strategies to solve problems as they explore the blanket.

3. Sit near the babies as they crawl on and touch the blanket. Comment on what they are feeling: "Oh, the satin is so soft, isn't it?" "The corduroy is scratchy. It feels bumpy too." "Feel this furry part."

4. Wash the blanket frequently.

More to Do: Extensions and Adaptations

Support infants as they touch other things in the room every day. Talk about how objects, skin, or food feels and looks—*rough, smooth, shiny, scratchy, bumpy, furry.* (But not too much furry food!)

Suggested Book: *Geraldine's Blanket* by Holly Keller

Opportunities for Learning
· · · • · · · •

- Emotional development: The children will develop a positive sense of identity and confidence in what they do.

- Language development: The children will respond to and use a growing vocabulary as adults frequently read books and talk about what the infants are seeing and feeling.

- Cognitive development: The children will use their senses to construct knowledge about the world as they touch different types of fabrics.

- Physical/Motor development: The children will develop large- and small-muscle control as they move and touch the fabrics.

Texture Crawl

Materials

Fabric in a variety of textures: wool, velvet, corduroy, burlap, satin, terrycloth, fake fur

Scissors (adult use only)   Cardboard

Bubble wrap   Gauze pads

Contact paper   Duct or packing tape

Glue

What to Do

Ahead of Time:

1. Cut out large (10" x 10" or larger) squares from the fabric, bubble wrap, and gauze pads.

2. Glue the squares to matching pieces of cardboard.

3. Use tape to attach contact paper (sticky side up) to the other side of each cardboard square.

With the Children:

1. Lay the squares on the floor, texture side up, for the infants and crawlers to explore. Comment on what the children are feeling or wondering as they experience the textures.

2. Keep the squares clean by not walking on them.

3. Pick up the squares when the babies are not actively involved with exploring them. Place them along a wall for crawling infants and toddlers to explore.

Opportunities for Learning

- Emotional development: The children will develop a positive sense of identity and confidence in what they do.

- Language development: The children will respond to and use a growing vocabulary as adults talk about what the infants are seeing and feeling.

- Cognitive development: The children will use their senses to construct knowledge about the world as they touch different textures.

- Physical/Motor development: The children will develop large- and small-muscle control as they move and touch the fabrics.

Flashlight Watch

Materials

Flashlight

What to Do

1. Darken the room and turn on a flashlight or a penlight.

2. Let the infants, toddlers, and two-year-olds track the beam as it moves slowly around the room.

3. Talk quietly about where the beam is going—high, low, forward, backward, on the chair, under the table, and so on.

4. This can be very soothing for fussy children. Novel experiences support children's curiosity.

More to Do: Extensions and Adaptations

For Toddlers and Two-Year-Olds:

● Encourage toddlers to hold the flashlights and shine the lights around the room.

● Observe how they experiment with holding the flashlight and moving it where they want it to go.

● Wrap colored cellophane around the end of the flashlight. Encourage children to experiment with different colored cellophane and guess what color will show on the wall. **SAFETY ALERT:** Supervise closely.

● Encourage two children to move their flashlights and beams together in a dance.

● Play a language game. Ask one child to point to an object in the room with his flashlight beam. Everyone else can guess what the beam is shining on.

● Talk about light and dark. Encourage family members to talk with children about the words and concepts of light and dark.

Suggested Book: *Sam and the Firefly* by P. D. Eastman

What We Know

Each child will have a different comfort level with sensory experiences. Watch for children who enjoy them and for those who seem overwhelmed with textures, lights, noise, and smells. Some children can experience sensory overload. Some children need and enjoy more sensory experiences.

Opportunities for Learning

- Cognitive and Motor development: The children will problem solve and use their fine-motor skills as they struggle to figure out how to hold the flashlight and control where the beam goes.

- Language development: The children will learn new vocabulary, such as *up, down, backward, forward*, colors, and names of items in the room, as adults use these words often in context.

- Cognitive development: The children will develop spatial understandings as they adapt their movements to the space provided.

- Physical/Motor development: The children will develop eye-hand coordination and perceptual skills.

I Can Feel It

Materials

Large pieces of felt

Velcro dots and strips

Variety of textured material, such as wool, velvet, cotton, bubble paper, corrugated cardboard, gauze pad, tiles, corduroy, burlap, satin, terrycloth, or fake fur

Scissors (adult use only)

What to Do

Ahead of Time:

1. Toddlers and two-year-olds love to explore and touch things. Create a magnificent texture board for them to touch.

2. Attach a large piece of felt to the wall using Velcro strips. Be sure to place it low enough that it is within easy reach of infants and toddlers.

3. Cut small pieces of a variety of textured materials.

4. Attach the textured pieces to the felt using the sticky hook side of the Velcro dots.

With the Children:

Observe how toddlers and two-year-olds explore the different textures. Do children gesture or talk to each other? As they explore, the children will show interest in and curiosity about objects and materials. Ask, "Does the velvet feel rough or smooth?" "Does the tile feel soft or hard?" "Which one would you like to take to bed with you?" "Which ones feel soft?" "Which ones feel rough?"

More to Do: Extensions and Adaptations

- Cut pieces of felt to cover each of the attached textured material pieces and make it a "Peekaboo Feel It" board.
- Extend the activity into other parts of the room and different times of the day by encouraging children to touch items in each area of the room and describe the textures.

Suggested Books:

My First Opposites by Max and Sid

Opposites by Sandra Boynton

What's Up, Duck? A Book of Opposites by Tad Hills

Opportunities for Learning

- Social development: The children will show interest in, interact with, and develop personal relationships with peers.

- Language development: The children will use nonverbal communication and language to engage others to learn and gain information. They will learn the names of textures, *same, different, rough, smooth, soft,* and *hard*.

- Cognitive development: The children will actively explore objects and learn the names of different textures. They will recognize differences between familiar and unfamiliar objects, which are memory and sorting skills. They will use matching and sorting of objects to understand similar and different characteristics, which is emergent mathematical thinking.

- Physical/Motor development: The children will use perceptual information to direct their own actions, experiences, and interactions.

Texture Box

Materials

Large shoe box with lid

Various sensory materials, such as duct tape, Velcro, cotton, fake fur, velvet, and playdough

Scissors (adult use only)

What to Do

Ahead of Time:

1. Cut a hole in the top of the box large enough for a child to put his hand inside the box.

2. Place various objects inside the box.

With the Children:

1. Place the box in the sensory area of the room. Observe how children play with the box. Do they guess what the object is or do they peek inside? What do children say to each other about the objects?

2. On another day, sit in the area and encourage children to try to guess what they are feeling. Encourage them to use descriptive language to describe what they are feeling. If they cannot, then ask them a choice question: "Is it soft or hard?" "Is it rough or smooth?" "Where would you use it?"

3. As the children investigate the box and explore the textures, they will demonstrate interest in and curiosity about objects. They will manage feelings and emotions with the support of familiar adults.

More to Do: Extensions and Adaptations

- Extend the activity into other parts of the room and times of the day by encouraging children to touch items in each area of the room and describe the textures.
- Notice and document what descriptive words toddlers and two-year-olds use. Do they say, for example, *pretty, hot, cold, soft*, or *hard*?

Suggested Books:

Tails by Matthew Van Fleet

Fuzzy, Fuzzy, Fuzzy! By Sandra Boynton

- Emotional development: The children will show confidence in their own abilities.

- Social development: The children will interact with others as several children sit by each other to play the game.

- Language development: The children will increase vocabulary, such as the names of items in the box, *hole, in, out,* the phrase "pull it out," and texture words—*rough, smooth, bumpy, soft, hard.*

- Literacy development: The children will recognize pictures and some symbols, signs, or words when teachers read books to them.

- Cognitive development: The children will actively explore objects to understand themselves, others, and objects. They will use matching and sorting of objects to understand similar and different characteristics, which is mathematical thinking. They will use reasoning to solve problems as they describe the objects and guess what they are.

- Physical/Motor development: The children will use perceptual information (touch, hearing, and vision) to understand objects.

Let's Dance

Materials

Recordings of music from different cultures

Colorful scarves or streamers

What to Do

Ahead of Time:

1. Ask families to contribute CDs or send links to songs on YouTube that are representative of their cultures, explaining that the songs will be used to begin building awareness of the different sounds and rhythms of music.

2. Download music from different genres and a variety of cultures.

With the Children:

1. Play some music for a short time each day.

2. Involve infants and young toddlers by holding them and moving them around or swaying with them to the beat of the music.

3. Provide older children with scarves and streamers to wave and sway to the rhythm of the music.

4. Ask if two older children want to hold hands as they dance. Small groups of older toddlers and two-year-olds can dance together.

5. Provide full-length mirrors so infants can see themselves dancing with adults and children can see themselves dancing.

More to Do: Extensions and Adaptations

- Take the music and scarves outside so children can move freely with their scarves blowing in the wind.

- Invite family members to visit and play music so that children can dance to it.

- Provide posters of people of different cultures dancing.

Suggested Books:

Giraffes Can't Dance by Giles Andreae

Barnyard Dance! by Sandra Boynton

Opportunities for Learning

- Emotional development: The children will develop self-regulation (executive functioning) as they maintain focus and sustain attention with the support of familiar adults.

- Social development: The children will show interest in, interact with, and develop personal relationships with peers as they dance together and possibly hold hands while dancing.

- Language development: The children will respond to the rhythm of the music.

- Cognitive development: The children will use spatial awareness to understand movement in space.

- Physical/Motor development: The children will develop both gross-motor and fine-motor skills as they use the large muscles in their body to dance and their small muscles to hold on to scarves and streamers.

Water Table Fun—Flotation Experiment

Materials

Water table or individual bins

Assortment of objects that sink or float: corks, sponges, plastic lids, plastic animals, rocks, small toy boats, rubber tubes, and so on

Water

What to Do

1. Fill the water table or individual bins with water. **SAFETY NOTE:** Always supervise children closely around water.

2. Explain the safety rules that go along with water play. Remind the children that the water stays in the bins or table. Explain that if water gets on the floor, children and teachers could slip and fall.

3. Put all the objects within the children's reach and observe as they experiment with the objects. Comment occasionally to describe what they are doing: "Sherard, the rock sank to the bottom." "Denise, that leaf is floating."

4. After the children have played for a while, ask them, "Which items float?" "Which items sink?"

5. The children will maintain focus and sustain attention with support as they play with the water and experiment with floating and sinking. They will show interest in and curiosity about objects, materials, events as objects appear (bob up) and disappear (sink). They will use a variety of strategies to solve problems as they experiment with objects.

More to Do: Extensions and Adaptations

For Toddlers and Two-Year-Olds:

● Some children will need their own bin of water because of sensory issues. Place four bins in a square so children can see and talk with each other as they experiment.

● On most other days, continue providing unique materials for children to use to pour, dump, fill, sieve, pick up, move, and experiment with water.

For Two-Year-Olds:

Provide two empty containers near the water table. On one, tape to the side a picture of objects floating and the word *float* written on paper. On the other container, tape a picture of objects sinking and the word *sink*. After children decide that an object floats or sinks, ask them to place it in the float or sink container. Provide duplicates of objects. Children probably will test each item even though a duplicate item has been determined to float or sink. They are testing their theory about which items float or sink. Count the items that sink and those that float.

Opportunities for Learning

- Emotional development: The children will show confidence in their own abilities through relationships with others.

- Social development: The children will learn to use adults as resources to meet their needs as they want hands wiped or want utensils. They will imitate and engage in play with other children.

- Language development: The children will understand and use an increasing number of words in communication with others: *water table, up, down, appear, disappear, sink, float, blocks, boat, corks, sponges, lids.*

- Literacy development: The children will recognize pictures and some symbols, signs, or words.

- Cognitive development: The children will explore people and objects to understand themselves, others, and objects. They will develop a sense of number and quantity. They will sort objects to understand similar and different characteristics, which is mathematical thinking. They will use memory as a foundation for more complex actions and thoughts.

- Physical/Motor development: The children will develop fine-motor control as they use the small muscles in their hands to adjust their reach and grasp to hold objects.

Sand Table Fun—Animal Hunt

Materials

Sand

Sand table or small bins inside or a sandbox outside

Plastic animals

Shovels, cups

What We Know

Unexpected outcomes about objects or events enhance young children's learning and information seeking (Stahl and Feigenson, 2015). Children will be surprised when they find animals buried in the sand table. They will wonder, "What will I find next?"

What to Do

Ahead of Time:

Hide plastic animals in the sand. Choose plastic animals that represent the animals in the books suggested below. Provide enough animals so that each child in the small group can find one or two.

With the Children:

1. Read one or more of the books about animals to small groups of children.

2. Let them play in the sand and discover the animals. As they play, they will demonstrate emerging initiative and curiosity.

3. Document their surprise, curiosity, and desire to explore. Record the language that they use for their portfolios or for a documentation panel.

4. Talk about the names of the animals: "Shamonda, you found a cat!"

More to Do: Extensions and Adaptations

- Add or hide animals that enhance the content of books that you read to children. For example, add dinosaur figures if you are reading a book about dinosaurs.

- In the room or outside on the playground, hunt for stuffed animals represented in the books.

Suggested Books:

We're Going on a Bear Hunt by Michael Rosen and Helen Oxenbury

Baby Touch and Feel Animals by DK Publishing

Song: (Sing to the tune of "The Farmer in the Dell.")

> *A-hunting we will go,*
> *A-hunting we will go.*
> *Heigh-ho, the derry-o,*
> *A-hunting we will go.*
>
> (Child's name) *finds a cat.*
> (Child's name) *finds a cat.*
> *Heigh-ho, the derry-o,*
> *A-hunting we will go.*

Opportunities for Learning

· ·· · ● ● · · · ·

- Emotional development: The children will demonstrate positive feelings about themselves.

- Social development: The children will develop relationships and a sense of belonging with other children.

- Language development: The children will learn new vocabulary, such as the names of animals, *in, out, under, sand, hidden,* and *hiding.*

- Cognitive development: The children will recall information as they remember the names of animals. They will use objects or symbols to represent something else (plastic animals and pictures of animals in books represent real animals). They will learn about object permanence—that objects still exist even when they are out of sight.

- Physical/Motor development: The children will develop perceptual skills as they look for animals. They will develop fine-motor skills as they use the small muscles in their hands to handle toys and use shovels to find animals.

Section 3
ROUTINES

- Arrival
- Fingerplays, Songs, and Rhymes
- Transitions
- Snack Time
- Nap Time
- Cleanup
- Departure

Arrival

· • ● ● ● ● ● •

Terrific Today

Materials

Whiteboard

Dry-erase markers (adult use only)

What to Do

1. Hang the whiteboard outside your classroom door, or just inside the door, at the adults' eye level.

2. Each morning, write information to the families about the day. For example, you could write:

   Terrific Tuesday
   - Choice/play time
   - Singing a new song—"Twinkle, Twinkle, Little Star"
   - Silly Shoe Mixup
   - Walk outdoors

3. Family members can talk with their child about what to expect for that day. Also, encourage family members to point to specific letters and words: "Look, Sarai. This word *sing* starts with the same letter as your name! *S* for *Sarai* and *s* for *sing*.

More to Do: Extensions and Adaptations

For Infants:

Sing the song if you know it. Wait for the infant to take a turn making sounds.

What We Know

The number of words that infants and toddlers know predicts their language, behavior, and early reading as preschoolers. Children need to have interactive, turn-taking conversations to learn language.

For Toddlers and Two-Year-Olds:

- Read the words on the board to the child.

- Find the letters on the board that are in the child's name.

- Ask the child what he or she would like to do today.

- Greet a peer by name while talking about the day. "Oh look! Reggie is here today. Hello, Reggie."

Suggested Book: *Twinkle, Twinkle, Little Star* by Caroline Jayne Church

Opportunities for Learning

· · ● · ● ● ● · ● · ·

- Language development: The children will develop the ability to communicate. They need rich communication interactions to learn to communicate well.

- Literacy development: The children will develop foundations for reading and writing as they learn that those squiggly lines have meaning, begin to learn the names of letters, and begin to recognize a few familiar words in a natural, meaningful way.

Welcome Bulletin Board

Materials

Photograph of each child

Scissors (adult use only)

Marker

Stapler or tape

Colorful paper

Glue

Bulletin board by entrance

What We Know

Children usually do not recognize themselves in a mirror until between eighteen and twenty-four months of age. Many toddlers have practice seeing and naming themselves in photos on a smartphone, so this skill may appear earlier than recognizing themselves in a mirror.

What to Do

1. Take a photograph of each child or ask families for one.

2. Decide on a theme, such as flowers, snowflakes, or leaves. Make one theme-related shape for each child.

3. Attach each child's picture to a shape. Write the child's first name under the photo.

4. Add the photographs to the bulletin board with a catchy title, such as "Friendships Are Blooming," "Each Snowflake Is Special," or "Fantastic Fall Friendships."

5. Encourage families to go to the bulletin board with their child each morning. Talk about the children's names, flowers, leaves, and snowflakes. Say to an infant, "(Child's name) is your friend." For older children, say, "Tell me about your friends."

6. The children will build their memory skills as they begin to remember the names of familiar peers.

More to Do: Extensions and Adaptations

For Infants:

Point to the child's photo and say the child's name. Point to photos and say the names of other children in the room.

For Toddlers:

Encourage the child to point to his or her photo. Talk about the other children in the room.

For Two-Year-Olds:

Use Velcro to attach the photos to the shapes. Place the photos on a felt board below the bulletin board. Encourage the children to find their photo and place the photo by their name on the shape. More advanced—match another child's name to his or her photo. If the bulletin board is within children's reach, it can be used for "Who's Here Today?"

Opportunities for Learning

· • · ● · • ·

- Emotional development: The children will begin to develop a sense of self as they recognize their photos and say their names.

- Social development: The children will begin to develop a sense of self with others and relationships with peers as they look at the photos on the bulletin board.

- Literacy development: The children will build foundations for reading when they see their printed names under each photo. Older toddlers and two-year-olds may begin to recognize their names and learn their letters for a purpose.

- Cognitive development: The children will begin to learn about symbols—that shapes, photos, pictures, or words represent something real (a child, a leaf, a snowflake).

Welcome Song

Materials

None

What to Do

1. Sing the following song to the tune of "Mary Had a Little Lamb." You can sing it when each child arrives.

2. Encourage the children to clap and give a cheer when prompted by the song.

> (Child's name) *came to school today,*
> *School today, school today.*
> (Child's name) *came to school today,*
> *We are so glad (she's, he's) here.* (clap or give a cheer)

More to Do: Extensions and Adaptations

For Infants:

Sing to the infant. Change the last line of the song to, "I'm so glad you're here." Smile at and cuddle the infant.

For Toddlers and Two-Year-Olds:

- Sit on the floor and invite toddlers and two-year-olds to join you. Sing the song as you point to each child. Other toddlers and two-year-olds may come over to join the group. Let a child leave as she pleases. As a child waits to hear the song about her, she will learn to wait for a turn and attend to other children. This is difficult for many young children.

- Comment on how each child seems to feel. "Carl seems happy right now. Look, he is smiling."

- After singing about a child, ask, "How are you feeling today?" Use the feeling words that the children in your group may understand; for example, ask, "Are you feeling happy or sad?" as you make a happy or sad face.

- Change the last line of the song to, "We're so glad we're friends."

- Create a laminated photo of each child that is large enough for a child to hold. Give the child her photo or hold it up as you sing the song.

Animal Adventure

Materials

Play tunnel or chairs and a sheet

Flashlights

Stuffed animals

What to Do

Ahead of Time:

1. Set up a play tunnel near the door for arrival times. If you don't have a tunnel, use chairs with a sheet over them. Do not block the doorway. Provide room for children to enter the room who do not want to go through the tunnel.

2. Put a few stuffed bears and other animals in the tunnel and a few at the end for the children to find.

With the Children:

1. When each child arrives, ask whether he wants to go through the tunnel on an adventure and look for stuffed bears and other animals.

2. Give each child a flashlight as he enters the tunnel.

What We Know

Many older infants and toddlers can understand simple directions, such as, "Go get your coat." Two-year-olds can understand more complex directions, "Get the ball and take it to Henry."

The Encyclopedia of Infant and Toddler Activities for Children Birth to 3

3. After the child has gone through the tunnel, ask her what she saw. Encourage the children to tell you the names of the animals they find. The children may want to do this repeatedly.

4. Some children may want to hold a stuffed animal rather than leave it in the tunnel. Provide enough animals so that each child can hold one.

5. As the children investigate the tunnel, they will show curiosity, which is supported by novel experiences. Some children will be fearful of entering the tunnel. They will be taking a risk as they enter it.

More to Do: Extensions and Adaptations

For Toddlers and Two-Year-Olds:

- If a child is fearful of entering the tunnel, look in from the other end so the child can see you.
- Make the tunnel shorter for children who may be fearful.

For Two-Year-Olds:

- Make the tunnel longer with some curves so children can't see the end.
- Count the number of animals that they saw.

Suggested Books:

We're Going on a Bear Hunt by Michael Rosen and Helen Oxenbury

Baby Touch and Feel: Animals by DK Publishing

Rhyme:

We're Going on a Bear Hunt
We're goin' on a bear hunt.
We're going to catch a big one.
I'm not scared!
What a beautiful day!
Uh-uh!
Grass!
Long wavy grass.
We can't go over it.
We can't go under it.
Oh no!
We've got to go through it!
Swishy swashy! Swishy swashy! Swishy swashy!

Add verses for water, rocks, trees, and so on.

Matching Photos

Materials

2 copies of a photograph of each child with a family member

Construction paper

Scissors (adult use only)

Clear contact paper

Child-size table and chairs

What to Do

Ahead of Time:

1. Make sure you have two of each photograph. **Note:** Let the families know that you will be covering the photographs with contact paper. If needed, make a copy and return the original photo to them.

2. Mount each photograph on a piece of construction paper. Cover the photo and construction-paper backing with contact paper, sealing them together. Trim the contact paper as needed.

3. Lay the photos on the table in a mixed-up pile.

With the Children:

1. Give each child her photograph and ask her to find a photo on the table that is the same. You may first need to demonstrate how to find the matching photo.

2. Encourage the child to talk about what she sees in the photo.

More to Do: Extensions and Adaptations

For Infants:

- Show infants the two photos that are alike, and talk about how they are alike. Imitate the sounds that the infant makes and wait for the infant to take a language turn.

- Point out the infant's nose and eyes in the picture and your own nose and eyes. Say the rhyme listed below while gently pointing at the infant's nose and eyes.

For Toddlers and Two-Year-Olds:

- Encourage several toddlers or two-year-olds to come to the table together and find the photos of their friends.

- Talk about how families may differ; for example, "Here is Jake with his dad." "Here is Tamara with her mother." "Here is Gabe with his dog, cat, mother, and father."

- Read the story listed below in an interactive way to children. Encourage conversation about noses and ears.

- Place an upright mirror next to the table. Encourage toddlers and two-year-olds to compare how they look in the photo to how they look today. While infants and younger toddlers often will not recognize themselves in a mirror, it is important to give them opportunities to look at themselves while an adult names them. As you look in the mirror, you can say, "Look, there is Zoey," as you point to the child.

Suggested Book: *Toes, Ears, and Nose! A Lift-the-Flap Book* by Marion Dane Bauer and Karen Katz

Fingerplay:

> *Here are* (child's name)*'s eyes.* (gently touch eyelid)
> *Here is* (child's name)*'s nose.* (gently touch nose)
> *Touch the part that sees.*
> *Touch the part that blows.*

Opportunities for Learning

- Emotional development: The children will begin to develop a sense of self as they look at the photos of themselves (and others) and look in the mirror.

- Social development: The children will build relationships with others as they interact with peers and adults. They will build trust with adults who are responsive to them.

- Language development: The children will develop receptive language skills as they listen to language and participate in conversations. They will increase vocabulary as they learn the names of body parts and the concepts of same and different. They will use language skills as they participate in conversations.

- Cognitive development: The children will construct knowledge, think, and reason as they recall the names of their family members, pets, and friends. They will begin to learn about symbols—that words and pictures in books represent their real toes, ears, and nose.

Fingerplays, Songs, and Rhymes

Where, Oh Where?

Materials

Light blanket

What to Do

1. Infants love to play peekaboo. Here is a variation of the traditional game.

2. Hide the infant's toes with a light blanket. Sing the song to the tune of "Way Down Yonder in the Pawpaw Patch."

    Where, oh where are (infant's name)*'s toes?*
    Where, oh where are (infant's name)*'s toes?*
    Where, oh where are (infant's name)*'s toes?*
    Way down yonder under the blanket.

    Come on (infant's name)*, let's go find them.*
    Come on (infant's name)*, let's go find them.*
    Come on (infant's name)*, let's go find them.*
    Way down yonder under the blanket.
    Wiggle your toe-toes, now put 'em back under.
    Wiggle your toe-toes, now put 'em back under.
    Wiggle your toe-toes, now put 'em back under.
    Way down yonder under the blanket.

3. Cover the infant's hands with the blanket. Sing the song again, changing the word *toes* to *hands.*

4. Substitute other body parts, such as feet, fingers, knees, arms, and so on.

More to Do: Extensions and Adaptations

- Sing the song and look for Mommy, Daddy, brothers, sisters, pets, friends, relatives, and so on.

- Toddlers and two-year-olds may enjoy hiding your toes and singing the song with you.

Suggested Books:

Where Is Baby's Belly Button? by Karen Katz

Where Is Baby's Mommy? by Karen Katz

Stars Shining

Materials

None

What to Do

Recite the following rhyme, making the necessary gestures when indicated.

> *Stars shining*
> *Number, number one,* (stroke child's cheek with index finger)
> *Number two,* (stroke child's cheek with index and middle fingers)
> *Number three,* (stroke cheek with index, middle, and ring fingers)
> *Oh, my!*
> *Bye and bye, bye and bye.*
> *Oh, my! Bye and bye.*

Bunny Kiss

Materials

None

What to Do

Recite the following rhyme, rubbing noses with the child at the end of the rhyme.

> *Bunny kiss. Bunny kiss.*
> *Gotta give baby a bunny kiss.*
> *Bunny kiss. Bunny kiss.*
> *Gotta give baby a bunny kiss.*

More to Do: Extensions and Adaptations

Consider giving the child a stuffed animal to rub noses with at the end of the activity.

Baby's Little Nose

Materials

None

What to Do

Sing the following song to the tune of "Mary Had a Little Lamb." Older toddlers can sing along.

> (Child's name) *had a little nose,*
> *Little nose, little nose.*
> (Child's name) *had a little nose.*
> *It's oh so nice to touch.* (touch the child's nose)

Autumn Leaves Song

Materials

None

What to Do

Sing the following song to the tune of "London Bridge Is Falling Down."

> *Autumn leaves are falling down,* (wiggle fingers and slowly lower hands)
> *Falling down, falling down.*
> *Autumn leaves are falling down,*
> *All through the town.*

Red, yellow, orange, and brown,
Orange and brown,
Orange and brown.
Red, yellow, orange, and brown,
All through the town.

More to Do: Extensions and Adaptations

If you live in an area where leaves change and fall in the autumn, consider taking a walk to look at the leaves.

Suggested Book: *Red Leaf, Yellow Leaf* by Lois Ehlert

Tiny Worm

Materials

None

What to Do

Say the following rhyme, using your finger as the worm.

I saw a tiny worm wriggling on the ground.
He wriggled around, making not a sound.
He wriggled here,
He wriggled there,
And then he turned around.
He wriggled one more time then went into the ground! (hide finger inside fingers of opposite hand)

Snow Action Rhymes

Materials

None

The Encyclopedia of Infant and Toddler Activities for Children Birth to 3

What to Do

Recite the following rhymes, making the gestures when indicated. If appropriate, encourage the children to say the rhymes with you and/or move their hands to the words.

Snowflakes falling on the ground, (wiggle fingers from high to low)
Snowflakes falling all around, (wiggle fingers around body)
Snowflakes falling, one, two, three (count with fingers)
Snowflakes fall on you and me! (point to child, point to self)

One little snowflake fell on my hat. (show one finger, point to head)
Two little snowflakes fell on my cat. (show two fingers)
Three little snowflakes fell on a tree. (show three fingers)
Four little snowflakes fell on me! (show four fingers, point to self)

Suggested Book: *The Snowy Day* by Ezra Jack Keats

Where, Oh Where? Boo!

Materials

12" to 24" squares of sheer fabric (one per child)

What to Do

1. Give a scarf to each child. Show them how to put the scarves over their heads to cover their faces.

2. Sing the following song to the tune of "Way Down Yonder in the Pawpaw Patch."

   Where, oh where, oh where is (child's name)?
   Where, oh where, oh where is (child's name)?
   Where, oh where, oh where is (child's name)?
   Boo! I see you! (help children pull scarves from their heads)

3. The children will delight in this game and want to play over and over again.

More to Do: Extensions and Adaptations

For Infants:

Hold a scarf over the infant's head. Sing the song, and move the scarf away on the last line.

Willow Tree

Materials

None

What to Do

Invite the children to recite the following rhyme with you. Make the appropriate actions where indicated.

Bend your branches down (bend over at the waist)
To touch the ground. (touch your toes)
Wiggle your long limbs (wave your arms side to side)
And wave to the sky. (look up at the ceiling and wave)
A gust of strong wind (blow air through your lips)
Blows leaves all around. (fall to the ground)

Firefighter

Materials

None

What to Do

Recite the following rhyme with the children.

I'd like to be a firefighter
And drive my truck so fast. (pretend to drive)
I think I'd be too busy
To wave as I go past. (wave hand)

I'd hurry with the fire hose
And hear the people shout. (cup hand to ear)
I'd help squirt the water (pretend to hold hose)
And put the fire out.

Police Officer

Materials

None

What to Do

Say the following rhyme with the children. Encourage them to do the actions with you.

> *I'm a police officer.*
> *I stand just so.* (stand straight and tall)
> *Telling cars to stop,* (hold out hand to signal *stop*)
> *Telling cars to go.* (move hand to wave cars forward)

Where Is My Knee?

Materials

None

What to Do

1. Invite the children to sing the following song with you. Sing to the tune of "Frère Jacques." Encourage the children to make the gestures.

   > *Where is my knee?*
   > *Where is my knee?*
   > *It's right here.* (point to knee)
   > *It's right here.*
   > *Isn't it so wonderful?*
   > *Isn't it so wonderful?*
   > *I can bend.* (bend the knee)
   > *I can bend.*

2. Sing the song again, using other body parts. Be sure to add a function for the last two lines. For example:

   > *Where is my eye? . . . I can see.*
   > *Where is my finger? . . . I can point.*
   > *Where is my mouth? . . . I can chew or smile.*
   > *Where is my nose? . . . I can sniff or smell.*
   > *Where is my foot? . . . I can stand or step.*
   > *Where is my hand? . . . I can wave.*

Sharing Song

Materials

None

What to Do

Invite the children to sing with you. Sing to the tune of "Row, Row, Row Your Boat."

> *Share, share, share your toys.*
> *Share them every day.*
> *Happily, happily, happily, happily*
> *This is how we play.*

Snow

Materials

None

What to Do

Invite the children to do the actions of the following rhyme with you.

> *Snow is falling all around* (wiggle fingers and bring hands down)
> *Like sugar on the leaves and ground.*
> *Put on mittens, boots, and hat,* (pretend to put on mittens, boots, hat)
> *And build a snowman, round and fat.* (puff out cheeks, make a circle with arms)
> *Tromping around through swirling snow* (march around)
> *My fingers are frozen, my nose aglow.* (rub hands together, rub nose)

Until at last I am so frozen, (wrap arms around yourself and shiver)
I rush inside my cozy home. (run in place)
From the window I watch the storm. (peek through hands)
Wrapped in my blankie, snug and warm. (wrap arms around yourself)

Suggested Book: *The Snowy Day* by Ezra Jack Keats

Helpers

Materials

None

What to Do

Encourage the children to look at their hands as they recite the following rhyme with you.

> *My hands are helpers all day long.*
> *They help me do things; they are strong.*
> *They stay with me throughout the day*
> *To help me work and help me play.*

Hat Song

Materials

Hat for each child

What to Do

1. Invite a small group of children to sit in a circle.

2. Choose a child to start with. Recite the following rhyme, performing the actions when prompted.

> (Child's name) *has a hat,*
> *What do you think of that?*
> (He or she) *takes it off* (his or her) *head*

And puts it back on again.

3. Continue until each child gets a turn.

4. When the last child in the group takes off his hat, say:

> *Everybody* (say names of children) *has a hat.*
> *What do you think of that?*
> *They take them off their heads.*
> *And that's the end of that!*

5. The children will probably want to sing the song again. Sing it until you see that the children are ready for a new song. Ask the children to take their hats and put them back by their coats.

Jack in the Box

Materials

Large cardboard box

Markers or nontoxic paint and paintbrushes

What to Do

1. Invite the children to paint or draw on the outside of the box.

2. When the paint is dry, invite one child to get inside the box and crouch down so the flaps can be closed overhead.

3. As the first child hides, the other children can recite the following rhyme.

> (Child's name) *in the box,*
> *Oh so still.*
> *Will (he or she) come out?*
> *Yes, (he or she) will!* (child in box pops up)

4. This is a good activity to use at the beginning of the year to help the children learn each other's names.

More to Do: Extensions and Adaptations

Take photographs of the children as they pop out of the box. Create a class *Jack in the Box* book, and place it in the book area. Look at it with the children.

Splash!

Materials

Bar of soap

Washcloth

Shampoo bottle

Bath toy (optional)

What to Do

Invite the children to recite the following rhyme and make the gestures.

> *I love to take a bath each night*
> *In water bubbly, warm, and wet.* (pretend to feel the water with fingers)
> *I step in one foot* (pretend to step into bath)
> *Then the other.*
> *I wash my legs, my knees, and my back.* (pretend to wash these parts)
> *I scrub my ears, my arms, and my hair.*
> *Then I sit back and kick my feet!* (sit down and kick feet in air)
> *Splash! Splash! Splash!*

Houses

Materials

None

What to Do

1. Talk about different animal homes with the children. You might say, for example, that birds live in nests, bunnies live in holes in the ground, and bees live in hives.

2. Do the following fingerplay with the children.

> *This is a nest for the bluebird.* (cup hands, palms up)
> *This is a hive for the bee.* (put fists together, palm to palm)
> *This is a hole for a bunny rabbit.* (make a hole with fingers)
> *And this is a house for me.* (put fingertips together to make a peak)

Mary Wore Her Red Dress

Materials

None

What to Do

1. Invite the children to sit in a circle.

2. Tell the children to clap as you chant the following rhyme.

   Mary wore her red dress,
   Red dress, red dress.
   Mary wore her red dress
   All day long.

3. Invite the children to take turns standing in the middle of the circle. The child in the circle chooses an article of clothing to chant about. For example, if the child says, "Purple shirt," say, "We're going to sing about JaQuan's purple shirt!"

4. As the children clap, say:

   JaQuan wore his purple shirt, (child in the center can jump up and down)
   Purple shirt, purple shirt.
   JaQuan wore his purple shirt
   All day long.

5. Continue until all the children who want to have had a turn in the center of the circle.

What Are We Doing?

Materials

None

What to Do

1. Gather a small group of children in a circle.

2. Ask one child to stand in the center and do an action, such as jumping.

3. Invite the rest of the children to copy the child's action. As they do, ask, "What are we doing?"

4. Encourage them to answer, "Jumping! We're jumping!"

5. As the children jump, sing the following song to the tune of "Frère Jacques."

> *We are jumping.*
> *We are jumping.*
> *Yes, we are. Yes, we are.*
> *Now we are done.*
> *Now we are done.*
> *We just jumped.*
> *We just jumped.*

6. Ask for another volunteer, and repeat with a different action.

Puppet Sing-Along

Materials

Farm-animal puppets, one for each child

What to Do

1. Give each child a puppet.

2. Sing one verse of "Old MacDonald Had a Farm." Make sure to sing about an animal represented by one of the puppets.

3. Ask the children, "Who has the (animal name) puppet?" The child with that puppet will hold it up.

4. Encourage the child to make the animal noise for that puppet as you sing the verse again.

5. Repeat with other animals.

Transitions

Transition Alerts

Materials

Bell with a soft tone

Clear contact paper

Camera

Clearly defined spaces to place toys
and equipment (outdoors)

Shelves and/or bins (indoors)

Packing tape

Printer

What to Do

Ahead of Time:

1. Take photos of toys and materials that the children use in the classroom. Print these out, and cover them with contact paper for durability.

2. Tape the photos securely to the shelves and bins to indicate where these toys and materials belong.

3. Establish places outdoors where children are to put the outside toys before returning to the classroom. These might be bins for balls, sand toys, and trucks or parking spaces for riding toys.

With the Children:

1. Young children need to be alerted before a transition from one activity to another, so that they can finish what they are doing and prepare to change. Show the children the bell, and tell them that when they hear it, they will need to stop the activity they are doing in five minutes. It will take a little time to get the children accustomed to this. Give them practice.

2. Shortly before a transition, alert the children that you all will be going to (for example) the snack table in five minutes. Young children don't know what five minutes is, but if they hear it every day, then they will begin to understand.

3. Use the signal consistently to help the children understand that a transition is coming. A bell with a pleasant, soft tone will alert them without making an obnoxious noise that may cause them to feel stressed.

4. Show the children the bins and shelves indoors and the bins and parking spaces outdoors where they should put toys and materials when they hear the signal. Walk around the room or outdoors, move to the children's level, and support them as they clean up and prepare to transition. Remind them of what happens next.

5. Make a game out of picking up toys and, if needed, be specific in your directions. Say, "Meira, please pick up the red blocks. Now, put the red blocks on the shelf."

6. You can say, "When you are finished putting toys away, you can go stand by the door."

More to Do: Extensions and Adaptations

For Young Toddlers:

- Young toddlers often will need emotional and verbal support to pick up a toy or two and put it away. Use encouraging words, such as, "You are picking up the truck. Thank you!"

- Keep directions very simple and use gestures as you point to an object. Say, "Sawyer, see the red truck?" as you point to the truck. "Let's put it on the shelf." Then point to where the truck goes.

- Understand that young toddlers and children with autism may feel stressed unless they know what will happen next. Be emotionally available to these children. Sometimes a hug, a pat, or holding a hand will help a child feel safe during times of change.

For Toddlers:

- Toddlers may have difficulty stopping one activity and moving to another. Be patient. Toddlers need understanding words: "I know it is hard to stop playing with the blocks. Let's go see what we are having for snack."

- Encourage toddler peers to help each other and work together in a cooperative way.

Song: (Sing to the tune of "London Bridge Is Falling Down.")

> *It is time to have our snack,*
> *Have our snack, have our snack.*
> *It is time to have our snack.*
> *Let's all jump to the snack table.*

Change the lyrics to fit the next activity. For example, ". . . time to go outside," "Let's all walk . . . ."

If You Are Listening

Materials

None

What to Do

1. To capture children's attention and indicate that there will be a transition, chant the following:

   If you are listening to me, touch your head. (touch head)
   If you are listening to me, touch your head.
   If you are listening to me, touch your foot. (touch foot)
   If you are listening to me, touch your foot.
   If you are listening to me, raise your hands. (touch hands)
   If you are listening to me, raise your hands.

2. Continue to add body parts until all the children are listening. Then, give a simple direction about what will happen next.

3. Model the movements for the children. Wait after each line of the chant to scan the room to see who is listening. The children will increase their attention skills when adults help make transitions easier and fun.

What We Know

Older infants, toddlers, and two-year-olds are competent imitators. It is a primary way that they learn in interactions with adults and peers (Meltzoff, 2011).

More to Do: Extensions and Adaptations

For Toddlers and Two-Year-Olds:

- Substitute a child's name for the word *you*: "If Sarah is listening to me, touch your head."

- If you know that a child has a hearing impairment or difficulty transitioning, move close to that child so that you can provide physical support.

- Sing the song listed below until all the children are listening.

- Use specific admiration of children's listening and skills. For example, say, "Elijah is touching his head."

Song:

Head, Shoulders, Knees, and Toes
Head, shoulders, knees, and toes, knees and toes (touch each body part)
Head, shoulders, knees, and toes, knees and toes
Eyes and ears and mouth and nose.
Head, shoulders, knees, and toes, knees and toes

Opportunities for Learning

- Emotional development: The children will control their emotions and impulses as they stop one activity and get ready for a second activity. Young children are just learning how to do this and often need adult support to be successful.

- Social development: The children will develop the social and behavioral skills needed to participate successfully in groups. Social development with adults and peers blossoms as children experience the joy of participating together in an activity.

- Language development: The children will develop receptive and expressive language skills as they listen to the directions from the teacher and sing the songs. They will learn the names of their body parts and that words correspond with actions.

- Cognitive development: The children will observe and imitate sounds, words, gestures, actions, and behaviors.

- Physical/Motor development: The children will develop the small muscles in their hands and the large muscles in their arms and legs as they follow the different motor actions.

Off We Go

Materials

Train whistle

Conductor's hat

What to Do

1. When children need to move from one activity to another, put on a conductor's hat and use a train whistle.

2. Whistle gently and tell the children that it is time to go outdoors to play. Do not expect children to line up. Rather, ask them to follow you in a group. Say, "All aboard! We are going outside. Stay together."

3. Pretend that you and the children are a train. Model how to chug, chug and toot, toot like a train as you move. The children will use their imaginations as they pretend to be part of a train. They will develop curiosity and attention as they learn a new way to move together to go outside.

4. Remind the children of the safety rule: We keep ourselves and our friends safe.

More to Do: Extensions and Adaptations

For Infants:

Adults can hold children as they move together to go outside.

For Toddlers:

- Read books about trains so that children know what a train does.
- Young toddlers will need both verbal and physical support as they learn how to follow directions.
- Teachers can hold up a sign with a picture of a train on it.

For Two-Year-Olds:

- Teachers can hold up a sign with a picture of a train and the word *train*. This helps build literacy skills and a foundation for learning to read.
- Toddlers can form a line and hold on to a knotted (safe) rope.
- Toddlers can take turns pretending to be the engine and the caboose.

Suggested Book: *Here Comes the Train* by J.K. Ha

Song: (Sing to the tune of "The Wheels on the Bus.")

> *The wheels on the train go 'round and 'round,*
> *'Round and 'round, 'round and 'round.*
> *The wheels on the train go 'round and 'round,*
> *As we go outside.*
> *The children on the train say, "Toot, toot, toot,"*
> *"Toot, toot, toot, toot, toot, toot."*
> *The children on the train say, "Toot, toot, toot,"*
> *As we go outside.*

Opportunities for Learning

- Emotional development: The children will practice impulse control as they control their bodies to be a part of a group. Flexible but predictable routines help children feel safe.

- Social development: The children will enjoy how they feel when interacting with peers and will develop a sense of self with others.

- Language development: The children will learn new words and sing them as they hear a song repeated many times. When the book is read, they will learn color and counting words.

- Literacy development: The children will develop emergent literacy skills. Reading books, providing a photo of a train, or using the word *train* helps children learn that there are levels of representation from the real to the abstract. Levels of representation include, for example, a real train, a photo of a train, a drawing of a train, the sound of a train, a puzzle of a train, and the word *train*. Experiences with materials at different levels of representation provide a foundation for children learning to read the word.

- Physical/Motor development: The children will develop the large muscles in their bodies as they participate in a physical activity. They will learn to control their movements to be safe in a group and to keep their friends safe.

Gathering Together

Materials

None

What to Do

1. When you need to gather the children together, repeat the following rhyme several times.

   Point to the window,
   Point to the door,
   Point to the ceiling,
   And point to the floor.
   Point to your elbow,
   Point to your knee,
   Point to your shoulder,
   And walk to me.

   You can also use the chant when you are outdoors.

   Point to the sky,
   Point to the ground,
   Point to the tree,
   And walk to me.

2. This activity will increase children's attention skills.

More to Do: Extensions and Adaptations

For Toddlers:

- Toddlers may need you to repeat the chant many times and model where to point. As the children walk to you, say, "Thank you, Charlie. You walked to me."
- For children who have difficulty hearing or attending, move close to them to chant.

For Two-Year-Olds:

Say the chant without modeling to see where the children will point. Do this only if they are familiar with the chant. If they do not know where to point, then model pointing to the correct part of the room, outdoors, or a body part. When you do not model by pointing, then the children must listen closely to the words.

Opportunities for Learning

- Social development: The children will develop a sense of self with others and build relationships with peers when they gather together in small groups.

- Language development: The children will increase receptive language as adults use new and different words for body parts and say the words *sky, ground,* and *tree.* They will increase expressive language as they learn the words to the chants. They will increase vocabulary: *point to, window, door, ceiling, floor, elbow, knee, shoulder, sky, ground, tree,* and "walk to me."

- Physical/Motor development: The children will develop small-motor skills as they point and large-motor skills as they move toward you and with groups.

The Magic Wand

Materials

Rhythm stick or paper towel tube

Streamers

Glitter

Glue

What to Do

Ahead of Time:

Make a magic wand by decorating a rhythm stick or paper towel tube with glitter and streamers.

With the Children:

1. This is a great activity during transitions. It seems very simple, but works like magic! When you need children to listen and prepare for a new activity, wave your wand and say:

   Abracadabra
   Alla ka zogs
   All the children will now be dogs.
   Poof!

2. The children will start barking and acting like doggies.

3. Wave your wand and ask them to freeze!

4. Wave your wand again, and have them become another animal or object (just change the rhyme). For example, *zunkeys/monkeys*, *zair/chair*, and so on.

5. Be sure to turn them back into children when it is time to stop.

6. The children will show imagination in play and interactions with others as they pretend to be something that they are not.

More to Do: Extensions and Adaptations

For Toddlers:

- Toddlers may have a difficult time pretending to be a dog, cat, chair, and so on. Model for them what you want them to do.
- Read books with photos of dogs, cats, and other animals that you use in this game, so that children will begin to learn the names of animals. Practice the sounds that the animals make as you read the books.

For Toddlers and Two-Year-Olds:

- Hold up a picture of the animal or object that you are asking them to pretend to be.
- Many toddlers and two-year-olds will find it challenging to freeze and hold very still. They are just learning to control their bodies in this way. You can say, "You are trying so hard to stand very still."

For Two-Year-Olds:

- Many two-year-olds will be ready to pretend to be different animals and objects.
- Create peer cooperation by encouraging peers to work together to be a chair or a dog.

Song: "Old MacDonald Had a Farm" Say the sounds that each animal makes as you sing the song.

Suggested Books:

Animals and Their Sounds by Kim Berry

My Big Animal Book by Roger Priddy

My Very First Book of Animal Sounds by Eric Carle

My First Animals: Let's Squeak and Squawk! by DK Publishing

Opportunities for Learning

- Emotional development: The children will develop impulse control and self-regulation when they stop being one animal and become another and when they stand still when the teacher says, "Freeze."

- Social development: The children will interact with peers and build friendships when teachers ask the children to work together.

- Language development: The children will increase vocabulary by learning the names of the animals and objects.

- Literacy and Cognitive development: The children will learn about symbols—a photo of an animal is a representation or symbol of the real animal. Understanding symbols provides a basis for learning to read.

- Physical/Motor development: The children will develop perceptual skills when they look at a picture of an animal and then try to make the movement and sounds. Gross-motor skills grow as children use their large muscles in their arms and legs to move like different animals.

Yes or No

Materials

None

What to Do

1. Tell the children that they are going to play the Yes or No Game. This is a great game to play when children need to wait.

2. Start asking questions, but make sure the questions can only be answered with a yes or a no. In the beginning, try to use questions that have obvious answers.

   Some examples are:

   - Is the sky green?
   - Do you have two eyes?
   - Is snow hot?
   - Do you wear a coat when you take a bath?
   - Do dogs have tails?
   - Do your knees bend?
   - Does a bear say, "Meow"?

- Do you wear mittens on your feet?

3. The children will show interest, curiosity, and eagerness to learn as they listen for silly questions. Attentiveness develops as children listen to the questions.

More to Do: Extensions and Adaptations

For Toddlers:

If there are toddlers in the group, pair them with an older two-year-old. Some older toddlers may answer and some may imitate their older peers.

For Toddlers and Two-Year-Olds:

Take time to help children learn the meaning of the words in the questions. Go to the window and ask again, "Is the sky green?"

Suggested Book: *Down by the Bay* by Raffi

Song:

> **Down by the Bay** (adapted)
> *Down by the bay where the watermelons grow,*
> *Back to my home I dare not go.*
> *For if I do, my mother will say,*
> *"Have you ever seen a cat wearing a hat, down by the bay?"*
> *Down by the bay where the watermelons grow,*
> *Back to my home I dare not go.*
> *For if I do, my mother will say,*
> *"Have you ever seen a dog kissing a frog, down by the bay?"*

Make up easy rhymes that the children in your group will understand.

Opportunities for Learning

- Emotional development: The children will express a variety of emotions. Children will have fun and laugh as they say no or yes to silly questions. They will develop self-regulation as they learn to become quiet for the next question.
- Social development: The children will enjoy interacting with their peers.
- Language development: The children will develop receptive language abilities. These blossom as children listen to the words of the questions or to the words in the book and see a picture or a demonstration of the content of the questions.
- Cognitive development: The children will develop scientific knowledge as they learn about why we don't wear a coat when we take a bath or why we don't wear mittens on our feet.

Snack Time

Finger Foods

Materials

Small finger foods

Muffin tin

What to Do

1. Put a variety of foods in different sections of the muffin tin. Use finger foods that are safe and nutritious for the age of the children and that have been approved by the parents.

2. Name each food while encouraging the children to pick them up.

More to Do: Extensions and Adaptations

For Older Infants:

If a child is likely to throw a muffin tin, then definitely use plastic or silicone ones or place the food in different groups on the child's high-chair tray.

For Toddlers and Two-Year-Olds:

Group the foods by color, shape, or texture, and then talk about the differences as the child eats the food. Say, "You are eating an orange, soft carrot." "You are eating a green, soft bean."

Suggested Book: *Baby Touch and Feel: Mealtime* by DK Publishing

- Language development: The children will increase vocabulary if teachers emphasize color, shape, and texture words.

- Cognitive development: The children will begin to learn words that help them sort objects by shade of color, shape, length, width, and texture.

- Physical/Motor development: The children will develop fine-motor skills as they use the small muscles in their hands and fingers.

Wishy Washy Time

Materials

Terry washcloths

Water

What to Do

1. This is a fun way to clean up the children after snack or any other time of the day.

2. Tell them what you are going to do before you do it. This helps them feel safe with you.

3. Using a soft, warm, wet washcloth, rub parts of the child's face gently and sing the following song to the tune of "Row, Row, Row Your Boat."

   Wash, wash, wash your cheeks,
   Wash them every day.
   When you do it every day,
   The dirt will wash away.

4. Rub the child's lips, ears, toes, nose, and forehead. Touch the children gently and be responsive to their communication cues.

5. Change the song for each of the body parts.

What We Know

Older toddlers often experience a **language explosion** around fifteen months. They begin to say many words after hearing them several times while seeing or touching the object or person.

More to Do: Extensions and Adaptations

For Infants:

Place a second infant where he can see you clean the face of the first infant. Be sure to say the name of each body part as you wash it.

For Toddlers and Two-Year-Olds:

Give them the washcloth, and ask them to wash different parts of their faces. Model with your own washcloth on your face.

Suggested Books:

The Eye Book by Dr. Seuss

The Foot Book by Dr. Seuss

Toes, Ears, and Nose! A Lift-the-Flap Book by Marion Dane Bauer and Karen Katz

Opportunities for Learning

· • · • ● • · • ·

- Emotional development: The children will develop a sense of self as they learn their body parts. First, they can point to their body parts, and later they can say the names of them. They will build a positive self-identity if you smile, show affection, and have fun. Your face and voice are mirrors for them to know how to feel about themselves. They will learn to trust their primary caregivers to feel secure.

- Language development: The children will develop receptive language skills as they listen to the words of the song and learn new vocabulary.

- Cognitive development: The children will develop memory skills as they recall the names of their body parts.

Nap Time

Sleepy Time for Infants

Materials

Glider or rocking chair

What to Do

1. Observe for cues that an infant is ready to nap—yawning or rubbing eyes.

2. Rock the infant in the glider, and feed the baby if this is part of the routine.

3. Sing lullabies to the baby. Almost any song sung softly and slowly will work as a lullaby.

4. Hold the infant in a way that soothes her.

5. When the baby is asleep, place her on her back in a crib with no blankets, pillows, or stuffed animals.

6. As the child listens, she will focus her attention as the adult looks into her eyes, sings, and takes language turns with her.

Song:

Hush, Little Baby
Hush, little baby, don't say a word.
Papa's gonna buy you a mockingbird.
And if that mockingbird won't sing,
Papa's gonna buy you a diamond ring.
And if that diamond ring turns brass,
Papa's gonna buy you a looking glass.
And if that looking glass gets broke,
Papa's gonna buy you a billy goat.
And if that billy goat won't pull,
Papa's gonna buy you a cart and bull.
And if that cart and bull turn over,

What We Know

Infants learn to trust others who are kind and responsive to their needs. This leads to secure attachments. Children who feel secure enjoy interactions with adults, are happier, and can focus on learning. Too much stress leads to impaired brain development in infants.

According to the American Academy of Pediatrics, infants must sleep on their backs to avoid SIDS (American Academy of Pediatrics, 2016).

Infants remain calmer for longer when adults sing to them. Listening to singing helps infants regulate their emotions (Corbeil, Trehub, and Peretz, 2015).

Papa's gonna buy you a dog named Rover.
And if that dog named Rover won't bark,
Papa's gonna buy you a horse and cart.
And if that horse and cart fall down,
You'll still be the sweetest little baby in town.

Wee Sing Nursery Rhymes and Lullabies is a charming collection of lullabies for wee ones. Available at http://weesing.com/Books-Music/Wee-Sing-Nursery-Rhymes-and-Lullabies

Suggested Book:

Baby's Lullaby by Jill Barber and Hilda Rose

Opportunities for Learning

• • • • • ● • • •

- Emotional development: The children will develop expectations of consistent, positive interactions through secure relationships with familiar adults. Infants feel valued when adults are responsive to their cues of tiredness. They learn to control their emotions when adults help them relax.

- Social development: The children will develop a positive sense of self with others.

- Language development: The children will enjoy and use language. When infants hear singing, they are listening to sounds and the rhythm of language.

- Physical development: The children will develop healthy sleeping behaviors. Infants need sleep for healthy brain development.

Sleepy Time for Toddlers and Two-Year-Olds

Materials

Stuffed animals or snuggle items

Small blankets

What to Do

1. Give each child a stuffed animal or snuggle item at nap time.

What We Know

Encourage toddlers and two-year-olds to talk by asking them open-ended questions such as, "How did your dolly sleep?" rather than closed questions such as, "Did your doll sleep?"

2. Recite the following poem. Very young toddlers may just listen, and older toddlers can do the actions. Repetition of the poem supports children's ability to attend.

> *Now we lay our babies down* (children lay animals down)
> *And tuck them into bed.* (children cover animals with small blankets)
> *We give their cheeks a little kiss* (children kiss animals)
> *And pat their little heads.* (children pat animals)
> *Now we lay our own heads down,* (children lay down, teacher turns off lights)
> *Nearby our little friends.*
> *We close our eyes and rest a while* (children close eyes)
> *And dream 'til nap time ends.*

3. The children will use their imaginations as they put their stuffed animals to sleep. They will maintain attention and focus when they feel safe.

More to Do: Extensions and Adaptations

- Ask the children how their dolls or stuffed animals feel. You may need to offer choices for toddlers. For example, you could ask, "Does your animal feel happy or sad?"

- Make a book with pictures of the children with their stuffed animals at each stage of the poem. Show the pictures as you say the poem. In a calm voice, say, "Sammy is closing his eyes. Mara is closing hers."

- For children who have a difficult time covering the doll with the blanket, use a smaller blanket that Velcros to the doll.

- Read a bedtime story in a quiet, calm voice. Reading the picture book supports children's ability to attend.

- Demonstrate affection by patting a child who needs gentle touch to fall asleep.

Suggested Books:

Time for Bed by Mem Fox

Goodnight Moon by Margaret Wise Brown

Song:

Frère Jacques
Are you sleeping?
Are you sleeping?
Brother John, Brother John? (substitute the name of a child)
Morning bells are ringing.
Morning bells are ringing.
Ding ding dong,
Ding ding dong.

To learn the song in French, see https://www.youtube.com/watch?v=BC6rvbxdywg.

Opportunities for Learning

- Emotional development: The children will increase vocabulary as they learn emotion words.

- Social development: The children will experience empathy for others as they learn to take gentle care of their stuffed animals and dolls. This is good practice for taking care of each other.

- Language development: The children will develop understanding and use of language as they listen to the poem and learn new vocabulary. Emphasize the concept words of *down, up, into,* and *near.*

Waking Up

Materials

Variety of board books

Basket

Paper and crayons

What to Do

1. Waking up from naps is easy for some children and harder for others. Some children need a longer amount of time to fully wake up and join the group. Others wake up before most of the other children and need something quiet to do.

2. Place a basket of board books and paper and crayons close to the nap time area.

3. When children start to wake up, let them look at books or color quietly. This gives those who wake up earlier a quiet activity to do. Ask one teacher to remain with this group.

4. Approximately fifteen minutes before you need all the children to wake up and join the group, turn on part of the lights and lift the shades.

5. Slowly start talking in a normal tone of voice.

6. If you move into the wake-up routine as slowly as you move into the nap-time routine, you will have a happier group of children.

What We Know

Toddlers and two-year-olds need adult support to control their emotions. If they wake up sad, irritable, or afraid, they need their special adults to soothe, calm, and comfort them. Consistent routines help young children feel safe.

Very young children hold a crayon overhand and use their whole arm. Children may use an adult grip on a crayon when they are three or four years old.

More to Do: Extensions and Adaptations

For Infants:

When infants wake up, they will need snuggle time and probably a diaper change with their special adults.

For Toddlers and Two-Year-Olds:

- Use adaptive crayons for children who have difficulty with fine-motor control.
- Waking up sometimes causes toddlers and two-year-olds to miss their parents. Some children will need to be held when they wake up until they feel like hopping off your lap to play.
- Teachers can encourage peers to help a child who is having a difficult time. Ask the child having difficulty if he would like a peer to pat his back.

Song: (Sing to the tune of "London Bridge Is Falling Down.")

> It is time to wake up now,
> Wake up now, wake up now.
> It is time to wake up now,
> And start to play.

Opportunities for Learning
· · ● ● ● ● ● · ·

- Emotional development: The children will manage feelings and emotions with the support of familiar adults.

- Social development: The children will learn empathy as their special adults demonstrate empathy for how hard it can be to wake up. The children feel the kindness and learn how to be kind themselves.

- Language development: The children will increase vocabulary when they learn the meaning of the words "wake up now."

- Cognitive development: The children will understand cause and effect as they use crayons and make marks and scribbles on a piece of paper. They will increase problem-solving skills as they figure out how to make marks of different colors. They will demonstrate self-expression and creativity as they experiment with color and different marks.

- Physical/Motor development: The children will develop their fine-motor skills as they use the small muscles in their hands and fingers to play with the crayons and paper.

Cleanup

Cleanup Songs

Materials

None

What to Do

1. Give signals that it is cleanup time at five minutes and one minute before it is time. This helps children understand the routine, respects their play, and prepares them for the transition.

2. Choose one of the following songs to sing as you put toys away with an infant or as toddlers and two-year-olds help clean up the room after play time.

3. As the children help clean up, they will learn how to attend, persist at challenging tasks, and demonstrate initiative.

Songs:

> **Cleanup Song** (Sing to the tune of "Mary Had a Little Lamb.")
> *Who is going to pick up the blocks?*
> *Pick up the blocks, pick up the blocks?*
> *Who is going to pick up the blocks*
> *And be a classroom helper?*
>
> *(Child's name) is picking up the blocks,*
> *Picking up the blocks, picking up the blocks.*
> *(Child's name) is picking up the blocks.*
> *She is a classroom helper.*
>
> **Clean Up the Room** *(Sing to the tune of "Mary Had a Little Lamb.")*
> *We will all clean up our room,*
> *Clean up our room, clean up our room.*

What We Know

Comment on children's effort rather than saying, "Good work," or "Good boy." Instead say, "You are working so hard," or "You are a hard worker." Praising outcomes instead of effort can cause children to not take risks in learning because they do not want to fail.

We will all clean up our room,
Until we are all done.

More to Do: Extensions and Adaptations

For Infants:

Walk around the room carrying a child or holding a child's hand while you sing the song and pick up toys. You can encourage older infants to pick up a toy and place it in a box or on a shelf.

For Toddlers and Two-Year-Olds:

- Provide symbols (both pictures and words) on bins on a shelf or on the shelf itself so that children know where to put toys as they clean up.

- Use spatial vocabulary (*on, under, over, through, up, down, around*) and talk about colors as children put toys on shelves or in bins.

- Count toys such as blocks.

Another Cleanup Song

Materials

None

What to Do

1. Give signals that it is cleanup time at five minutes and one minute before it is time. This helps children understand the routine, respects their play, and prepares them for the transition.

2. Choose a song to sing as you put toys away with an infant or as toddlers and two-year-olds help clean up the room after play time.

3. As they help, the children will learn how to attend, persist at challenging tasks, and demonstrate initiative.

Song:

Do You Know It's Cleanup Time? (Sing to the tune of "Mary Had a Little Lamb.")
Do you know it's cleanup time?
Cleanup time, cleanup time?
Do you know it's cleanup time?
So, everyone come and help.

It was fun to work and play,
Work and play, work and play.

It was fun to work and play.
And, now it's time to say. . .
(Repeat first verse)

More to Do: Extensions and Adaptations

For Infants:

Walk around the room carrying a child or holding a child's hand while you sing the song and pick up toys. You can encourage older infants to pick up a toy and place it in a box or on a shelf.

For Toddlers and Two-Year-Olds:

- Provide symbols (both pictures and words) on bins on a shelf or on the shelf itself so that children know where to put toys as they clean up.
- Encourage two toddlers to cooperate and move a big toy.
- Use spatial vocabulary and talk about colors as children put toys on shelves or in bins. Count toys such as blocks.

Opportunities for Learning
· · • • • ● • • · ·

- Emotional development: The children will learn to regulate their bodies and desires with help from supportive adults.

- Language development: The children will learn from communication and language experiences with others as teachers model and children say *in, out, up, down, over, through, top, bottom,* and color words.

- Literacy development: The children will recognize pictures and some symbols, signs, or words if the pictures or words are on a bin or shelf. This promotes readiness for reading.

- Cognitive development: The children will use spatial information as they fit toys into spaces on shelves. They will develop emergent mathematical thinking and develop a sense of number and quantity if teachers count objects, such as blocks, as they are placed on shelves.

- Physical/Motor development: The children will use perceptual information to understand objects and to direct their own actions. As they pick up toys, they are using their eyes and hands together.

Crayon Catcher

Materials

Shoe box with lid

Scissors (adult use only)

Marker

Contact paper

Crayons

What to Do

Ahead of Time:

1. Make cleanup time fun by designing a container to hold crayons. Decorate the sides of the container with contact paper.

2. Decorate the lid, but be sure that it will fit on and come off the box easily.

3. Write the word *crayons* on the side of the container.

4. Cut a hole in the lid large enough to drop a crayon in vertically.

With the Children:

1. Encourage the children to put the crayons in the container. Emphasize the word *in*.

2. Open the lid and show them where the crayons end up. Say, "The box is open." Close the lid, and say, "The box is closed."

3. Encourage the children to take the crayons out when they want to use them or if they want to repeat the activity. Emphasize the word *out*.

More to Do: Extensions and Adaptations

For Young Toddlers:

- Some young toddlers may need the hole to be quite large to ensure their success. They may find it difficult to turn the crayon so that the crayon goes in vertically.

- Let children experiment. If a child is frustrated, scaffold his learning by modeling how to put the crayon in the container. If the child is still frustrated, place your hand gently on the child's hand and show him how.

- Use specific encouraging words. For example, say enthusiastically, "You put the crayon in the box!"

For Toddlers and Two-Year-Olds:

- Provide opportunities for classification by making several containers and coloring each lid a different color. Encourage the children to place crayons in the container that matches the color of the crayon.
- Count the crayons as they go into the container.
- Say the name of the color as it goes into the container.

Suggested Book: *Harold and the Purple Crayon* by Crockett Johnson

Song: (Sing to the tune of "Head, Shoulders, Knees, and Toes.")

> *Crayons, crayons, in the box, in the box.*
> *Crayons, crayons, in the box, in the box.*
> *Black and blue and other colors, too*
> *Crayons, crayons, in the box, in the box.*

Opportunities for Learning
• • • • ● • • • •

- Language development: The children will increase their vocabulary as they learn the words *closed, open, in, out,* number words, and the names of colors.
- Literacy development: The children will use objects or symbols to represent something else. If the word *crayon* is written on the container, children are learning that there are symbols for objects. This supports children's readiness for reading.
- Cognitive development: The children will develop emergent mathematical ability as they learn about counting and one-to-one correspondence when the adult counts the crayons as they go in the container.
- Physical/Motor development: The children will develop the small muscles in their hands and eye-hand coordination as they pick up a crayon, figure out which direction they need to turn the crayon, and then put it in the hole.

Departure

Goodbye, Room

Materials

None

What to Do

1. Children often have difficulty saying goodbye when they are busy having fun. One way to transition them to go home is to say goodbye to things. Parents often pick up their children at different times of the day, so you may be able to do this with each child.

2. Model saying goodbye to someone or something in the room. For example, say, "Goodbye, chair," "Goodbye, rug," and "Goodbye, Cezanne."

3. Encourage each child to wave or say goodbye to their friends and favorite things.

More to Do: Extensions and Adaptations

For Toddlers:

- Young toddlers are just beginning to learn the names of objects and other children. Be sure to point at the objects or children when you name them. This helps young toddlers focus on the object that goes with the word.

- Encourage a family member to go around the room with the child to say goodbye. Encourage them to point to the objects as they name them.

For Two-Year-Olds:

- Use more complex sentences with many two-year-olds. Instead of just naming the objects, add descriptive words. For example, say, "Goodbye, red block," "Goodbye, blue block." After doing this several times, two-year-olds will begin to name the objects and children themselves.

What We Know

Pointing is a very important stage of language development. When toddlers point to objects, they often want you to look at and/or name the object. They seem ready to learn the name of that object. It also is important for adults to point to objects when children are learning the names of them. Nine- to fourteen-month-old infants learn words significantly better when adults use a gesture such as pointing (Rader and Zukow-Goldring, 2012). This directs their attention to the exact object or person adults are talking about, thus helping the infants make the connection between the word and its referent.

- If a child is having a difficult time leaving, you can comment on what you think the child may be feeling: "You feel sad when you say goodbye to your friends."

Suggested Book: *Goodnight Moon* by Margaret Wise Brown

Opportunities for Learning

- Emotional development: The children will manage difficult emotions with the support of caring, familiar adults. They will learn to express a range of emotions when the teacher or other adults comment on the children's feelings.

- Social development: The children will develop friendships with other children. Saying goodbye is what friends do with each other.

- Language development: The children will communicate needs and wants nonverbally and by using language. They will increase vocabulary when they learn the names of toys, objects, and other children.

- Cognitive development: The children will develop memory skills as they learn the names of objects and children.

- Physical/Motor development: The children will develop both fine-motor and gross-motor skills when they learn to point (often by one year of age), when they move around the room, and when they wave goodbye.

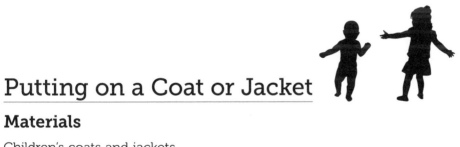

Putting on a Coat or Jacket

Materials

Children's coats and jackets

What to Do

1. Invite the children to lay their coats or jackets on the floor.

2. Prop up the armholes of each child's coat.

3. Have each child stand at the top of her coat (near the collar), squat down, and put her hands and arms into the armholes.

4. Have the child stand up and raise her arms over her head then push her arms into the sleeves. The coat will slide right on.

5. You might want to pair up the children so they can help each other. The children will develop focus, sustained attention, and persistence with adult support as they learn how to put on their coats.

More to Do: Extensions and Adaptations

- For children who have difficulty, model how to do this with your own coat.

- Help the child by guiding her arms into the jacket, raising her arms above her head, and sliding the jacket down on her back. Then ask, "Do you want to try it?"

- Place different types of coats (firefighter, astronaut, small parents' coats) in the dramatic play area. Children will try them on, and older toddlers will pretend they are someone else, such as a mom, dad, or firefighter.

What We Know

Besides physical needs, the need to belong is very strong (Maslow, 1954).

Chant:

> *Lay your coat out on the floor.*
> *Stretch your arms up toward the door.*
> *Put your arms into the sleeves.*
> *And pull it over your head. Hooray!*

Opportunities for Learning

- Emotional development: The children will learn that they can use adults as resources to meet needs. They will develop skills for managing frustration. Encourage the frustrated child to try again with your assistance. If the child is too frustrated, try again later. The child might be hungry or tired.

- Social development: The children will develop a sense of belonging as friends help each other.

- Language development: The children will increase vocabulary as they learn *in* and *out* when adults say, "Put your arms in the sleeves." "Look, here come your hands out of the sleeve." They may learn the words *first* and *last* as the adult gives clear directions.

- Cognitive development: The children will use problem-solving skills as they learn a new strategy for putting on a coat.

- Physical/Motor development: The children will develop gross-motor skills as they use the large muscles in their legs to balance and their arms to put on the coat.

Section 4
WORKING WITH FAMILIES

The Importance of Working with Families

Positive relationships among teachers and program staff and the children and families are key both to children's success and well-being and to parents' satisfaction with a program. Develop positive relationships by honoring the parents' role. For example, on your intake form, ask parents about their goals for their child, the family's cultural experiences and wishes, and family concerns. Learn about the child's food preferences and needs, sleep habits, temperament, likes and dislikes, needs, interests, and strengths. This is all important information about the child that will help teachers provide responsive care. Parents also can fill out a brief form each morning about how the child slept the previous night, any food the child has eaten that day, and any special information that will help teachers respond to the child's individual needs. Teachers can complete a form for parents concerning the child's diapering, eating, playing, and sleeping experiences that day. Provide a parent handbook to inform families of important program policies, such as when to keep their children home during illness. When challenges arise with the child and/or family, a relationship of trust provides the foundation for dialogue. When parents and teachers constantly share information about children's development, it is more likely that children's physical and emotional needs will be met.

Family engagement can take many forms, depending on the families and the program.

- Provide a survey for parents so they can let you know how they want to be involved. Offer a list of opportunities for family engagement and a newsletter or bulletin to inform families of upcoming events.

- Provide a file of resources and links with the community to help families who may want more information concerning health and development issues.

- Offer bulletin boards or a page on your website to inform parents of program events and child-development news.

- Invite family members to join advisory boards to help them feel a part of the program community and provide valuable input.

"Every day, the relationship way" (Wittmer and Petersen, 2017) applies both to teacher-child interactions and teacher-parent interactions. When teachers and family members experience positive relationships and interactions with each other, children are more likely to thrive.

My Family

Materials

Large three-ring binder

Glue

Paper

Page or photo protectors

Marker

Labels

What to Do

1. Ask family members to send in a photo of the child's family (including pets, if desired). Place this on the cover of the binder. **Note**: Be sure to tell the families that you will be gluing the photos into an album. Offer to make copies of the photos, and send the originals back home.

2. Ask family members to send in photos of family events throughout the year. Glue each photo onto a sheet of paper.

3. Print who is in the photo on the label and place it at the bottom of the paper.

4. Slide the paper in the sheet protector and place it in the binder.

5. Leave binders in the literacy area for the children to see themselves and their families often.

More to Do: Extensions and Adaptations

For Infants:

Place the photos in small photo albums so that an older infant can hold the album. Many older infants will be able to turn the pages. Make sure there are no sharp corners or loose pieces or pages, in case infants put them in their mouths.

For Toddlers and Two-Year-Olds:

Place the binders on a low shelf or along the wall. Glue a photo of the child on the end of the binder so that children can see whose family is in the binder. You will want to use clear contact paper to cover the photo.

Calendar/Schedule for Families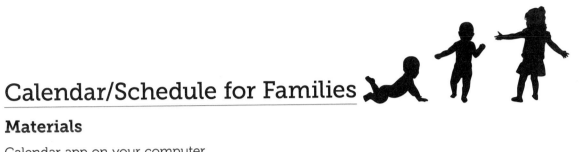

Materials

Calendar app on your computer

What to Do

1. Use a calendar app. For each month, add important dates, such as days that the center or family child care is closed or the date for a family meeting.

2. Add special projects that you may do with the children during the month, such as taking a nature walk.

3. Add any concepts that you are exploring each week, such as on and off, caterpillars and butterflies, light and dark, shadows, friends, family, and so on. Add a note to the bottom explaining why you are exploring that topic, such as, "Matias is interested in exploring light and heavy."

4. Add storybooks and a special song that you will emphasize that month.

5. Make copies and give one to each family.

6. This tool for communication helps parents feel connected and gives them information about your classroom or family child care home.

7. Family members can help by bringing in supplies, puzzles, and books that support a concept that a child or the group is exploring.

Family Night—Paper-Bag Stories

Materials

Large paper bags

What to Do

1. Invite families to come into the classroom with their children. Gather everyone together and put a paper bag in front of you. Ask the children to pick one item from the classroom to place in the bag.

2. Once all the objects are in the bag and children are with their families again, pull one of the items out of the bag and ask, "Who put this block in the bag?" Hand the block to the child and ask, "What do you like about blocks?" or "What do you like to do with blocks?" If a child doesn't speak, do not pressure the child. You talk about what you've seen the child do with the object.

3. Pull out each item one at a time, encouraging the children to talk, until the bag is empty.

4. When you are finished with the bag, ask the children to take their families to a place in the room where they like to play, eat, or sleep. Everyone can begin playing with the items in that area.

5. Gather the children together and sing one of their favorite songs to the families. "The Wheels on the Bus" is always a favorite. Have the children hold props, such as a hat for the driver, a purse for the mama, a stuffed dog toy, a stuffed cat toy, and a baby doll. Each child can hold up the prop when that part is sung.

Appendix: Activities by Children's Ages

· · · ● · · ·

Infant Activities

Emotional Development
What Are You Feeling?
Baby Faces Books
Mirror Face
Describing Emotions

Cognitive Development/ Discovery
Peekaboo
Did I Do That?
Where Did the Monkey Go?
How Things Work—An
Adventure Walk in the Room
Discovery Bottles
Instrument Fun

Fine- and Gross-Motor Development
Eyes, Hand, and Feet
Prone Play
Saucer Spin
Bumpy Lumpy Locomotion
Obstacle Course
Stacking Cups
Magic Surprise
Wall Puzzles
Sticky Crawl or Walk
Fun with Balls
Amaze Me

Language Development
Baby Conversations
Babbling: Echo Me, Echo You
Self-Talk, Parallel Talk, and
Expansion
Two or More Languages
Picture Wall
Rhyming Time
Where Is It?

Social Development
I Want to See You
Friendship Book

My Friend, My Friend, Who Do
You See?
Handprint Friendship Collage

Blocks/Construction
Dump It Out and Fill It Up
Baby Stacking Blocks

Creative Explorations
My Baby Footprints

Literacy
Read Books to Me—The
Important First Year
All about Me Book

Math
Let's Count Your Fingers and
Toes

Outdoor Play/Nature
Explore a Tree

Sensory/Science
Feeling Feet, Feeling Good, and
Gentle Touches
I Can Make It Move
Senses on the Move: See, Feel,
Listen, Smell, and Maybe
Even Taste
Baby Mirrors
Texture Blanket
Texture Crawl
Flashlight Watch
Let's Dance

Arrival
Terrific Today
Welcome Bulletin Board
Welcome Song
Animal Adventure

Fingerplays, Songs, and Rhymes
Where, Oh Where?

Stars Shining
Bunny Kiss
Baby's Little Nose
Autumn Leaves Song
Tiny Worm
Snow Action Rhymes
Where, Oh Where? Boo!

Snack Time
Finger Foods
Wishy Washy Time

Nap Time
Sleepy Time for Infants

Cleanup
Cleanup Songs
Another Cleanup Song

Departure
Goodbye, Room

Working with Families
My Family
Calendar/Schedule for Families

Toddler Activities

Emotional Development
Baby Faces Books
Mirror Face
Describing Emotions
How Do You Feel Today?

Cognitive Development/ Discovery
Where Did the Monkey Go?
How Things Work—An
Adventure Walk in the Room
Discovery Bottles
Give Me Eggs—It's Eggciting!
Boxes Galore—Where's the Toy?
On/Off, In/Out, Up/Down
Instrument Fun
Sorting the Groceries

265

Clothespin Drop
Bubble Fun and Sculptures
Color and "Just Like Me" Search
Who Lives Here?
Who Says *Moo*?

Fine- and Gross-Motor Development
Saucer Spin
Bumpy Lumpy Locomotion
Obstacle Course
Stacking Cups
Magic Surprise
Wall Puzzles
Sticky Crawl or Walk
Fun with Balls
Caterpillar/Butterfly Collection
Pull Me Fast, Pull Me Slowly
Happy Trails
Rocks in the River
Amaze Me
Squeeze Me Tight
Scientists at Play
Balance Beam
Cereal Pour
Beanbag Fun
Bowling Away
Butterfly Catchers
Baby Doll Bath Time
Laundry Time

Language Development
Babbling: Echo Me, Echo You
Self-Talk, Parallel Talk, and
    Expansion
Two or More Languages
Picture Wall
Rhyming Time
Where Is It?
Yo-Ho: A-Spying We Go
Pack 'n' Go
Photo Finish
Surprise Box
Flip the Flap

Social Development
Friendship Book
My Friend, My Friend, Who Do
    You See?
Handprint Friendship Collage

Color Hands—Making Green
    Together
Row, Row, Row Your Boat
    Together
Look What I Can Do

Construction
Dump It Out and Fill It Up
Baby Stacking Blocks
Hammering
Weighty Block Building

Creative Explorations
My Toddler Footprints
Painting Like a Painter
Making and Playing with
    Playdough
Super-Soft Playdough to Cut
All about the Process
Tear It Up
Contact Paper Art
Yarn Painting
It Looked Like Spilt Milk
Creative Creating

Dramatic Play
Dress Me Up
Pet Week
Oh, My Baby
Going to the Farm
On the Go
My Special House
Camping

Literacy
The Love of Books
All about Me Book
Color Shopping
Squeeze Us In

Math
Matching in Many Ways
Sort Us Out and Classify Us,
    Too

Outdoor Play/Nature
Explore a Tree
No-Mess Painting

Sensory/Science
Flashlight Watch
I Can Feel It
Texture Box
Let's Dance
Water Table Fun—Flotation
    Experiment
Sand Table Fun—Animal Hunt

Arrival
Terrific Today
Welcome Bulletin Board
Welcome Song
Animal Adventure
Matching Photos

Fingerplays, Songs, and Rhymes
Where, Oh Where?
Stars Shining
Bunny Kiss
Baby's Little Nose
Autumn Leaves Song
Tiny Worm
Snow Action Rhymes
Where, Oh Where? Boo!
Willow Tree
Firefighter
Police Officer
Where Is My Knee?
Sharing Song
Snow
Helpers
Jack in the Box
Splash!
Houses
Mary Wore Her Red Dress
What Are We Doing?
Puppet Sing-Along

Transitions
Transition Alerts
If You Are Listening
Off We Go
Gathering Together
The Magic Wand

Snack Time
Finger Foods
Wishy Washy Time

Nap Time
Sleepy Time for Toddlers and
Two-Year-Olds
Waking Up

Cleanup
Cleanup Songs
Another Cleanup Song
Crayon Catcher

Departure
Goodbye, Room
Putting on a Coat or Jacket

Working with Families
My Family
Calendar/Schedule for Families
Family Night—Paper-Bag Stories

Two-Year-Old Activities
Emotional Development
Mirror Face
Describing Emotions
How Do You Feel Today?

Cognitive Development/ Discovery
How Things Work—An
Adventure Walk in the Room
Discovery Bottles
Give Me Eggs—It's Eggciting!
Boxes Galore—Where's the Toy?
On/Off, In/Out, Up/Down
Instrument Fun
Sorting the Groceries
Clothespin Drop
Bubble Fun and Sculptures
Color and "Just Like Me" Search
Who Lives Here?
Who Says Moo?
Function Junction
Something's Different

Fine- and Gross-Motor Development
Wall Puzzles
Sticky Crawl or Walk
Fun with Balls

Caterpillar/Butterfly Collection
Pull Me Fast, Pull Me Slowly
Happy Trails
Rocks in the River
Amaze Me
Squeeze Me Tight
Scientists at Play
Balance Beam
Cereal Pour
Beanbag Fun
Bowling Away
Butterfly Catchers
Baby Doll Bath Time
Laundry Time
Scoop Out the Ice Cubes
Lacing Shapes

Language Development
Self-Talk, Parallel Talk, and
Expansion
Two or More Languages
Picture Wall
Rhyming Time
Where Is It?
Yo-Ho: A-Spying We Go
Pack 'n' Go
Photo Finish
Surprise Box
Flip the Flap

Social Development
Friendship Book
My Friend, My Friend, Who Do
You See?
Handprint Friendship Collage
Color Hands—Making Green
Together
Row, Row, Row Your Boat
Together
Look What I Can Do
Silly Shoe Mix-Up

Construction
Dump It Out and Fill It Up
Hammering
Weighty Block Building
Animal Houses

Creative Explorations
Painting Like a Painter

Making and Playing with
Playdough
Super-Soft Playdough to Cut
All about the Process
Tear It Up
Contact Paper Art
Yarn Painting
It Looked Like Spilt Milk
Creative Creating
Snow in the Night
Easels for Two

Dramatic Play
Dress Me Up
Pet Week
Oh, My Baby
Going to the Farm
On the Go
My Special House
Camping

Literacy
The Love of Books
All About Me Book
Color Shopping
Squeeze Us In
ABC Ticket

Math
Matching in Many Ways
Sort Us Out and Classify Us,
Too
Shape Me Up

Outdoor Play/Nature
Explore a Tree
No-Mess Painting
Nature Hide and Seek
Transition with a Red Caboose
Stop and Go Signs

Sensory/Science
Flashlight Watch
I Can Feel It
Texture Box
Let's Dance
Water Table Fun—Flotation
Experiment
Sand Table Fun—Animal Hunt

Arrival
Terrific Today
Welcome Bulletin Board
Welcome Song
Animal Adventure
Matching Photos

Fingerplays, Songs, and Rhymes
Where, Oh Where?
Stars Shining
Bunny Kiss
Autumn Leaves Song
Snow Action Rhymes
Where, Oh Where? Boo?
Willow Tree
Firefighter
Police Officer
Where Is My Knee?
Sharing Song
Snow
Helpers
Hat Song
Jack in the Box
Splash!
Houses
Mary Wore Her Red Dress
What Are We Doing?
Puppet Sing-Along

Transitions
Transition Alerts
If You Are Listening
Off We Go
Gathering Together
The Magic Wand
Yes or No

Snack Time
Finger Foods
Wishy Washy Time

Nap Time
Sleepy Time for Toddlers and Two-Year-Olds
Waking Up

Cleanup
Cleanup Songs
Another Cleanup Song
Crayon Catcher

Departure
Goodbye, Room
Putting on a Coat or Jacket

Working with Families
My Family
Calendar/Schedule for Families
Family Night—Paper-Bag Stories

Glossary

Active listening: The act of listening carefully to another person to understand the meaning of that person's language and then stating the meaning back to the person for clarification

Alphabetic principle: The understanding that letters represent sounds, which form words

Attachment: A child's feelings of safety derived from proximity to his or her most familiar adults; a strong emotional relationship between two people, characterized by mutual affection and a desire to maintain proximity

Cardinal number: A number indicating quantity, such as one, two, three, and so on

Cause and effect: The relationships between actions or events indicating that one or more are the result of the others

Classify, classifying, classification: Ordering, organizing, and sorting objects

Cognitive disequilibrium: The uncertainty that a person feels when confronted with new information that doesn't fit into existing schemas

Contingency, contingently: In infancy research, terms used to describe an adult's responses and language that are dependent on and follow the child's movements, gestures, or language

Dialogic reading: A technique in which an adult asks a child questions about a book they are looking at together, such as "Why do you think he is wearing a hat?" "Where is the bear?" and so on; this technique prompts the child to engage with the images and content

Emotional refueling: Term used by physician Margaret Mahler to describe the positive energy and emotional satisfaction that a child obtains when checking in with a familiar caregiver

Emotionally available: With a young child, the state of an adult being emotionally present and accessible to the child

Executive functioning: Term used when describing the brain's ability to plan, stay focused, process information, and filter out distractions

Expansion talk: Adult talk that includes oral-communication responses to children's language that extends the meaning, vocabulary, or grammar of their language; for example, a child says, "Ball." The adult responds, "The ball is green."

Expressive language: A term that refers to spoken language; compare *receptive language*

Eye-hand coordination: Use of visual information to perform smooth, coordinated, and precise movements

Joint attention: When two or more people are focused on the same person, object, or animal; joint attention between an adult and child facilitates both language and emotional development

Language explosion: Term used to describe the extensive and rapid increase in expressive language development that occurs with older toddlers

Levels of representation: The levels include the following:

- **Object level:** gives children experiences with real objects and places, such as touching, seeing, hearing, smelling, and/or tasting a real duck
- **Index level:** children remember the whole object even though they only see, hear, touch, taste, or smell one part of the object, such as recognizing the footprint of a duck as a duck
- **Symbol level:** includes pictures, models, and forms of play, such as recognizing a picture of a duck as a duck
- **Sign level:** arbitrary signs or symbols are used to represent objects, actions, animals, or persons, such as recognizing the symbols D-U-C-K as representing a real duck

Object permanence: The realization that objects continue to exist even though they may not be visible or detected through another sense

One-to-one correspondence: The act of matching one object to one object or person; for example, a child who puts one plate on a table for each child in the group is practicing one-to-one correspondence

Ordinal number: A number indicating position, such as first, second, third, and so on

Overgeneralization: The use of a word, such as *cat*, for all animals with four legs; also, the error of using a language rule with many other words to which it doesn't apply. For example, a child learns that in English an *s* is added to words to indicate plurality. However, the child may apply the rule to the word *foot* and say *foots* instead of *feet*. Overgeneralizing indicates that children are not just imitating language, they are processing language.

Parallel talk: Adult talk that describes what a child is presently doing, to help a child learn language

Parentese: A universal language used with young infants that includes utterances that are shorter, repeated, spoken in a higher pitch, and directed at the infant

Perceptual skills: Skills that a person has in order to interpret or process sensory information

Person permanence: The realization that people continue to exist even though they may not be visible or detected through another sense

Pincer grasp: Picking up objects between the thumb and forefinger

Print referencing: Technique in which an adult points out and asks questions about print on a page; for example, the adult asks the child to point to a letter on the page that is in the child's name; the adult points to words as she reads them; or the adult comments about a detail on the page, such as, "The sign on the bear's store says *Grocery*."

Prone: Lying flat or prostrate

Prosocial: Term that refers to the skills and tendency of a child to be kind, empathic, caring, helpful, thoughtful, considerate, compassionate, and supportive with others. When a child helps another child, we may say, "That child is prosocial."

Raking grasp or motion: Using all the fingers to collect or gather items; a raking grasp occurs before scissors grasp, which occurs before pincer grasp

Receptive language: Language that is comprehended but not necessarily produced. Children birth to three years often understand the meanings of more words than they can express.

Scaffold: Term used by psychologist Lev Vygotsky to refer to a process by which adults or more skilled children help a learner acquire knowledge or skills through coaching or supplying needed information

Schema: A cognitive framework or concept that helps organize and interpret information. For example, an older infant who learns to bang on object on the floor to make it work will try that action with other objects.

Scissors grasp: Using the thumb with the fingers to pick up objects

Self-efficacy: The feeling that one's efforts are effective; the perception that one can succeed

Self-recognition: With children from birth to three years of age, this term refers to the ability to recognize oneself, for example, in a mirror

Self-regulation: The ability to monitor and control one's own behavior, emotions, and thoughts. It can describe the ability of a person to adapt behavior in an appropriate way for the setting, such as whispering in a library

Self-talk: Talk by a person describing what the person is doing or thinking; for example, when an adult is changing a baby's diaper, the adult might say, "I am changing your diaper. First, I pull the tape open on the dirty diaper. Next, I'm going to lift your legs and pull that old diaper off of you. . . ."

Semantic responsive talk: Adult talk with children that expands on the meaning of a child's language and stays on the same topic

Sensory overload: Situation in which one or more of the body's senses is overstimulated. Sensory overload occurs when the individual's nervous system cannot successfully process information from the sensory experience.

Seriation: When discussing the cognitive skills of children, refers to placing objects, animals, or persons in order based on a dimension of the item; for example, placing rods in order based on size, length, or width

Spatial relations: How one object is located in space in relationship to other objects. Spatial relationship terms include *above, below, before, after, high, low, in front of, in back of, behind, inside, outside, on top of*, and *under*.

Sudden infant death syndrome (SIDS) or sudden unexpected infant death (SUID): Terms that refer to the unexpected death of a baby, usually during the first year of life, which cannot be explained or is undetermined

Supine: On the back, lying faceup

Syntax: The grammar and structure of a language system

Theory of mind: The ability to know that other people have feelings, thoughts, and desires that are different from your own

Toxic stress: Refers to a level of stress that is damaging to a person. With children from birth to three years of age, the term often refers to a level of stress that is damaging to a child's brain and learning capabilities

Undergeneralization: A child's use of a general term to refer to a more specific object, situation, or category; for example, a child using the word *cat* to refer only to his black cat and to no other cats

Zone of proximal development: Refers to the level of concept development that is too difficult for the child to accomplish alone but can be achieved with the help of adults or more skilled children through scaffolding

References

Adolph, Karen, et al. 2012. "How Do You Learn to Walk? Thousands of Steps and Dozens of Falls per Day." *Psychological Science* 23(11): 1387–1394.

American Academy of Pediatrics. 2016. "American Academy of Pediatrics Announces New Safe Sleep Recommendations to Protect Against SIDS, Sleep-Related Infant Deaths." https://www.aap.org/en-us/about-the-aap/aap-press-room/pages/american-academy-of-pediatrics-announces-new-safe-sleep-recommendations-to-protect-against-sids.aspx.aspx

Amsterdam, Beulah. 1972. "Mirror Self-Image Reactions before Age Two." *Developmental Psychobiology* 5(4): 297–305.

Begus, Katarina, and Victoria Southgate. 2012. "Infant Pointing Serves an Interrogative Function." *Developmental Science* 15(5): 611–617.

Bertenthal, Bennett, Gustaf Gredebäck, and Ty Boyer. 2013. "Differential Contributions of Development and Learning to Infants' Knowledge of Object Continuity and Discontinuity." *Child Development* 84(2): 413–421.

Brownell, Celia, Geetha Ramani, and Stephanie Zerwas. 2006. "Becoming a Social Partner with Peers: Cooperation and Social Understanding in One- and Two-Year-Olds." *Child Development* 77(4): 803–821.

Brownell, Celia, et al. 2013. "Socialization of Early Prosocial Behavior: Parents' Talk about Emotions Is Associated with Sharing and Helping in Toddlers." *Infancy* 18(1): 91–119.

Cirelli, Laura, Kathleen Einarson, and Laurel Trainor. 2014. "Interpersonal Synchrony Increases Prosocial Behavior in Infants." *Developmental Science* 17(6): 1003–1011.

Conboy, Barbara, and Patricia Kuhl. 2011. "Impact of Second-Language Experience in Infancy: Brain Measures of First- and Second-Language Speech Perception." *Developmental Science* 14(2): 242–248.

Cooper, Shelly. 2010. "Lighting Up the Brain with Songs and Stories." *General Music Today* 23(2): 24–30.

Corbeil, Mariève, Sandra Trehub, and Isabelle Peretz. 2015. "Singing Delays the Onset of Infant Distress." *Infancy* 21(3): 373–391.

Crivello, Cristina, et al. 2016. "The Effects of Bilingual Growth on Toddlers' Executive Function." *Journal of Experimental Child Psychology* 141: 121–132.

Duff, Fiona, et al. 2015. "Do Infant Vocabulary Skills Predict School-Age Language and Literacy Outcomes?" *Journal of Child Psychology and Psychiatry* 56(8): 848–856.

Dunfield, Kristen A., and Valerie A. Kuhlmeier. 2013. "Classifying Prosocial Behavior: Children's Responses to Instrumental Need, Emotional Distress, and Material Desire." *Child Development* 84(5): 1766–1776.

Engel de Abreu, Pascale, et al. 2012. "Bilingualism Enriches the Poor: Enhanced Cognitive Control in Low-Income Minority Children." *Psychological Science* 23(11): 1364–1371.

Fletcher, Kathryn L., and W. Holmes Finch. 2015. "The Role of Book Familiarity and Book Type on Mothers' Reading Strategies and Toddlers' Responsiveness." *Journal of Early Childhood Literacy* 15(1): 73–96.

Fukuyama, Hiroshi, et al. 2015. "Infant's Action Skill Dynamically Modulates Parental Action Demonstration in the Dyadic Interaction." *Developmental Science* 18(6): 1006–1013.

Gainsley, Suzanne. 2011. "Look, Listen, Touch, Feel, Taste: The Importance of Sensory Play." *Highscope Extensions* 25(5): 1–4.

Gershkoff-Stowe, Lisa, and Erin Hahn. 2007. "Fast Mapping Skills in the Developing Lexicon." *Journal of Speech, Language, and Hearing Research* 50(3): 682–697.

Gerson, Sarah A., and Amanda L. Woodward. 2014. "Learning from Their Own Actions: The Unique Effect of Producing Actions on Infants' Action Understanding." *Child Development* 85(1): 264–277.

Goldstein, Michael H., and Jennifer A. Schwade. 2008. "Social Feedback to Infants' Babbling Facilitates Rapid Phonological Learning." *Psychological Science* 19(5): 515–523.

Hart, Betty, and Todd Risley. 1995. *Meaningful Differences in the Everyday Experience of Young American Children*. Baltimore, MD: Paul H. Brookes.

Honig, Alice. 2015. *Experiencing Nature with Young Children: Awakening Delight, Curiosity, and a Sense of Stewardship*. Washington, DC: NAEYC.

Honig, Alice, and Donna Wittmer. 1982. "Teacher Questions to Male and Female Toddlers." *Early Child Development and Care* 9(1): 19–32.

Howes, Carrollee. 1987. "Social Competency with Peers: Contributions from Child Care." *Early Childhood Research Quarterly* 2(2): 155–167.

Howes, Carrollee. 1996. "The Earliest Friendships." In *The Company They Keep: Friendship in Childhood and Adolescence*. New York: Cambridge University Press.

Justice, Laura M., et al. 2009. "Accelerating Preschoolers' Early Literacy Development through Classroom-Based Teacher-Child Storybook Reading and Explicit Print Referencing." *Language, Speech, and Hearing Services in Schools* 40(1): 67–85.

Kaplan, Louise. 1978. *Oneness and Separateness: From Infant to Individual*. New York: Simon and Schuster.

Kawakami, Kiyobumi, and Kiyoko Takai-Kawakami. 2015. "Teaching, Caring, and Altruistic Behaviors in Toddlers." *Infant Behavior and Development* 41: 108–112.

Kluger, Jeffrey. 2013. "The Power of the Bilingual Brain." *Time* 182(5): 42–47.

Liddle, Mitzi-Jane E., Ben S. Bradley, and Andrew Mcgrath. 2015. "Baby Empathy: Infant Distress and Peer Prosocial Responses." *Infant Mental Health Journal* 36(4): 446–458.

Løkken, Gunvor. 2000. "The Playful Quality of the Toddling 'Style.'" *International Journal of Qualitative Studies in Education* 13(5): 531–542.

Maslow, Abraham. 1954. *Motivation and Personality*. New York: Harper and Row.

McFadden, Karen E., and Catherine S. Tamis-Lemonda. 2013. "Maternal Responsiveness, Intrusiveness, and Negativity during Play with Infants: Contextual Associations and Infant Cognitive Status in a Low-Income Sample." *Infant Mental Health Journal* 34(1): 80–92.

Mcquaid, Nancy E., Maximilian B. Bibok, and Jeremy I. M. Carpendale. 2009. "Relation between Maternal Contingent Responsiveness and Infant Social Expectations." *Infancy* 14(3): 390–401.

Meltzoff, Andrew. 2011. "Social Cognition and the Origins of Imitation, Empathy, and Theory of Mind." In *The Wiley-Blackwell Handbook of Childhood Cognitive Development*, 2nd edition. Malden, MA: Wiley-Blackwell.

Morgan, Paul, et al. 2015. "24-Month-Old Children with Larger Oral Vocabularies Display Greater Academic and Behavioral Functioning at Kindergarten Entry." *Child Development* 86(5): 1351–1370.

National Scientific Council on the Developing Child. 2005/2014. "Excessive Stress Disrupts the Architecture of the Developing Brain." Working Paper No. 3. Cambridge, MA: Center on the Developing Child, Harvard University. http://developingchild.harvard.edu/resources/wp3/

Needham, Amy, et al. 2014. "Effects of Contingent Reinforcement of Actions on Infants' Object-Directed Reaching." *Infancy* 19(5): 496–517.

Newman, Rochelle, Meredith Rowe, and Nan Ratner. 2015. "Input and Uptake at 7 Months Predicts Toddler Vocabulary: The Role of Child-Directed Speech and Infant Processing Skills in Language Development." *Journal of Child Language* 43(5): 1158–1173.

Newton, Emily K., Ross A. Thompson, and Miranda Goodman. 2016. "Individual Differences in Toddlers' Prosociality: Experiences in Early Relationships Explain Variability in Prosocial Behavior." *Child Development* 87(6): 1715–1726.

Nielsen, Mark, and Cheryl Dissanayake. 2004. "Pretend Play, Mirror Self-Recognition, and Imitation: A Longitudinal Investigation through the Second Year." *Infant Behavior and Development* 27(3): 342–365.

North Carolina Foundations Task Force. 2013. *North Carolina Foundations for Early Learning and Development.* Raleigh, NC: North Carolina Foundations Task Force. ncchildcare.nc.gov/pdf_forms/NC_foundations.pdf

Office of Head Start. 2015. *Head Start Early Learning Outcomes Framework: Ages Birth to Five.* Washington, DC: Administration for Children and Families, US Department of Health and Human Services. https://eclkc.ohs.acf.hhs.gov/hslc/hs/sr/approach/pdf/ohs-framework.pdf

Piaget, Jean. 1977. *The Development of Thought: Equilibration of Cognitive Structures.* New York: Viking.

Rader, Nancy, and Patricia Zukow-Goldring. 2012. "Caregivers' Gestures Direct Infant Attention during Early Word Learning." *Language Sciences* 34(5): 559–568.

Ramirez-Esparza, Nairán, Adrián García-Sierra, and Patricia K. Kuhl. 2014. "Look Who's Talking: Speech Style and Social Context in Language Input to Infants Are Linked to Concurrent and Future Speech Development." *Developmental Science* 17(6): 880–891.

Raver, Cybele, Clancy Blair, and Patricia Garrett-Peters. 2014. "Poverty, Household Chaos, and Interparental Aggression Predict Children's Ability to Recognize and Modulate Negative Emotions." *Development and Psychopathology* 27(3): 695–708.

Roseberry, Sarah, et al. 2009. "Live Action: Can Young Children Learn Verbs From Video?" *Child Development* 80(5): 1360–1375.

Rowe, Meredith L. 2012. "A Longitudinal Investigation of the Role of Quantity and Quality of Child-Directed Speech in Vocabulary Development." *Child Development* 83(5): 1762–1774.

Saffran, Jenny R., Michelle M. Loman, and Rachel R. W. Robertson. 2000. "Infant Memory for Musical Experiences." *Cognition* 77(1): B15–B23.

Sanefuji, Wakako, Hidehiro Ohgami, and Kazuhide Hashiya. 2006. "Preference for Peers in Infancy." *Infant Behavior and Development* 29(4): 584–593.

Selby, Jane, and Benjamin Sylvester Bradley. 2003. "Infants in Groups: Extending the Debate." *Human Development* 46(4): 247–249.

Spelke, Elizabeth. 2011. "Natural Number and Natural Geometry." In *Space, Time, and Number in the Brain: Searching for the Foundations of Mathematical Thought.* Cambridge, MA: Academic Press.

Stahl, Aimee, and Lisa Feigenson. 2015. "Observing the Unexpected Enhances Infants' Learning and Exploration." *Science* 348(6230): 91–94.

Tamis-LeMonda, Catherine, Yana Kuchirko, and Lulu Song. 2014. "Why Is Infant Language Learning Facilitated by Parental Responsiveness?" *Current Directions in Psychological Science* 23(2): 121–126.

Twomey, Katherine E., Samantha L. Ranson, and Jessica S. Horst. 2014. "That's More Like It: Multiple Exemplars Facilitate Word Learning." *Infant and Child Development* 23(2): 105–122.

Vouloumanos, Athena, et al. "The Tuning of Human Neonates' Preference for Speech." *Child Development* 81(2): 517–527.

Vygotsky, Lev. 1978. *Mind in Society: The Development of Higher Psychological Processes.* Cambridge, MA: Harvard University Press.

Whitehurst, Grover, et al. 1999. "Outcomes of an Emergent Literacy Intervention from Head Start through Second Grade." *Journal of Educational Psychology* 91(2): 261–272.

Wittmer, Donna, and Sandra Petersen. 2017. *Infant and Toddler Development and Responsive Program Planning: A Relationship-Based Approach.* 4th ed. New York: Pearson.

Zhao, Christina, and Patricia Kuhl. 2016. "Musical Intervention Enhances Infants' Neural Processing of Temporal Structure in Music and Speech." *Proceedings of the National Academy of Sciences* 113(19): 5212–5217.

Index

• • • • • ● • • • •

Q

Quantity, 61–62, 65–66, 73–74, 76–77, 82–83, 126–128, 176, 207–208

R

Raking grasp or motion, 245–246, 269

Receptive language, 2, 177–179, 215–216, 218–220, 234–237, 239–241, 243–244, 246–247, 268–269

Risk taking, 65–66, 100–101

Routines, 2, 211–260

S

Safety, 5, 47–48, 54–55, 60, 70, 73, 79, 81, 84, 122, 141, 154, 157, 185, 194, 201, 207

Scaffolding, 5, 70–71, 128–129, 269

Schema, 29–30, 59–60, 269

Scissors grasp, 137–139, 245–246, 269

Seasons, 184–185, 187–188, 223–224

Self-efficacy, 8, 29–30, 32, 36–37, 43–44, 53–54, 56–57, 62–63, 73–74, 76–77, 98–99, 194–195, 200, 269

Self-recognition, 11–13, 18–19, 47, 51, 92–94, 107–109, 168–169, 197–198, 213–214, 218–220, 262, 269

Self-regulation, 1, 14, 17–18, 49–52, 58–59, 67–68, 70–74, 82–83, 94–98, 113–117, 128–129, 132–134, 157–158, 161–162, 181–182, 185–189, 197–198, 204–206, 236–237, 241–244, 248–249, 251–255, 258–260, 269

Self-talk, 87–88, 269

Semantic responsive talk, 87–88, 269

Sensory challenges, 110

Sensory overload, 8, 172, 193–194, 201, 269

Seriation, 40–41, 175, 269

Shapes, 175, 181–182, 245–246

Sign level of representation, 268

Signaling, 234–236, 238–241, 253–257

Spatial relations, 21, 23, 27, 40–41, 47–48, 51–52, 65–66, 68–69, 109–111, 113–114, 122–123, 159–161, 171–172, 175–176, 201–202, 205–206, 216–218, 253–255, 269

Sudden infant death syndrome (SIDS), 47–48, 248, 269

Supine, 47–48, 104–105, 166, 269

Symbol level of representation, 5, 33, 42, 55–57, 65–72, 76–79, 82–83, 99–103, 107–111, 157–162, 171–174, 187–188, 190–191, 204–205, 207–210, 213–214, 218–220, 241–243, 253–257, 268

Symbolic play, 156

Syntax, 185–186, 269

T

Theory of mind, 215–216, 269

Toxic stress, 8, 193–194, 269

U

Undergeneralization, 65–66, 97, 269

Z

Zone of proximal development, 3, 70–71, 269